The United States and the International Criminal Court

The United States and the International Criminal Court

National Security and International Law

Edited by Sarah B. Sewall
and Carl Kaysen

AMERICAN ACADEMY OF ARTS AND SCIENCES

ROWMAN & LITTLEFIELD PUBLISHERS, INC.
Lanham • Boulder • New York • Oxford

ROWMAN & LITTLEFIELD PUBLISHERS, INC.

Published in the United States of America
by Rowman & Littlefield Publishers, Inc.
A wholly owned subsidiary of The Rowman & Littlefield Publishing Group, Inc.
4501 Forbes Boulevard, Suite 200, Lanham, Maryland 20706
www.rowmanlittlefield.com

PO Box 317
Oxford
OX2 9RU, UK

Copyright © 2000 The American Academy of Arts and Sciences

British Library Cataloguing in Publication Information Available

Library of Congress Cataloging-in-Publication Data

The United States and the international criminal court : national security and international law / edited by Sarah B. Sewall and Carl Kaysen.
    p. cm.
    Includes index.
    ISBN 0-7425-0134-5 (alk. paper) — ISBN 0-7425-0135-3 (pbk. : alk. paper)
    1. International Criminal Court. 2. International criminal courts. 3. International offenses. 4. National security—United States. 5. Criminal jurisdiction—United States. I. Sewall, Sarah B. II. Kaysen, Carl.
    KZ6310.U55   2000
    341.7'7 21—dc 21   00-038736

Printed in the United States of America

♾™ The paper used in this publication meets the minimum requirements of American National Standard for Information Sciences—Permanence of Paper for Printed Library Materials, ANSI/NISO Z39.48—1992.

To Susan Duncan Thomas
an extraordinary mother
who believes in justice and peace

The American Academy of Arts and Sciences

Founded in 1780, the American Academy of Arts and Sciences is an international learned society with headquarters in Cambridge, Massachusetts. The Academy is composed of 3,300 fellows and 600 foreign honorary members representing the academic disciplines as well as the arts, business, and government. Through its multidisciplinary research projects, the Academy addresses major issues of both scholarly and public concern, including international affairs, economic and environmental issues, and the changing nature of higher education, science, and scholarship. The Academy publishes a quarterly journal, *Daedalus;* has regional offices at the University of Chicago and the University of California, Irvine; and oversees U.S. participation in the International Institute for Applied Systems Analysis (IIASA), located in Laxenburg, Austria, outside of Vienna.

The Academy's Committee on International Security Studies (CISS), founded in 1982, oversees a diverse research program focusing on global security issues. Current and previous projects have included Small Arms and Light Weapons, Environmental Scarcities, State Capacity, and Civil Violence, and Emerging Norms of Justified Intervention. CISS oversees the activities of the U.S. Pugwash Committee, part of the international Pugwash Conferences on Science and World Affairs, which received the 1995 Nobel Peace Prize.

Among the Academy's CISS publications are:

Light Weapons and Civil Conflict, edited by Jeffrey Boutwell and Michael T. Klare (1999)

Lethal Commerce: The Global Trade in Small Arms and Light Weapons, edited by Jeffrey Boutwell, Michael T. Klare, and Laura Reed (1995)

Israeli-Palestinian Security: Issues in the Permanent Status Negotiations, by Jeffrey Boutwell and Everett Mendelsohn (1995)

Collective Responses to Regional Problems: The Case of Latin America and the Caribbean, edited by Carl Kaysen, Robert A. Pastor, and Laura W. Reed (1994)

Emerging Norms of Justified Intervention, edited by Laura W. Reed and Carl Kaysen (1993)

Transition to Palestinian Self-Government: Practical Steps toward Israeli-Palestinian Peace, by Ann Mosely Lesch (1992)

To order publications or for more information, please contact CISS at American Academy of Arts and Sciences, 136 Irving Street, Cambridge, MA 02138. Phone: 617-576-5024; e-mail: *ciss@amacad.org*; World Wide Web: *www.amacad.org*

Contents

Acknowledgments

The origins of this effort can be traced to the fall 1997 meeting of the American Academy of Arts and Sciences Committee on International Security Studies (CISS), where Matthew Meselson asked whether the proposed International Criminal Court (ICC) might be used to enforce criminal prohibitions regarding the production or transfer of chemical and biological weapons. Meselson's question catalyzed a much broader discussion about the proposed Court and its relationship to U.S. national security. What goals would an international criminal court advance? Could such a court work—or would individual states block action when it was most needed? How would a court dealing with individuals interact with states and international institutions, most importantly the U.N. Security Council? Would a court complicate the efforts to promote international peace and security? Could an international criminal court independently create laws or impose restrictions that would impinge on American interests?

The complexity and importance of these questions bore the marks of a CISS research project, which also would help address the marked absence of public discussion about the proposed court. Although international lawyers and a handful of nongovernmental organizations cared deeply about the ICC, the broader policy community—and in particular the security community—seemed unaware of the prospect of a new international court that American foreign policy would have to take into account.

CISS believed that the role and the impact of the prospective ICC deserved detailed consideration by foreign policy and security experts, as well as by international legal scholars, and wanted to make this work accessible to a broader public. Fortunately, an anonymous donor agreed. The John D. and Catherine T. MacArthur Foundation then generously funded the bulk of the CISS project on the ICC.

The United States was an initial proponent of an ICC. Many expected the Rome diplomatic negotiations to affirm a Court that had been shaped to American satisfaction. But a majority of states wanted to grant the ICC a degree of independence that proved unacceptable to the U.S. government. Understanding the Clinton administration's objections and placing them in a larger context thus became the central challenge for this book.

Meeting this challenge required an amalgam of political, security, and international legal expertise. In joining CISS as associate director to run the project, Sarah Sewall brought a background in security and politics. Michael Scharf, a former State Department legal adviser and now professor at the New England School of

Law, served as the project's codirector, covering the effort through international legal issues. CISS Chairman and MIT Professor Emeritus Carl Kaysen, who was engaged in this work throughout, had served on President John F. Kennedy's national security staff.

Many contributors to this volume are distinguished international legal experts; some participated in the efforts to shape the Court. Two contributors are retired members of the U.S. military—one served as chief judge on the U.S. Court of Military Appeals and the other was commanding general of the first U.S. peace-keeping division in Bosnia. *New Yorker* staff writer Lawrence Weschler and other former journalists contributed chapters, as did the former chief prosecutor of the International Tribunal for the Former Yugoslavia, now a justice of South Africa's Constitutional Court. All have done a terrific job of addressing aspects of the Court from divergent perspectives, helping to create a comprehensive picture of the ICC's relationship to U.S. national security.

To launch the project, CISS held a two-day workshop on the heels of the Rome Conference finalizing the ICC Statute. In August 1998, at the American Academy of Arts and Sciences in Cambridge, Massachusetts, project participants reviewed the Court's history and debated many issues that became the core of this book. The second workshop was held in Chicago in January 1999. The two days of discussion, hosted by the Chicago–Kent College of Law, greatly improved the work in progress. CISS plans to hold a major public conference in Washington, D.C., in fall 2000 to bring the results of this work to a wider policy audience.

Each contributor is alone responsible for his or her chapter's content. The views of the contributors are independent of institutional affiliation, the American Academy of Arts and Sciences, and the Committee on International Security Studies, which does not take positions on matters of public policy.

CISS is grateful for the participation of the many experts who informed and shaped the volume, including academics, judges, retired and active-duty members of the military, U.S. and foreign government representatives, members of nongovernmental organizations, prosecutors, security analysts, and scientists. Special thanks are due to M. Cherif Bassiouni, Lieutenant Colonel William K. Leitzau, Minna Shrag, and John Washburn.

For their encouragement of this project, CISS would like to thank Kennette Benedict and Mary Page of the MacArthur Foundation. Chicago–Kent's dean Henry Perritt and Charles Rudnick contributed greatly through their enthusiastic sponsorship of the Chicago workshop.

Tracy Sanderson's professionalism and organizational skills proved critical throughout the course of this project. Jeffrey Boutwell and Monica Toft provided helpful comments on the first chapter, and Martin Malin helped bring the volume to closure. Jennifer Knerr, our patient editor at Rowman & Littlefield, also provided crucial support.

On a personal note, I am grateful that my best friend and husband, Thomas Conroy, not only understood, but encouraged me throughout and that our Madeleine, Cashen, and Emma remain magical.

These are difficult times to address U.S. national security issues rationally. America's unprecedented security surplus has pushed most security issues off the public radar screen. Where debate does occur, it is either poisoned by political partisanship or reduced to meaningless sound bites. In either case, the result is unsatisfactory—particularly for an issue as complex and significant as the ICC. This volume should help those who wish to look beneath reflexive politics or simplistic slogans to understand the ICC and its relationship to American security interests.

Sarah B. Sewall
Cambridge, Massachusetts
April 2000

Acronyms

AAAS	American Academy of Arts and Sciences
ABA	American Bar Association
CICC	Coalition for an International Criminal Court
CISS	Committee on International Security Studies
ECJ	European Court of Justice
GATT	General Agreement on Tariffs and Trade
HRW	Human Rights Watch
ICC	International Criminal Court
ICJ	International Court of Justice
ICT	International Criminal Tribunal
ICTR	International Criminal Tribunal for Rwanda
ICTY	International Criminal Tribunal for the Former Yugoslavia
ILC	International Law Commission
IMF	International Monetary Fund
IMT	International Military Tribunal
MIT	Massachusetts Institute of Technology
NAFTA	North American Free Trade Agreement
NGO	nongovernmental organization
NATO	North Atlantic Treaty Organization
PCA	Permanent Court of Arbitration
POW	prisoner of war
PrepCom	Preparatory Committee

SOFA	Status of Forces Agreement
U.N.	United Nations
U.S.	United States
WTO	World Trade Organization

The United States and the International Criminal Court: An Overview

Sarah B. Sewall, Carl Kaysen, and Michael P. Scharf

PURPOSE AND ORIGINS OF THE COURT

The creation of an International Criminal Court (ICC) is the natural culmination of two trends in world politics, one of which began late in the nineteenth century and the other after World War II. The first was an increasing recognition of individual human rights as a legitimate subject of international law. The Geneva Conventions on the laws of war began this process, which was reinforced by the proceedings of the Nuremberg and the Tokyo tribunals and was expanded through the Genocide Convention and the Universal Declaration of Human Rights. The second trend was the creating of a variety of international institutions to bring within a more universal and lawlike framework matters that previously had been left to unilateral state action or ad hoc diplomacy. From the United Nations (U.N.) to the International Monetary Fund (IMF) and the World Bank and most recently the World Trade Organization, these organizations have become essential features of the international landscape. The United States helped expand international law and led efforts to create international institutions in the belief that this work was in the national interest. Today, that international legal framework supports U.S. efforts ranging from controlling weapons proliferation, to combating terrorism, to regulating global trade.

International norms and institutions have had a significant impact on states and individuals, but many of the worst human rights abuses have gone unpunished in recent decades. Bold international prohibitions against mass atrocities have withered as states have failed to enforce these norms. Now a large majority of nations have decided to create an international court to uphold laws banning genocide, war crimes, and crimes against humanity. The ICC will prosecute individuals who commit the most egregious crimes. By helping end impunity for the worst violations of human rights, the Court will breathe new life into the norms that states have long proclaimed. The ICC will help establish historical records, respond to ongoing crises, and deter future gross abuses. Even modest contributions toward these ends will contribute to international stability and, by extension, American security.

The ICC's emergence poses a particular dilemma for today's preeminent global military and political power. The Court's central purpose—ending impunity for those who commit mass atrocities—clearly reflects U.S. values. By providing an opportunity to strengthen and enforce international law, the ICC can reinforce fifty years of U.S. efforts to make global behavior consistent with U.S. interests. Yet today, the United States stands—virtually alone among its allies[1]—in opposition to the Court.

This confounding state of affairs must be placed in context. The post–Cold War security regime remains undefined. The zero-sum paradigm of superpower conflict has not been replaced by a cooperative framework to ensure common security. Even as U.S. security planners attempt to focus on traditional military balances, their attention is diverted toward nonstate actors and unconventional threats to citizens, domestic infrastructure, and interests overseas. Unilateral military force has a distinctly limited utility for confronting many future threats. Nonmilitary measures, including improving the monitoring of technology, arms, and money flows; expanding civilian law enforcement; and isolating and imposing sanctions may be increasingly important for U.S. national security. These approaches will be most effective if coordinated among concerned nations and undertaken collectively.

During the Cold War, U.S. governments simultaneously increased the nation's military strength and worked to empower international norms and institutions in an effort to constrain Soviet behavior and to shape the international environment. The apparent ascendance of Western values has rendered ideological competition with the Soviet bloc a distant memory. With this "victory" in hand, it is easier to downplay the utility of international law and to instead stress the constraints it imposes on the United States. The Cold War's end may foster the belief that the United States no longer needs allies to confront security challenges effectively, emboldening those who prefer that the United States pursue unilateral military solutions to security challenges. Despite apparent support in Congress for this hegemonic approach, it is an increasingly difficult and doubtfully effective long-term security strategy. It risks undermining the larger normative framework, however imperfect, that regulates state behavior and enhances global security.

The United States is grappling with competing routes toward realizing national security. The Clinton administration, buffeted by conflicting approaches and their attendant politics, has been equivocal about America's course. Its stance with respect to the ICC is one manifestation of the tension between enhancing an international normative framework and preventing encroachment on a nation's unfettered right to use force.

It is virtually certain that the ICC will become a reality during the first decade of this century. During the 1998 negotiations in Rome, U.S. officials had registered a panoply of objections to the Court even as they assiduously shaped virtually every element of its governing Statute. After the Statute's overwhelming approval in 1998, the United States more clearly prioritized its concerns in order to influence the subsequent Preparatory Commission (PrepCom). The PrepCom process shapes not only the Court's rules and procedures, but also more importantly, the substantive law that will serve as the basis for the Court's jurisdiction in the elements of crimes. U.S. officials continued to pursue jurisdictional accommodations intended to address the administration's core concern that the ICC might indict and try a U.S. citizen. Obviously, the United States did not take issue with the Court's central purpose of punishing egregious human rights abuses. The United States previously had fought to create international tribunals to hold individuals accountable for massive crimes in former Yugoslavia and Rwanda.

Concern about Americans being tried by the ICC flowed from an underlying fear that the Court could become politicized, used by hostile states as a vehicle for challenging U.S. foreign policy. U.S. negotiators sought an exception for the prosecution of Americans. However, plainly demanding an exemption for Americans was not politically feasible. Thus, the United States promoted various proposals to allow the Permanent Members of the U.N. Security Council or, in other proposals, all states to protect their nationals from the ICC's reach.

U.S. leaders imply that because the United States is exceptional in international affairs today—assuming a unique responsibility for promoting international security—it deserves some exemption from rules applied to other states. This assumption of exceptionalism colors U.S. attitudes toward multilateral institutions generally—even those such as the U.N. Security Council, which grants special rights to more powerful states. The ICC vexes the United States because all individuals (and, by extension, states) stand before it as equals.

Under the principle of "complementarity" embodied in its Statute, the Court must defer to state sovereignty, acting only when states have failed to administer justice. ICC jurisdiction extends only to the most heinous international crimes, and various procedural safeguards protect state prerogatives. Because the United States has a functional judicial system, the ICC would investigate the actions of Americans only if the United States were unwilling to investigate or to prosecute a case. But the determination of whether a state has "genuinely" investigated or prosecuted an alleged offense ultimately rests with the ICC judges. Therefore, states take a significant step in accepting the ICC's right to judge actions or motivations regarding national prosecutions. In joining the Court, they agree to be bound by a process with defined rules but no guarantees. They accept this degree of risk in order to advance a larger goal of ending impunity for the worst international criminals. For current U.S. leaders, at least at this writing, it is a step too far.

This volume aims to help Americans evaluate their government's decision to refrain from joining the ICC. The chapters provide historical context for evaluating the Court, both as an evolution of international law and as an example of the changing manner in which international norms and institutions are being created. Contributors offer insights into why the Court assumed its current contours and explain the Court's proposed workings. They explore some prospective dilemmas, considering the Court's role in relation to national efforts to provide justice in times of transition. Finally, the volume examines U.S. objections to the Statute finalized in Rome, exploring in greater detail the constitutional, military justice, and operational military concerns related to the ICC.

The volume focuses on the ICC's relationship to U.S. national security. The definition of national security interests obviously shapes perceptions of the Court. This work suggests the need to view national security broadly, not in narrow military terms. National security interests of the United States fundamentally concern the creation of a peaceful, liberal democratic, and economically integrated international system that allows America to flourish. Military strength, and the role of force in regulating this system, is critical. But the economic, legal, and political elements and tools are equally important. Objectives such as halting the proliferation of weapons of mass destruction or preserving access to oil cannot be promoted by military might alone. Nonmilitary means, as well as the support of other states and institutions, are critical for an effective response. The United States must play a leading role in galvanizing other nations and organizations and coordinating a variety of tools to shape the international environment. Maintaining a broad and integrated view of security objectives and sustaining U.S. authority to lead will be key components of U.S. security in the twenty-first century.

Seen from this perspective, the ICC is important for two reasons: first, it provides an alternative means of advancing a consistent goal of post–World War II American foreign policy—upholding norms regarding egregious violations of human rights in order to improve security for individuals and among states. The ICC underscores the importance of international law and offers substantial hope of extending its reach. As such, it is another tool that can be used to promote the behaviors and international system that best suit the United States.

The ICC also is linked to U.S. national security in its effect on the legitimacy of U.S. leadership. Sustaining legitimacy can be viewed as part of Joseph Nye's "soft power" construct, and as a matter of intuition: a state that relies on the power of its political ideals can only stray so far from those ideals without losing the ability to inspire confidence internally and internationally. To the majority of the world's nations, including many of the closest allies of the United States, the ICC represents an acid test of U.S. commitment to justice and human rights and of its willingness to be bound by the rules it establishes for others. The reluctance of the United States to back the Court thereby undermines its ability to strengthen norms and to sustain the international relationships that are critical for its future security and prosperity.

INTERNATIONAL JUSTICE

To many legal scholars, the ICC represents the logical evolution of efforts to define and to enforce international justice. In chapter 2 of this volume, Leila Sadat argues that the ICC's emergence from the "shadowland" of normative construct is surprising nonetheless. The chapter details why the Court is both an obvious progression toward enforcement of existing norms and the result of a unique confluence of political events.

Laws governing interstate conflict began to emerge at the turn of the nineteenth century and gradually embraced a host of prohibitions (both customary and treaty-based) that came to be known as international humanitarian law. Although states pledged themselves to regulate the means of conflict, they notably refrained from providing enforcement mechanisms at the international level. Enforcement of humanitarian law in war primarily was ignored and residually was left to the victorious. Competing interests often could be relied on to divert states from pursuing charges of criminal action in the context of war. Even when dispensed with an aim of establishing legitimacy, as at Nuremberg, victor's justice raised concerns about motivations and fairness.

Nuremberg, Sadat explains, affirmed the primacy of international law and the notion that individuals should be held accountable for their crimes. It thereby reinvigorated efforts to define and to promote an international mechanism to accomplish this objective. Sadat details the post–World War II conceptual and legal variation in proposals for a court and the accompanying bureaucratic maneuvering in international forums. The lack of progress demonstrated that Nuremberg had not fundamentally altered states' attitudes; they viewed an international court as an infringement of their sovereignty.

Meanwhile, those who committed mass crimes in Cambodia, Uganda, and elsewhere made a mockery of the pledge "never again." It was not until the Cold War ended that the U.N. Security Council decided to respond to genocide and mass atrocities through the creation of ad hoc tribunals. The Yugoslav and the Rwanda tribunals provided a tangible model for the ICC and suggested that states had come to recognize the need for an international court. They helped propel the efforts of the International Legal Commission, that had been stalled for decades, toward a formal treaty. The U.N.-sponsored process culminated in Rome with the adoption of a Statute creating the ICC.

Richard Goldstone and Gary Bass believe that the ICC may reveal a nascent consensus that deference to state sovereignty can no longer override attention to gross violations of human rights. In chapter 3 on the ad hoc international criminal tribunals (ICTs) for the former Yugoslavia and Rwanda, they contend that the tribunals' demonstrable fairness should mitigate fears about an overreaching ICC. Rules of precedent and procedure bounded ICT actions almost to a fault, they argue, but proved that an international tribunal could execute "ordinary law in extraordinary circumstances." Yet the tribunals were hobbled by the challenge of starting from scratch after a crisis erupted. A standing ICC should have significant advantages, being able to respond more swiftly and effectively to charges of criminal actions. Goldstone and Bass believe the ICC will, like the tribunals, make a significant contribution simply by compiling a definitive historical account of criminal actions. Truthtelling can mitigate forgetting and the creation of historical fiction, they argue, thereby helping to prevent recurring violence that undermines both internal and international stability.

Goldstone and Bass highlight a central dilemma facing the new Court. The moral strength of an international institution can also be a practical weakness when it comes to enforcement of the Court's will. Tribunals of the victorious may be partial, but they are powerful. The ICC may purchase its impartiality at the cost of impotence.

The ICTs illustrate this point by occupying a middle ground between Nuremberg and the ICC. Many viewed the ICTs as politically biased institutions because of their origins in the U.N. Security Council, where they obtained expansive mandates and the nominal support of the world's leading powers. The breadth of their legal mandate was supported by substantial force on the ground. Sixty thousand forces of the North Atlantic Treaty Organization (NATO) occupied Bosnia; the new Rwandan government leaders had defeated the genocidaires. Yet even under such auspicious conditions, the ICTs had difficulties carrying out their work. NATO has been reluctant to arrest major indicted criminals in Bosnia. Neither tribunal has had meaningful recourse when states chose to withhold evidence or suspects. It is almost certain that some of the criminals indicted by the International Criminal Tribunal for the Former Yugoslavia (ICTY) will never face a tribunal.

The ICC will have no direct means of enforcing its will. It will be strongest when authorized by the U.N. Security Council, which retains the authority to compel state action under Chapter VII of the United Nations Charter. But the ICC often may act without the Security Council's formal support. Obligations to cooperate with the ICC are imposed only on signatories. However, the ultimate threat against recalcitrant states will be referral of the matter to other states (back to the United Nations or to the Assembly of States Parties), with unspecified (and unlikely) consequences. Enforcement remains the Court's Achilles' heel; the ICC ultimately must rely on state power. Accordingly, the United States has both less to fear and more to offer the Court than if the Court possessed an independent source of power. Skepticism of the United States toward the Court not only undermines the U.S. claim to moral authority, but also appears to increase the like-lihood that justice will be divorced from power.

Even in instances where leading states support it, the ICC's quest for justice may confront the competing interest of peace. Some contend that even a weak Court could undermine efforts to promote peace, particularly if the ICC were to act independently of the U.N. Security Council, which is charged with ensuring international peace and security. Negotiations with criminals are sometimes nec-essary to end conflict; there are many cases in which peace and justice will be at odds. But recent events in Kosovo suggest that the pursuit of justice is not always antithetical to a settlement of conflict. When the ICTY indicted Serbian leader Slobodan Milosevic, some, including American officials, feared that the Tribunal's actions would make it more difficult to end the NATO air campaign. Instead, the ICTY appears to have increased the pressure on Milosevic, possibly hastening his capitulation to NATO forces. In that case, pursuit of justice may have comple-mented efforts to settle the conflict. Nonetheless, NATO valued making a deal with Milosevic more than it did apprehending the indicted Serb leader—so much that NATO appeared to be ignoring the tribunal that it had created. Justice took second place.

In chapter 11 Michael Scharf argues that sometimes it will be appropriate for an ICC to forgo prosecutions in order to allow nations to achieve peace. This chapter focuses on the ICC's proper relationship to national amnesties, which are so often critical for resolving a civil conflict. The ICC Statute is ambiguous on the issue of the Court's ability to defer to amnesties in deciding whether to pros-ecute alleged criminals. Scharf concludes that the ICC can and should do so un-der certain circumstances.

The underlying international agreements or customary law regarding crimes covered in the ICC Statute allow states to prosecute specified crimes but require national prosecution in only two cases: genocide and the most serious war crimes (the grave breaches of the Geneva Convention). Scharf argues that the ICC should respect those obligations to prosecute and should not respect national amnesties that cover such crimes. But in other cases, Scharf urges the ICC to consider both the character of the amnesty and its contribution to peace when contemplating whether to forgo prosecutions. The recent transitions in Haiti and South Africa, he argues, offer examples of amnesties that an ICC should respect. Neither am-nesty involved crimes for which prosecution was required under international law; both amnesties averted almost certain military conflict and were linked to alter-native mechanisms for providing accountability and redress. Scharf argues that when possible under international law, the ICC should defer to amnesties that contribute significantly toward peace and promote accountability for criminal actions.

In chapter 12, Madeline Morris also considers how an ICC will affect the pur-suit of justice by national governments. Morris believes that the principle of complementarity (that the ICC should complement, not replace, national judicial efforts) begs important policy questions regarding the type of person and crime with which the ICC should be concerned. Morris fears that in making decisions about ICC strategy, the Prosecutor will be most responsive to the majority of States Parties—at the expense of the victim populations or of the state most directly affected by the crimes at issue.

Specifically, an ICC seems likely to prosecute only a limited number of leaders in the context of the commission of mass crimes. This will trouble the affected state and victims, who will prefer prosecution of a larger number and a wider cross section of human rights violators. A state that decides to conduct its own prosecutions simultaneously with those of the ICC may be undermined if the ICC claims the right to prosecute the key "big fish," Morris warns. Deprived of the chance to administer justice to the worst violators, the national government could lose legitimacy and could face difficulty in implementing plea bargaining arrangements.

Simultaneous national and international proceedings will be rare because the Court will act only when a national judicial system is unwilling or unable to do so. Assuming state willingness, the Court must find that a total or substantial collapse or the unavailability of a national judicial system renders the government unable to obtain the accused or the necessary evidence or otherwise carry out its proceedings. A state with a collapsed justice system that proceeds to prosecutions creates a different set of problems. If it is simply the case that the state cannot obtain physical custody of the accused, then the ICC or another state might have more success. In such cases, some attempt to ensure justice probably is better than none.

The ICC, whether it acts alone or alongside national courts, can provide a model for the deliberate and fair administration of justice. The ICC may not satisfy popular passions or political agendas; but by conducting transparent proceedings that provide due process, the ICC may mitigate the desire for revenge arising from perceptions of a victor's tainted judgment.

The ICC faces a host of uncertainties regarding its ability to enforce justice, to weigh the interests of justice against those of peace, and to define the interests that justice will serve. How the Court addresses these issues will have a significant impact on international security. Yet these are not the major issues of U.S. concern.

U.S. CONCERNS ABOUT THE COURT

Administration Views

David Scheffer, ambassador-at-large for war crimes, summarizes the Clinton administration's position toward the ICC in chapter 6. Scheffer lauds the ICC as an effort to promote important U.S. values and stresses a continuing desire by the United States to achieve an effective Court. But he warns that, as currently conceived, the Court may fall short of its potential because it lacks U.S. support.

Scheffer argues that the Court may deter states from acting to protect international peace and security because states may fear that well-intentioned interventions that yield unintended consequences such as civilian casualties could result in prosecution. Valid actions to enforce international law should not be subject to investigation by an ICC, nor should states feel compelled to investigate what they regard as legitimate uses of force. The credibility of the Court, he notes, will rest on its relations with states and its support of international peace and security.

Concern about the Court's implications for U.S. military and political power is implicit, but Scheffer places explicit objections in legal framework. He criticizes the ICC's claim to be able to act without a U.N. Security Council referral to assert jurisdiction over nonparty nationals. He also highlights concerns relating to signatories' abilities to "opt out" of war crimes prosecutions for seven years when nonsignatories cannot, as well as the process for amending ICC jurisdiction to become binding on all states. In Scheffer's view, the Court's concept of jurisdiction may be ineffective and he stresses that it risks dividing states on the already challenging issue of international justice.

The Statute

To understand the administration's reservations about the ICC, one must dive into the details of the Rome Statute.[2] In chapter 4, Bartram Brown guides the reader through the Statute's intricacies, highlights its key provisions, and outlines the significant challenges that lie ahead for the Court. Even as he calls the ICC the last great international organization of the twentieth century, Brown considers the Court unremarkable in its codification of international law and national practice. He describes a Court with relatively narrow jurisdiction and generally accepted procedures, one intended to act only to the extent necessary to prevent impunity.

The ICC's definitions of crimes—genocide, war crimes, and crimes against humanity—generally are narrower than those embodied in international law. The only other crime the Statute specifies is aggression, but the Court cannot assume jurisdiction over this crime until two-thirds of the Parties to the Treaty agree on a definition, which seems unlikely to occur in the foreseeable future.

The Statute provides extensive guidelines for selecting judges and prosecutors, establishes some internal checks and balances, and stipulates a mix of common law and civil law approaches to judicial proceedings. Brown explains how complementarity would work, detailing the series of steps and rulings that would have to occur in order for the Court to prosecute an American—the central and consistent U.S. objection during the Rome Treaty Conference.[3] Understanding this process is important in order to evaluate U.S. concerns about the ICC.

Any criminal allegation would have to involve a core crime under ICC jurisdiction. A genocide charge against an American acting in an official capacity (e.g., a member of the armed forces) seems impossible, given the definition of the crime.[4] Americans would more conceivably be charged with war crimes or crimes against humanity. The Court is to consider crimes against humanity when they form part of a known widespread or systematic attack against civilians, and war crimes "in particular" when they are committed as part of a plan or policy or a large-scale commission of such crimes. These thresholds are made stronger by linkage to the contextual requirements in the elements of crimes. Attacking a legitimate military target, even if the bombing resulted in civilian casualties, would not pass these tests.

Assuming that an allegation against an American met the substantive thresholds just described, a state could refer the case to the Court, or the Prosecutor could initiate an investigation (with the approval of the Pre-Trial Chamber). If an American were involved, the United States presumably would block the third route to the Court, a U.N. Security Council referral.[5] As a prerequisite to proceedings under the first two routes, ICC jurisdiction would have to be accepted either by the United States (again, unimaginable) or by the state in which the crime allegedly was committed. A state can accept ICC jurisdiction by being a Party to the Treaty or by accepting the Court's jurisdiction with respect to a specific situation. The ICC Prosecutor would then be required to notify the United States of the investigation's commencement. The United States would have a month in which to inform the Prosecutor of any U.S. investigation of the case. The Prosecutor would be required to defer to any U.S. investigation—and to respect a U.S. decision not to proceed to prosecution—unless a Pre-Trial Chamber nonetheless authorized the investigation.

This is the procedural nub of U.S. concerns, for without this ICC review of national action, any state automatically could remove its nationals from potential prosecution by asserting complementarity. A Pre-Trial Chamber's decision to overrule a U.S. claim to handle a case is the only circumstance in which an American could come before the Court over U.S. objections. For this to occur, a majority of Judges would have to determine that the United States "is unwilling or unable genuinely to carry out the investigation or prosecution." Because the literal ability of the United States to administer justice is unquestioned, the ICC's judgment would hinge on "willingness." The terms are further defined in the Statute: unwillingness can be found only where the proceedings or decisions not to prosecute were intended to shield the person from criminal responsibility, where there has been an unjustified delay inconsistent with an intent to bring the suspect to justice, or where the proceedings were not independent or impartial and were conducted in a manner inconsistent with an intent to bring the suspect to justice.

In other words, the United States would have to be so biased that it could not evaluate the question of international crime, had no intention of investigating the claim, or was investigating only to protect an individual. The seriousness with which the modern U.S. military justice system treats international humanitarian law makes this a virtual impossibility in the case of a military investigation. Moreover, actions—official or unofficial—of a U.S. citizen that approached the gravity of an international crime would be addressed within the U.S. judicial system. If the ICC were to bring to light previously unknown or unacknowledged crimes committed by Americans, such as those alleged at No Gun Ri during the Korean War, so much the better for ensuring national judicial attention. It is difficult to envision ICC Judges, who will be eminent international legal figures, concluding that the United States was unwilling to investigate in good faith allegations of egregious international criminal violations.

Yet such a scenario in theory is possible under the Rome Statute. If it were to occur, the United States could ask the U.N. Security Council to suspend the ICC investigation, but that decision would rest with other Security Council members. Therefore even if the United States investigated an alleged crime and decided that there was no cause for prosecution, the ICC nonetheless could assert jurisdiction over the case. U.S. officials assume that only a "politicized" Court intent on undermining U.S. foreign policy could reach such a decision. But these officials are unwilling to believe that the Court could never become so politicized. This is why, despite the many procedural and substantive hurdles to ICC prosecution, the United States has sought an ironclad guarantee that it can shield Americans from the ICC. The pursuit of such a guarantee seemed, to most other nations, contrary to the Court's central purpose: to hold all individuals accountable for massive international crimes.

The Rome Conference

America's approach toward the ICC is the focus of Lawrence Weschler's vivid journalistic account of the Rome Conference. In chapter 5, he reports that the U.S. delegation's thoughts and positions at Rome revolved around two major recurring themes: The first was the conception of "unique" political vulnerabilities that accompany the military role of the United States in ensuring international stability. The second theme was constant skepticism about the integrity of the proposed institution, the purposes of its mandate, and the ultimate intentions of its staff. Weschler believes that independent prosecutor Kenneth Starr cast a long shadow over U.S. conceptions of the ICC, fueling fears that an independent court would acquire its own political agenda contrary to U.S. interests.

Weschler's narrative reveals the extent to which the U.S. stance mystified and frustrated other national delegations. Many believed they had made sufficient changes in the Statute to accommodate U.S. demands and worried that their effort to woo the United States aboard risked compromising the integrity of the Court.

Other leading powers, like Germany and the United Kingdom, shared many U.S. concerns about perceived limits on their national power. Yet during the negotiations, they became satisfied with the trade-offs inherent in joining the Court (including, in the case of France, the need to amend its Constitution). Some political nemeses shared common concerns with the United States; Iran reportedly dreaded the prospect of its citizens facing an American ICC Judge. Weschler points out that the United States was exceptional not in its fears but in its demands.

He suggests that the Rome Conference, just like the U.S. Constitutional Convention, involved independent states loath to surrender sovereignty—for both well-intentioned and more suspect reasons. Providing intimate glimpses of key actors' motivations and objectives, Weschler details how substantive provisions were defined, refined, horsetraded, and ultimately jury-rigged into a Statute. This history makes it easier to understand specific elements of the Court, and it illuminates the political and psychological dynamics that ultimately cemented the Treaty.

Weschler suggests that President Clinton's "Whitmanesque" desire to encompass apparent contradictions helps explain why the United States worked so hard to shape, and then ultimately stood apart from, the ICC.

The Genocide Convention

In chapter 10, Samantha Power reminds readers that this chasm between U.S. rhetoric and deeds is not unique to the ICC. America's policy toward the Genocide Convention adumbrated U.S. views of the ICC, and Power argues that Americans are reluctant to endure risks to prevent genocide in distant lands. The United States was a driving force behind the 1948 Genocide Convention but waited forty years to ratify it, attaching conditions that transformed the ban into a symbolic condemnation of genocide. Power describes the reasons for the gap between signature and ratification, between a committed executive and a hostile Congress.

Early on, opponents of the Genocide Convention feared that it would be used to charge U.S. segregationists with genocide. Although the racial implications of genocide faded decades ago, senators came to fear that the genocide label could be applied to U.S. foreign policy. ICC opponents share the concern that legal terms—however straightforward or unobjectionable—can be reinterpreted and misapplied. Accordingly, there is great reluctance to submit the United States or its citizens to rules that would be interpreted by outsiders.

U.S. senators considering the Genocide Convention also evinced a fundamental suspicion of the capabilities and intentions of fellow states and international institutions. ICC skeptics voice a parallel concern, evoking images of hostile judges and prosecutors who would stand behind the Court's curtain like a manipulative Wizard of Oz. Power reminds us that it is virtually impossible to create new institutions or to achieve important goals with this set of assumptions.

Joining world efforts to regulate international justice (as distinguished from, say, trade) seems to pose a particular problem for U.S. policymakers. The United States has independent power to respond directly to tyrants and human rights abusers, and its officials therefore focus on the inherent risks—however small— of empowering institutions that could apply justice equally to all. Power argues that U.S. policymakers underestimate the importance of ending impunity for international criminals because the benefits are less tangible than the concrete costs suggested by the specter of an unjustly accused American sitting before the ICC. Power argues that the average American would accept the small risk of being judged by an ICC in exchange for a Court that could help rid the world of its worst human rights violators.

The Constitution

In the U.S. debate about the ICC, words such as *sovereignty* and *constitutionality* often are used as trump cards. But these words can obfuscate the underlying questions at issue. The constitutionality of the ICC has been flatly denied by many of the senators who would be asked to ratify the Treaty. But under the Clinton administration, one that is skeptical of the ICC, the Department of Justice has concluded that the Court is consistent with the U.S. Constitution. Clearly, something lies beneath the surface of these competing constitutional assertions, and that something may be the difference between a legal analysis of the Constitution and a political judgment about what feels constitutional to citizens. Although it might be tempting to dismiss the political concerns, the Senate—where many of these views will be strongest—plays an honored role in interpreting constitutional matters. Moreover, the Constitution's centrality in American political thought makes it essential to explore the ICC's relationship to the Constitution fully.

This is Ruth Wedgwood's mission in this volume. In chapter 7, she concludes that there is no forbidding constitutional obstacle to U.S. participation in the ICC Treaty. Although the practice may not be commonly understood, U.S. governments have long used treaty power to participate in international tribunals that affect the lives and the property of Americans. In addressing the question of the ICC Statute's compatibility with the Constitution, Wedgwood's analysis illuminates the underlying concerns of many Court skeptics.

The ICC's procedural protections closely follow the safeguards of the U.S. Bill of Rights. Wedgwood nonetheless identifies constitutional issues that may deserve clarification beyond that provided in the Statute. These include ensuring proper standards of confinement (prison conditions), clarifying the Statute's protections regarding double jeopardy, and further tightening complementarity, particularly with regard to conduct occurring within the United States. Some clarification will be provided in the Preparatory Commission as it refines the rules of evidence and procedure and defines the elements of crime; other issues may be clarified only by the Court's practice. Wedgwood suggests that remaining U.S. concerns could be addressed through various means: "understandings" on signature or ratification of the Treaty; conditions to any cooperation agreement with the Court; or conditions of transfer of an individual (should this even ever be at issue). In the context of any ICC Treaty ratification process, Wedgwood calls for recognizing Congress's leading role in addressing questions of substantive criminal law: before depositing an instrument of ratification, the president should ask both the House of Representatives and the Senate to approve the definitions of ICC crimes and elements of the offenses.

However important they may be, these issues do not motivate most critics of the ICC, who focus on the absence of a trial by jury and the very concept of Americans sitting before foreign judges. To such critics, these aspects of the Court simply do not feel constitutional. Wedgwood therefore establishes the proper point of comparison regarding these issues. For actions that occur abroad and otherwise would fall within foreign national jurisdiction, ICC proceedings should be compared with those of a foreign state, not a U.S. court. Americans abroad are subject to the jurisdiction of foreign courts; the Constitution does not travel with them. Americans now face the possibility of foreign prosecution for ICC-covered crimes. General Augusto Pinochet discovered this principle with some surprise. And his case may encourage similar prosecutions by other countries, including those more interested in challenging U.S. foreign policy than in upholding human rights. Depending on a nation's political motivation and legal system, foreign judicial proceedings may be far less hospitable to U.S. constitutional principles than proceedings of an ICC would be.

But Wedgwood points out that Americans need not be physically in the custody of another state for a foreign judicial system to apply to their actions. Extradition of American citizens for trial abroad has been common practice for two hundred years. The United States has chosen, by treaty, to delegate the trial of Americans to nations that do not provide American-style justice. Thus the ICC can be viewed as simply an alternative forum (significantly shaped by U.S. legal practice) to which the prosecution of Americans may be delegated.

An additional comparative basis for judging the ICC's constitutionality is the American military justice system. American servicemembers are subject to courts martial that employ procedures fundamentally different from those available in a civilian court. Some of the most cherished American rights (e.g., trial by jury) do not extend to active-duty members of the Armed Forces. Thus, while the constitutional objections voiced by several leading senators are understandable, they seem misplaced when placed in context.

The Clinton administration has paid relatively little attention to the question of the Court's constitutionality per se and has focused instead on the Court's possible jurisdiction over Americans. The Pentagon, the government agency that most values and benefits from international humanitarian law, also harbors the most vehement objections to the ICC because U.S. servicemembers are most exposed to foreign jurisdiction relating to the laws of war. In the military corridors, a key question is "Who speaks for Sergeant Jones?"

In chapter 8, Robinson Everett evaluates the ICC from the perspective of American servicemembers. He sees an edifying analogy in the U.S. creation of Status of Forces Agreements (SOFAs) to clarify legal jurisdiction over the U.S. military in foreign countries. Following World War II, U.S. officials were concerned about the legal status of forward-deployed American forces. The United States aimed to maximize the likelihood of due process for American servicemembers and to help prevent impunity for crimes committed against Americans. It therefore negotiated SOFAs within NATO, and subsequently with many countries, to divide and share jurisdiction over American forces with their "host" nations.

The NATO SOFA stipulates that sympathetic consideration be accorded requests by the United States to prosecute U.S. personnel for charges in areas of shared jurisdiction. Although the formula for shared jurisdiction allows for old-fashioned diplomacy to be applied in sorting out each case, it provides no guarantee that the U.S. request always will be accepted. SOFAs are not a perfect means of ensuring U.S. trial, but they now are widely regarded as far preferable to the alternative: no framework for recognizing the U.S. military justice system's relevance to alleged U.S. criminal activity overseas. As discussed earlier, Americans abroad are presumed to fall under the legal system of the host nation. Thus, even if imperfect, SOFAs establish those circumstances in which the U.S. judicial process has the primary responsibility, and they clarify other instances when the United States may request that it be accorded that responsibility. The United States proposed that language from SOFAs be used to change ICC jurisdiction, acceding jurisdiction to any nation that acknowledges as an "official act" the alleged criminal activity of a national. Everett's discussion suggests that the ICC's complementarity standard might be considered preferable to that embodied in SOFAs because the ICC is to defer to national jurisdiction in all cases. For the Clinton administration, that apparent certainty of complementarity must be weighed against the uncertainty associated with a new institution. After all, the actual practice of implementing SOFA procedures on jurisdiction has been established slowly, case by case, country by country.

Everett nonetheless recommends that the United States take all possible steps to create domestic legal authority to prosecute crimes that fall under ICC jurisdiction. He notes that the Uniform Code of Military Justice affords significant prosecutorial flexibility and that the War Crimes Act of 1996 is a step forward in expanding domestic jurisdiction over international crimes. He urges the United States to consider further ensuring that U.S. civil and military courts can try all crimes that fall within the ICC's jurisdiction.

This recommendation would have the added benefit of expanding U.S. legal options with regard to national prosecutions of international criminals. For example, when seeking to encourage the prosecution of Pol Pot for human rights abuses, U.S. officials struggled to identify U.S. and foreign laws that could hold him to account.

Everett also notes that the ICC might benefit Sergeant Jones in the event that he were apprehended during conflict. For both legal and political reasons, the ICC could be a welcome alternative to trial in a foreign country. Serbia's Milosevic was most obliging when three Americans were seized in Kosovo, but had the timing been different, so too might have been his calculation of interest. A rogue state that captured an American soldier or pilot might refuse to return him to the United States. Having the ICC as an option might provide a face-saving alternative to provoking a crisis and, given complementarity, also might be the most expeditious means to bring the American home. Alternatively, the United States might find suggesting that foreign criminal suspects be tried in an ICC more useful than engaging in protracted wrangling over the trial venue, as was true of the dispute with Libya over where to try the Libyan suspects implicated in the Pan Am bombing over Lockerbie, Scotland.

Although the Clinton administration repeatedly has expressed concern about the vulnerability of U.S. servicemembers to ICC prosecution, few observers believe that the action of a U.S. sergeant is the real issue. U.S. leaders worry that individuals—most likely military commanders or political leaders—could become a target of ICC challenge and a vehicle for critiquing U.S. leadership decisions about the use of force. As explained at the outset, the United States fundamentally fears that the Court could be used to undermine the legitimacy of U.S. military actions and, by extension, global leadership of the United States. This is not an academic point. Following the 1999 NATO bombing of Yugoslavia, private groups (e.g., Russian parliamentarians, North American law professors) asked the ICTY to investigate whether NATO pilots and commanders had committed war crimes. Although the ICTY staff compiled an internal assessment and submitted a raft of questions to the Pentagon, the Chief Prosecutor decided that there was ". . . no basis for opening an investigation into any of those allegations or into other incidents related to the NATO bombing."[6]

American Use of Force

Retired General William Nash, in chapter 9, addresses the potential impact of the ICC on U.S. use of force. As the preeminent military power acting on behalf of international security, the United States exposes its troops and its policy decisions to frequent—and, in particular, asymmetric—threats. Because the United States is so powerful, the ICC creates unique potential liabilities for Americans. The

United States may become a target of information warfare campaigns launched by weaker nations. Nash predicts that hostile states will bring trumped-up charges against the United States to the ICC. Possession of or policy toward the use of nuclear, chemical, or biological weapons will not fall under the Court's jurisdiction. But U.S. use of conventional military force could prompt allegations against Americans.

Were the ICC to take such charges seriously, the United States would be forced to justify or to explain its military policies in a legal context. Ambassador David Scheffer has condemned the prospect of states being forced to investigate the legality of military actions that they already regard as valid under international law. Nonetheless, if the ICC were formally to launch an investigation, the United States might well choose to investigate anyway, in order to trigger complementarity and to halt any ICC involvement in the matter. If the ICC frequently challenged U.S. military actions, Nash believes there could be impact at the strategic and the operational levels. Internal investigations routinely conducted to ward off an ICC would be demoralizing both for military personnel and for the public that supports them. Such actions ultimately could undermine the basis of domestic support for U.S. foreign policy. Constant investigations would be perceived as second-guessing of military decisions, which could undermine confidence in individual operational decisions—a particular strength of the U.S. armed forces. The argument is conjectural, but Nash lays it out.

The My Lai massacre in Vietnam demonstrated the legitimate need to hold Americans, like all other nationals, accountable for war crimes. Although many viewed the judicial outcome as unsatisfactory, the U.S. military justice system did investigate and prosecute. An ICC would have had no role in the case. Recently knowledge of apparent war crimes committed during the Korean War came to light. Fearing infiltrators in a crowd of refugees, American soldiers reportedly gunned down fleeing civilians. Had an ICC made these actions known, there is little doubt that the United States would have investigated the matter. The ICC thus would have enhanced the likelihood of appropriate national responses to possible international crimes committed by members of their military, which is precisely the Court's role.

Future debates regarding U.S. responsibility for war crimes are most likely to arise in cases akin to NATO's bombing of Yugoslavia. Several factors, including the objective of minimizing risks to coalition forces and confidence in precision weapons, shaped a strategy of bombing from high altitudes and targeting infrastructure. NATO consciously sought to avoid civilian casualties and was embarrassed by its tragic mistakes in specific cases. It is nonetheless a reality that bombing—even when conducted with great precision—predictably results in civilian casualties, particularly in urban areas. Many observers have criticized NATO's strategy, including target choice and use of weapons.[7] Yet Operation Allied Force was not a systematic attack against civilians nor was it part of a large-scale commission of war crimes. NATO's military campaign in Yugoslavia was intended to respect international humanitarian law. ICTY indictment of individuals involved in that campaign would have created a damaging precedent with regard to the interpretation of existing humanitarian law.[8]

Nash acknowledges the inherent difficulty of defining war crimes in the context of the ICC. U.S. negotiators addressed this problem by securing a provision that requires that the U.S.-drafted elements of crimes be applied with the ICC Statute. And even if it would theoretically remain possible for the ICC to focus on a case involving a hundred unintended deaths while ignoring a hundred thousand purposeful murders, complementarity remains the critical protection for any state concerned about the Court's ability to interpret or to apply law.

Therefore Nash warns against allowing overblown fears of the ICC to affect the conduct of U.S. military operations. Concerns about proportional uses of force might prompt the United States to become more cautious in its application of military power, risking the safety of U.S. military personnel. He implies that U.S. leaders should not overreact to fears that have yet to be realized, particularly when ICC action could be blocked by asserting national jurisdiction.

Some administration officials have argued that the simple existence of the ICC, regardless of its actions, could dampen U.S. participation in certain "nonvital" military operations (specifically peacekeeping and humanitarian efforts). Officials have implied that if forced to expose servicemembers to ICC jurisdiction, the United States might prefer to forgo that risk in interventions of marginal importance. Nash believes that those who oppose action will cite the Court as yet another reason but that it will be otherwise ignored.

Nash nonetheless wants to minimize the possibility of an irresponsible Court and therefore counsels that the United States should help shape the ICC. The Court requires more than political endorsement; it needs the resources, information, and implied muscle of leading powers. Most international institutions benefited from U.S. support that in turn strengthened U.S. influence within the organization. If the United States joined the ICC, it could help nominate, select, and dismiss ICC Judges and Prosecutors, better ensuring the competence of those who will carry out ICC responsibilities. Becoming a State Party also would allow the United States to participate in efforts to define the crime of aggression, or any potential new crime of ICC jurisdiction. And while the United States could not control the Assembly of States Parties, American influence certainly would be stronger if the U.S. supported the Court.

Nash sees little value in ignoring or isolating the Court—benign neglect by the United States would be unlikely to destroy the ICC, although it would render the Court less effective. Key congressional leaders have recommended that the United States adopt a policy of active opposition to the ICC, refusing to cooperate with the Court and penalizing other nations that join the ICC. Administration officials hinted that they would consider such an approach. But this would be counterproductive, costing the United States far more than it could gain—as illustrated by the administration's threats to withdraw U.S. forces from NATO countries that joined the ICC. As a practical matter, the ICC will exist and will seek to fulfill its mandate regardless of the U.S. position toward the Court.

Moreover, Michael Scharf contends that the ICC's reach will extend to Americans accused of committing relevant crimes abroad and therefore will affect U.S. policy, regardless of the U.S. posture toward the Court. By this logic, even an ICC critic should see value in the United States engaging, not abandoning, the Court.

Ambassador Scheffer stresses the U.S. concern about ICC jurisdiction over nonsignatories to the Statute in the absence of U.N. Security Council referral. It therefore may not be surprising that the administration has sought to reinterpret the reach of international law, asserting that the ICC cannot exercise jurisdiction over Americans if the United States is not a party to the Treaty. Scharf in chapter 13 argues that this position is inconsistent with historic precedent and contradicts the legal basis for other U.S. policies, such as those regarding the apprehension of terrorists. He concludes that the U.S. position on ICC jurisdiction both is unfounded and risks jeopardizing other U.S. objectives.

The U.S. claim to be excepted from the ICC bespeaks a larger arrogance, Nash believes, that is eroding the U.S. claim to international leadership and ultimately U.S. security. Effective U.S. leadership demands retaining the confidence and the cooperation of other states. Whether the issue is obtaining military base rights, recruiting an international military coalition, or passing a U.N. Security Council resolution, U.S. security is closely linked to the actions of other states. This will be increasingly true as the United States confronts emerging security threats that require collective and often nonmilitary responses. To retain legitimacy, U.S. leadership must be viewed as congruent with international interests, Nash argues. The United States therefore must recognize that it cannot always insist on its own way.

The U.S. position toward the ICC implies the opposite assumption; it is seen as a unilateral demand for exemption from international rules. The United States should soften this approach not simply because the Court will have some value in its own right, but also because U.S. support for the ICC enhances U.S. legitimacy as an international leader. The current U.S. position erodes U.S. credibility and so undermines the ability of the United States to lead. Nash argues that this trend will harm U.S. national security far more than an ICC could.

WEIGHING INTERESTS

The Court and the United States

This chapter's authors share some of the administration's concerns about the ICC, in that it is a yet untested proposition. The Court's structure raises important questions about how differences in state power should be reflected in future international institutions, including the proper role of the U.N. Security Council. In evaluating the Court's potential impact, we conclude that on balance it would be positive, recognizing that the calculation is crude and qualitative. A different evaluation cannot be ruled out as unreasonable, or inconsistent with the evidence, such as it is.

The Clinton administration has genuinely supported efforts to end impunity for gross abuses of human rights. Yet it has been so focused on the negative aspects of an ICC that it appears to have lost sight of the Court's value. Moreover, the United States appears blind to the significant costs of estrangement from the ICC. To be sure, "best case" effects of the ICC are indirect, longer-term, and at this moment, speculative. Yet the benefits of encouraging international justice seem more likely to be realized than the nightmare scenario of an overreaching ICC on which U.S. objections are based.

Although we doubt that the ICC will override state sovereignty by abandoning complementarity, it is legitimate for military and security experts to evaluate capability, not intent. Therefore, the United States may remain apprehensive until the ICC demonstrates its reasoning and intent over time. During that period, the Court's most negative effects on U.S. national security interests would likely be self-imposed. The United States could become more hesitant about peacekeeping or humanitarian operations. Operational planning could become more tentative, with resulting risks to members of the armed forces. American overreaction to possible ICC actions, resulting from worst-case analysis, could transform unlikely possibilities into predicted outcomes.

There is a further irony in the U.S. position. Ultimately, the United States is concerned that the ICC could become a forum for challenging U.S. foreign policy, using charges against Americans to undermine the legitimacy of U.S. power. Yet U.S. opposition to the Court, which includes apparent demands for preferential treatment under international law, currently damages U.S. foreign policy and undermines its legitimacy. The closest NATO allies of the United States, who are among the Court's strongest supporters, feel this most immediately.

American skeptics may remain unconvinced that prosecuting foreign mass murderers or war criminals is related to U.S. national security. They will argue that U.S. interests are unaffected by most mass atrocities occurring abroad and that when atrocities do matter, the United States will address them directly. Only in the most superficial sense is this true.

One does not have to believe Robert Kaplan's[9] prediction of a coming anarchy in order to recognize that the United States is affected in some measure by the dissolution of responsible government structures and the spread of violence worldwide. The effect can be multidimensional, affecting U.S. trade and investment, military security and access, or political objectives. Mass atrocities almost always have wider regional security repercussions, such as expanded armed conflict, massive refugee flows, and arms trafficking and organized criminal activity. Crises fueled by gross violations of international law will continue to occupy the attention of the United States. Furthermore, the lines between security interests and normative interests are blurring. When mass atrocities dominate the media, or when tyrants push too far, democratic societies may choose to stop them partly or purely for moral reasons. Some NATO leaders called the Kosovo operation a human rights intervention; U.S. government officials deemed it a matter of national interest. Future campaigns may not bother to dress up normative goals.

Looking at U.S. military operations during just the past decade, it is clear that stopping human rights abuses has been an integral part of both the impetus and the rationale for foreign military intervention. Even if one disputes the wisdom of the decisions, mass atrocities have had an undeniable effect on U.S. security policy.

In terms of the ICC's impact on U.S. security, there is a difference between the specific contributions of the Court and the systemic benefits of strengthening international norms and institutions to address a broader range of global challenges.

The ICC's specific contributions are hard to gauge because they are prospective and conjectural. Many supporters of the Court have oversold its potential impact. The ICC will not end human rights abuses nor will it bring about world peace. ICC practice will lag far behind its promise. But this also was true for the ad hoc tribunals, which the United States views as useful policy tools. As a standing institution, the ICC will be more professional, will respond more quickly, and will have wider legitimacy than the tribunals. The ICC therefore should be more effective in obtaining evidence, in gaining state cooperation, and ultimately in responding to international crises.

The ICC will prove a better alternative than doing nothing to punish criminal actions. In other cases, the ICC will substitute for more costly measures (some fear the Court will be used as an excuse not to take forceful action). Sometimes the ICC will complement and legitimize the use of force. It need not impinge on traditional methods of statecraft. Moreover, the United States must recognize that it cannot dismiss the ICC and then seek to create future ad hoc tribunals; U.N. members will not countenance creating additional courts that duplicate the function of the ICC. In the future, the options for prosecuting individuals responsible for mass atrocities will be either national courts or the ICC.

The ICC probably will prove unable to prosecute criminals who cling to power within states or who take refuge in states willing to provide protection. But even if the Court could reach criminals, its indictments would affect them. Indicted individuals would fear traveling abroad to shop, to seek medical treatment, to raise funds, or to otherwise enhance their personal and political standing. More importantly, the ICC's spotlight can isolate and discredit gross human rights violators, potentially undermining their local support and limiting their ability to cause further harm. These are modest benefits, but they are real.

Of course, the Court will prosecute and ultimately imprison some perpetrators of massive crimes who might otherwise enjoy impunity, and the ICC also may prompt national prosecutions where they might otherwise have been forgone. In helping establish the historical record and holding criminals accountable where states could not, the ICC may help end cycles of violence in particular conflicts. By reinforcing norms against the most egregious crimes, the ICC will have some deterrent value. And by helping to bridge the gap between promise and practice, the ICC strengthens norms of state and individual behavior that the United States has long supported, and it lends credence to the proposition that international laws matter, including laws that protect Americans overseas.

The Court and International Law

In chapter 14, the conclusion to this volume, Abram Chayes and Anne-Marie Slaughter argue that the U.S. posture toward the Court risks undermining international law. They begin by placing the ICC among a new breed of international institutions. Those created in the 1940s were state-centric and intergovernmental, with institutional arrangements that reflected the distribution of state power and focused on preventing state aggression. Newer international institutions like the World Trade Organization (WTO) focus on a different array of problems. They often are unwieldy, with a variety of participants at both the supranational, intergovernmental and nongovernmental level. Some are universal and legislative, rather than voluntary and contractual. They increasingly blur the line between domestic and international law.

The ICC, like the North American Free Trade Agreement (NAFTA) and the WTO, has a "mixed regime" in which individuals join state officials at the bar of international law. The ICC was shaped by the efforts of nongovernmental organizations, not just states. The Court's complementarity regime treats domestic jurisdiction as conditional on national comportment with certain standards. The ICC will expand the growing interrelationship between national and international courts. Of course the ICC itself is a hybrid of national judicial practice, which will in turn shape both national law and national legal proceedings. Witness Robinson Everett's suggestion that the U.S. broaden domestic criminal law to encompass the ICC's jurisdiction. Other nations currently are adopting the ICC's elements of crimes (replete with U.S. fingerprints) as their own. Chayes and Slaughter suggest that when viewed in the light of these emerging trends, the ICC is neither novel nor frightening.

The ICC cannot be judged only on the basis of its own strengths and weaknesses. It also must be placed in the larger context of a world shaped by law. U.S. foreign policy has consistently stressed the value of international law in creating a world more congruent with U.S. interests. International law today is no longer utopian rhetoric, Chayes and Slaughter argue, but rather "hardheaded realism." Efforts to regulate and fuel the global economy, to protect the environment, to manage weapons proliferation, and to defend against terrorism all rely on an international legal framework. Throughout past decades, the United States has played a leading role in strengthening international law in order to protect U.S. interests.

Every new international legal instrument or institution has entailed obligations and required concessions of some form. The price of the accommodation has been outweighed by the benefits of both the specific institution and the expansion of a legal framework hospitable to U.S. interests and values. An essential element of that legal framework is the idea of *equality under the law*. Seeking an exemption from that principle strikes a heavy blow against the international rule of law.

Furthermore, if it decides not to join the Court, the United States will lose an opportunity to shape the way future international institutions and laws address emerging legal issues, such as balancing state power and equal treatment, addressing nonstate actors, and managing intertwined international and domestic processes. Chayes and Slaughter conclude that opting out of the Court will have a negative impact on U.S. national interests far beyond the work of prosecuting war crimes.

The Larger Security Picture

The two most important national goals of the United States, peace and prosperity, are best served by an international order increasingly based on the rule of law, and the present moment provides a great opportunity to move the world in that direction. In the economic realm, the world is already far along the path of cooperative rather than competitive solutions to problems of clashing interests. In the area of trade, dispute resolution has been formalized in an international institution, the World Trade Organization, of nearly universal membership. It issues decisions that are binding on states. Its rulings have significant economic, and often political, impact. It seems ironic, in light of the current U.S. stance toward the ICC, that the United States led the way in creating a supranational WTO. In international finance, a variety of informal processes are at work in which the United States has played a dominant role. Their limitations and particularly the questions of legitimacy and equity that their workings have raised are creating pressures for a greater degree of institutionalization, transparency, and perhaps formalization of the processes in this realm.

Wherever one looks at the long-run evolution of international relations—in security, in other political problems, in trade and finance—the increasing limitations of unilateral national actions are apparent. There is a growing need for a framework for cooperative action, a framework that calls for institutionalization and legitimization such as only agreed systems of rules can provide.

At this time, the United States is the richest and by far the most militarily powerful country in the world. It is also in many ways the most admired, despite the considerable envy and hostility its wealth and power arouse. There are now no external threats to U.S. security of the traditional kind—nations or coalitions of roughly equal military and economic power, with strong interests that clash with those of the United States and that are likely to lead to war; nor are any in prospect for the next fifteen to twenty years. The European Union is the only coalition now existing with a high degree of integration, more people, roughly equal economic power, and the potential for creating comparable military power over a period of time. It shares both major interests and political culture with the United States, and its core countries are joined with it in NATO, a military alliance of fifty years.

The world's largest countries—India and China—are poor and a decade or two away from the capacity for achieving the level of military power that the United States and its allies now possess. Other large countries that could grow in economic and military power—Indonesia, Brazil, and Nigeria—are even farther behind in realizing their potential. The military power that Russia inherited from the much larger and more populous Soviet Union is now in decay, and the achievement of the economic and political strength to rebuild it is a distant prospect.

The United States today faces three types of major military threats. One is the possibility that rogue regimes—North Korea, Iraq, Libya—might engage in desperate military ventures against U.S. allies, perhaps with the hope that the United States would fail to respond because of internal political division. These seem highly unlikely and, in any event, would almost certainly lead to a devastating military response.

The second more likely threat is that of terrorism, in some cases sponsored by the rogue or other hostile states (or substate actors) and with the potential of involving nuclear, chemical, or biological weapons and correspondingly large American civilian casualties. The third threat feeds into the first two: the deterioration of controls on nuclear arsenals and the scientists who created them. The possibility that some small number of nuclear, chemical, or biological weapons might be transferred to either hostile countries or terrorists certainly exists—how remote or likely a possibility is very difficult to assess. So is the possibility of an accidental or unauthorized launch of nuclear weapons with more horrifying consequences.

The United States has ample military force to respond to threats of the first kind if deterrence somehow fails. Military force is of limited use in responding to the other threats.

However, the legitimacy of the dominant military role of the United States is in question. French concerns about an American "hyperpower" are not new; what is new is the wider resonance of the charge. Increasing international concern about the military role of the United States may become a major constraint on the ability of the United States to use force to defend its interests long before the United States is physically constrained by other nations' power. In this period of unchallenged military power, the United States should use its diplomacy and example to shape a world in which the United States can continue to be secure, regardless of whether it remains militarily dominant.

Moreover, military power, even if sustained, may well become less relevant. Emerging security threats, such as penetration of the U.S. information infrastructure, defy a traditional military response. A significant future challenge for the United States is the development of alternative domestic capabilities and international partnerships to confront these threats. This suggests another reason for the United States to look toward collective international action as a means to enhance national security.

In the longer term, the indirect costs of conflict abroad will increase. The prosperity of our own increasingly globalized economy is already heavily dependent on extensive peace. As more of what are now economically marginalized states are drawn increasingly into the world economy, the areas in which conflict is of little significance will diminish, and the wider extension of peace will be even more important.

Perhaps the United States simply has not yet felt the limits of unilateral military power. It seems to take its current monopoly of force for granted instead of viewing it as an unnatural state of affairs in international relations. The United States has taken such an absolutist approach to preserving its freedom to act that it can reject even proposed rules or institutions that largely reflect U.S. policy objectives.

CONCLUSION

In the twentieth century, the United States augmented its military might by building norms and organizations intended to shape international behavior to be congenial to U.S. interests. Relying too much on current military dominance and rejecting even minimal risks to create new legal institutions will undermine U.S. leadership and security in the longer run.

As a repository of certain values, the ICC will become an actor in its own right. Some nations will seek to use the ICC as a vehicle for advancing their own foreign policy. The states most affected by the emergence of a relatively independent institution will be those currently enjoying the widest latitude and influence in international politics. But after all, the NATO allies will be the leading powers behind the Court in its initial years. It is not accidental that European states are accustomed to acting collectively and are more comfortable with the trade-offs between preserving nominal sovereignty and strengthening institutions and rules that provide broader benefits. U.S. control of the ICC is unnecessary and is incompatible with the very purpose of the institution.

The ICC represents an international commitment to end impunity for the most egregious crimes, underscoring the rights and responsibilities of individuals in the modern age and thus has value in its own right. It has a larger value in reinforcing international norms and in reinvigorating a cooperative framework for solving security problems. The most compelling long-term interests of the United States lie in strengthening, not abandoning, this cooperative framework.

ORGANIZATION OF THIS VOLUME

Chapters 2 through 14 are structured into four parts. Part One explores the roots of the ICC, beginning with the history of the evolution of international humanitarian law and the efforts to create an international criminal court, and including the lessons of recent ad hoc international criminal tribunals. In addition to explaining the Court's structure and workings, the section includes background on the actors, issues, and processes at the Rome Conference that created the Court.

Part Two focuses on the Court's potential impact on the United States, examining key issues that frame the U.S. debate about the ICC. The section begins with a U.S. government view of the Court in relation to U.S. interests. It then evaluates the ICC from a constitutional perspective. It considers the potential impact of the Court on U.S. military servicemembers and U.S. use of force. Finally, it identifies parallels between the U.S. debate about the Genocide Convention and today's debate about the ICC.

Part Three, on the relationship of justice and peace, considers whether the ICC can and should defer to national amnesties and highlights possible tensions between international and national approaches to criminal prosecutions relating to a specific conflict.

Part Four considers issues pertaining to the scope and character of international law. It evaluates whether the ICC's jurisdiction can extend to states that are not a party to the Court's Treaty. Finally, it considers the Court in relation to emerging trends in international law.

This volume does not attempt to provide an authoritative history of the ICC. As discussed earlier, the reader can find the Statute's text and supporting documents elsewhere. It is also worth noting that several issues deserve greater attention than could be devoted to them in this volume. The role of nongovernmental organizations (NGOs), so critical in creating the ICC, are discussed in several chapters (Weschler, Chayes and Slaughter, Brown, and Sadat). But there certainly is scope for a more detailed analysis of the NGO role. Similarly, the relationship between the ICC and national efforts to prosecute international human rights abuses (in particular, the Pinochet case) undoubtedly will be the subject of future essays.

In exploring the Court's relationship to U.S. security interests, this volume does not purport to explain the political dynamics that have made it difficult to bring public attention to this issue and harder still to discuss it in a factual, dispassionate manner. Although Samantha Power's and Lawrence Weschler's chapters offer some insights into congressional and executive thinking, a deeper partisanship and greater disaffection with international affairs are at work. These trends are deeply disturbing, a largely unremarked challenge to the future of U.S. security. This volume can only hope to affect them indirectly by providing a thorough and considered discussion of the issues at stake for Americans in deciding whether the United States should join the ICC.

NOTES

1. Israel voted alongside the United States against the Statute during its finalization in Rome. However, the clarification of key provisions relating to crimes in occupied territories may open the way for Israel to join the Court. Such a decision would be particularly significant because Israel has significant security concerns and strong reasons to fear the politicization of an international criminal court. See Edith M. Lederer, "Compromise Reached on War Tribunal," *Associated Press*, December 18, 1999; available on Lexus Nexus wire service reports.

2. For a complete history and record of the Rome Statute, see M. Cherif Bassiouni, *The Statute of the International Criminal Court: A Documentary History* (Ardsley, N.Y.: Transnational, 1998).

3. For a schematic representation of this process, see Brown's chart in the appendix.

4. "The Statute requires that the relevant act of violence be committed with intent to destroy a national, ethnical [sic], racial or religious group; it is unimaginable that the U.S. government would sponsor such action."

5. It is conceivable that the United States could become involved in a situation over which the U.N. Security Council already had been given jurisdiction, in a process analagous to NATO's intervention in Kosovo, which then fell under the ICTY's jurisdiction.

6. Barbara Crossette, "U.N. War Crimes Prosecutor Declines to Investigate NATO," *New York Times,* 3 June, 2000, p. 4.

7. See, for example, "Civilian Deaths in the NATO Air Campaign," *Human Rights Watch* 12 (February 2000).

8. It is significant that the ICTY Chief Prosecutor concluded that ". . . there was no deliberate targeting of civilians or unlawful military targets by NATO during the bombing campaign." Crossette, "U.N. War Crimes Prosecutor Declines to Investigate," p. 4.

9. Robert D. Kaplan, "The Coming Anarchy," *Atlantic Monthly* 273 (February 1994): 44–76.

Part I

The Roots of the ICC

2

The Evolution of the ICC: From The Hague to Rome and Back Again

Leila Nadya Sadat

On August 24, 1898, Czar Nicholas II proposed to the diplomatic representatives accredited to the Court of St. Petersburg that their governments tackle the problems stemming from the arms buildup of recent years.[1] The result was a peace conference held in The Hague in 1899, involving twenty-six countries (of fifty-nine claiming independent sovereignty). Although the conference was unsuccessful with regard to general arms limitation, three conventions were adopted relating to the peaceful settlement of disputes,[2] the laws and customs of war on land, and maritime warfare.[3]

A second peace conference was held in 1907. Once again, the czar issued the invitation (although the United States actually proposed the meeting),[4] and the Netherlands acted as host. Forty-four countries sent delegates to The Hague this time, construction of the Peace Palace began, and the conference concluded with the adoption of thirteen conventions (three of which revised the 1899 conventions), including Convention (IV) Respecting the Laws and Customs of War on Land.

Almost one hundred years after The Hague conferences, representatives of 160 countries,[5] closely watched by more than 250 nongovernmental organizations (NGOs),[6] met in Rome to negotiate a treaty that would establish a permanent International Criminal Court (ICC). The delegates struggled to define, in a manner acceptable to all participating States, the parameters of an institution whose purpose was to respond to the atrocities that had occurred throughout the twentieth century. After five weeks of grueling negotiations, the Diplomatic Conference adopted a Statute for the Court in an emotional vote of 120 to 7, with 21 countries abstaining.[7] The United States, which had called for the vote, was among the countries voting "nay."[8]

Seen in historical context, the Rome Treaty was the natural destination of The Hague conferences, but the outcome was in no way inevitable. As the international legal regime matured, the need for laws prohibiting the use of force that went beyond civil liability became painfully obvious. The establishment of an international criminal justice system to prevent and to punish pathological breaches of the international peace was a logical next step, but conceptual, legal, and political obstacles to its adoption abounded.[9] Indeed, given the unsuccessful history of previous efforts to establish an international criminal court and the tepid support of many of the major powers during the Preparatory Committee meetings leading up to the Diplomatic Conference, the adoption of the Statute by the Diplomatic Conference came as a surprise. It can be credited, at least in part, to the tremendous lobbying and informational efforts of NGOs whose tireless campaign in support of the Court provided additional evidence of global civil society.[10] Another important factor was the emergence of a so-called "like-minded" group of states, which, although holding quite divergent national views on many issues, were united in their view that the Court's establishment was a priority.[11] European countries and other traditional U.S. allies were willing to rally behind the Court, even without U.S. participation.

More subtle factors were also at work. Proponents of the ICC throughout the twentieth century have possessed a certain utilitarian optimism and moral fervor. The journey from The Hague to Rome was guided by those who were able to see the outlines of what the Court might be and what the world, acting in its own self-interest, might require for its betterment, if not its very survival. As Richard Falk writes:

> If . . . the purpose of our endeavors is to create a better world . . . [w]e require . . . a special sort of creativity that blends thought and imagination without neglecting obstacles to change. We require, in effect, an understanding of those elements of structure that resist change, as well as a feel for the possibilities of innovation that lie within the shadowland cast backward by emergent potential structures of power. Only within this shadowland, if at all, is it possible to discern "openings" that contain significant potential for reform, including the possibility of exerting an impact on the character of the emergent political realities.[12]

The ICC has been in the "shadowland" (or perhaps in the gray mists on its borders) for the entire twentieth century. Indeed, the century is littered with never-used proposals for a permanent international criminal court. Only a coincidence of positive political events (such as the end of the Cold War[13]), strong and committed leadership of key individuals and states, and the strength of global civil society[14] made the ICC's emergence possible at this time. As the culmination of a century-long process, one can therefore think of the Rome Conference as a "Grotian moment"[15] in international law[16]—an opportunity to fulfill the normative potential of our time by establishing an ICC before the political winds change again.[17] This is perhaps why U.S. efforts in Rome to postpone the Statute's adoption were so poorly received. Proponents of the Court feared that if the opportunity to establish the Court were squandered, it would be lost for the foreseeable future.[18]

This essay traces the Court's evolution from The Hague to Rome, breaking the century-long journey into four phases: Conception, Emergence, Conflict, and Resolution. In each period, detailed plans for the Court's structure and operation were proposed. Most were discarded. With each new effort to draft a comprehensive statute for a permanent court, however, progress was achieved, albeit slowly. With the benefit of hindsight, we now realize how important each of these "failed" attempts was to the adoption of the Court's Statute. Whether the Court ultimately will be successful is not a judgment this essay claims to make. Indeed, although it is quite likely that the Court's record will, as a practical matter, be mixed, this should not obscure the fact that the ICC's establishment was a watershed event in international law—cause for celebration as well as reflection.

CONCEPTION: 1899–1945

The attempts to regulate warfare that emerged from the two Hague conferences were firmly linked to notions of state sovereignty prevalent at the time: first, that the ruler of a state exercises sole authority over the territory of that state; second, that all states are juridically equal; and third, that states are not subject to any law, other than their own, to which they do not consent.[19] Thus, Hague Convention IV contemplated that only the parties to the Treaty would be bound by the rules of war therein, and then only if "all the belligerents were parties."[20] In addition, the only remedy for breach was state responsibility for violations of the Conventions and a right to compensation inuring to the injured party, "if the case demands."[21] The Martens Clause provided that in cases not included in the Hague Regulations, "the inhabitants and the belligerents remain under the protection and the rule of the principles of the law of nations, as they result from the usages established among civilized peoples, from the laws of humanity, and the dictates of the public conscience."[22] This Clause appeared to concede that some law lay outside the four corners of the Treaty. Notwithstanding, no thought was given to criminal responsibility for those violating the Treaty's proscriptions.

By the end of World War I, when the "world lay breathless and ashamed"[23] by the devastation of a war characterized by bitter savagery and monstrous slaughter, the idea surfaced that some criminal liability might be imposed for acts of war beyond the pale. Over American objections, the Commission on the Responsibility of the Authors of the War and on the Enforcement of Penalties[24] proposed the formation of an international "high tribunal" for the trial of "all enemy persons alleged to have been guilty of offenses against the laws and customs of war and the laws of humanity."[25] After difficult negotiations, Articles 227, 228, and 229 of the Treaty of Versailles ultimately provided for a "special tribunal" that would try William II of Hohenzollern, the German emperor, for the "supreme offence against international morality and the sanctity of treaties."[26] The trial never occurred, however, for the Netherlands refused to extradite William II.[27] Indeed, the whole effort was generally considered a fiasco.

Following this attempt to establish an international criminal tribunal, proposals for the establishment of a permanent international criminal court issued from many quarters. None was ever officially considered.[28] During this phase of the ICC's history, three major obstacles arose. First, the question of sovereignty was omnipresent. An international court that could try and sentence individuals was simply incompatible with the conception that international law governed only the relations between States.

Second, critics pointed to the absence of positive law for violations of which potential defendants could be charged. Some argued that there could be no international criminal law because there was no international sovereign power, while others questioned whether an international criminal code would have to be adopted before an international criminal court could be established.[29]

Finally, not all agreed that an international criminal court could help to prevent war, the fundamental premise of the court's establishment. Of course, no one seriously suggested that the proposed court alone could prevent war. Rather, they hoped that the ICC's establishment would contribute to that goal. But some contended that the ICC would actually worsen international relations: "This Court would render a peace impossible. When the soldiers and sailors had finished fighting, when hostilities were over and the soldiers and sailors on both sides were ready to shake hands with one another, as they are today, the lawyers would begin a war of accusation and counter accusation and recrimination. Such a war would render a peace of reconciliation impossible."[30]

EMERGENCE: NUREMBERG

The atrocities of World War II rekindled interest in the establishment of an international criminal court. The model statutes proposed by jurists gave way to the pressure of political events, however, and the charters of the Nuremberg and Tokyo tribunals took their place. Although not the first international criminal trials in history,[31] the Nuremberg and Tokyo trials are the first major precedents of our time. Much less weight is generally accorded to the decision of the International Military Tribunal (IMT) for the Far East than to the IMT at Nuremberg for a variety of reasons, including the perception that the Tokyo proceedings were substantially unfair to many of the defendants. Therefore, Tokyo will not be discussed further here. Its example is primarily relevant in considering what a credible international criminal justice system ought not to look like.

Nuremberg, however, was a watershed event in the ICC's progression from the drawing board to concrete reality. As is well known, on winning the war, the victors decided to try the Axis leaders. The Allies had announced their intentions in the Declaration of St. James in 1942 and at Moscow in 1943, but the decision to hold a trial was not a foregone conclusion. It took a great deal of convincing, this time by the Americans of their British allies, to hold trials rather than to summarily execute the Nazi leaders.[32]

The IMT at Nuremberg was constituted by an international agreement[33] signed by the four Allied powers on August 8, 1945.[34] Known as the London Accord, the agreement stated the Allies' intention to try "war criminals whose offenses have no particular geographical location whether they be accused individually or in their capacity as members of organizations or groups or in both capacities."[35] Annexed to the London Accord was the Charter of the International Military Tribunal.[36] The thirteen short articles of the charter addressed the tribunal's composition, rules of procedure, and jurisdiction—they also defined, in summary fashion, the law to be applied.

In issuing its judgment after nine months of trial, the Tribunal addressed many of the defendants' objections to the Tribunal's jurisdiction and the law it was asked to apply.[37] First, in rejecting the defendants' arguments based on state sovereignty,[38] the Tribunal held that individuals, including heads of state and those individuals acting under orders, could be criminally responsible under international law.

Second, the Tribunal affirmed the primacy of international law over national law: "The very essence of the Charter is that individuals have international duties which transcend the national obligations of obedience imposed by the individual State."[39] Thus the Nuremberg judgment seemed to lay to rest, at least as a practical matter, the theory that the constitution of an international criminal tribunal contravenes the sovereignty of states per se.[40]

Third, by holding that individuals may be liable, not only for the means used in conducting a war but also for initiating the war itself, the IMT established the wrongfulness of aggression—at least in some cases. In this respect, war as well as offenses against the laws of war were criminalized—a quantum leap forward from the steps taken at The Hague half a century earlier.

The IMT Charter and Judgment are often criticized for being merely a (retroactive) droit ad hoc.[41] Indeed, as the defense argued before the IMT prior to the Charter's signature, in many cases no instrument specifically proscribed the defendants' conduct. Nonetheless, having embodied its judgment in a legal precedent, the Tribunal arguably created the positive law thought to be lacking prior to its existence. As Nuremberg chief prosecutor Robert Jackson noted (quoting Justice Benjamin Cardozo), the power of precedent is the power of the "beaten path."[42] Of course, that is not to say that the IMT's judgment is binding on either municipal or international courts. But, at the very least, if Nuremberg bequeathed a cloudy legal legacy, its moral force is clear. Freed from its original limitations, the

Nuremberg judgment has been understood to affirm the idea that war as a means of solving interstate conflict is morally, legally, and politically wrong.

CONFLICT: U.N. STRUGGLES FOLLOWING WORLD WAR II

Nuremberg helped overcome objections to an international criminal court on the basis of sovereignty. But several problems attend the creation and use of ad hoc tribunals, in spite of the flexibility they may offer states or the Security Council at the time.[43] Thus it is not surprising that the United Nations considered the establishment of a permanent international criminal court immediately after the war, in connection with the formulation and adoption of the Genocide Convention. But although the Genocide Convention was adopted relatively quickly, efforts to create the international criminal tribunal envisaged in Article VI of the Convention failed. Indeed, the reference to an international penal tribunal now found in Article VI of the Genocide Convention had been deleted from earlier drafts and was restored only after extensive debate.[44]

In a resolution accompanying the adoption of the Genocide Convention, the U.N. General Assembly invited the newly established International Law Commission (ILC) to "study the desirability and possibility of establishing an international judicial organ for the trial of persons charged with genocide or other crimes over which jurisdiction will be conferred upon that organ by international conventions."[45] It also requested that the Commission consider the possibility that this might be accomplished through the creation of a Criminal Chamber of the International Court of Justice.[46] Thus instructed, the International Law Commission embarked on what would prove to be a frustrating and long endeavor.

The ILC ultimately voted at its Second Session in 1950 to support the desirability and feasibility of creating an international criminal court. However, an examination of the summary records and reports on the topic shows that the Commission was deeply divided on this subject. Indeed, two separate reports were submitted to the Commission regarding the international criminal court, one supporting the court's establishment and a second rejecting it.[47] After heated debate, the ILC voted eight to one, with two abstentions, that it was *desirable* to establish an international penal judicial organ, and seven to three, with one abstention, that the establishment of an international criminal judicial organ was *possible*.[48]

Although the Commission ultimately adopted a Draft Code of Offenses Against the Peace and Security of Mankind in 1954,[49] the General Assembly removed the question of the court that might enforce such a code from the ILC and vested it in a committee composed of the representatives of seventeen Member States.[50] As was later pointed out, the General Assembly's action involved a reversal of roles that was curious, to say the least: it had asked a body of jurists a political question (whether the creation of the court was desirable) and had subsequently entrusted a political body with the technical task of elaborating a draft statute.[51.] The Committee on International Criminal Jurisdiction met in Geneva, Switzerland, during August 1951, by the end of which it had agreed to a draft statute (the Geneva draft) for an international criminal court.[52] It comprised many features that reappeared in the 1994 ILC draft statute and ultimately in the 1998 Rome Statute. First, the Committee believed it would be most satisfactory to establish the court as a United Nations organ. However, in light of the practical difficulties involved in amending the Charter and the legal difficulties of establishing the court by General Assembly Resolution, the Committee concluded that a multilateral convention would be the most appropriate mechanism for the court's creation.[53] This was the solution ultimately adopted at Rome. Although a multilateral convention was perhaps the only means to ensure the court's establishment, it placed the court and its operations outside the U.N. system, suggesting that political support for the court is in many ways quite weak. The Committee envisaged the Court as a "semi-permanent" institution that would hold sessions only when matters before it required consideration,[54] an idea that the ILC retained in subsequent incarnations of the court's statute, but that was ultimately discarded at Rome.

The court envisaged by the 1951 Committee would have heard cases against natural persons only, including heads of state or agents of government.[55] The question of the criminality of states thus disappeared permanently from the agenda. The court's subject-matter jurisdiction was limited to international crimes "provided in conventions or special agreements among States parties" to the statute. This seemed to exclude from the proposal many of the most serious international crimes, including aggression, although the opacity of the formula leaves the scope of the proposed court's jurisdiction quite unclear.[56] Finally, cases could proceed only if the state or states of the accused's nationality and the state or states in which the crime was alleged to have been committed expressly conferred jurisdiction upon the court.[57]

Very few governments commented on the proposed statute. The United Kingdom expressed the view that "the whole project [was] fundamentally unsound."[58] The French and the Dutch delegations were more optimistic, and the General Assembly requested the formation of another seventeen-member-state committee to reexamine several of the issues and to prepare another report.[59] The second Committee met in New York during the summer of 1953 and issued its report with an amended version of the statute annexed thereto.[60] The 1953 Committee modified the Geneva text in some respects, although not fundamentally.

The 1951 and 1953 Committee Reports were never implemented for lack of a political consensus on the desirability of creating an ICC. Instead, the idea stalled in the United Nations for the next thirty-five years. The General Assembly, which had postponed consideration of the Draft Code of Offenses until a definition of aggression could be adopted, took twenty years to complete its task, although the ILC produced several excellent reports on the topic.[61]

The Cold War rendered action on the Draft Code of Offenses and the ICC virtually impossible, although the Draft Code remained on the General Assembly's agenda. But with the gradual reopening of East–West relations, work on an international criminal court could resume,[62] and in 1989 the General Assembly specifically requested the ILC to address the question of establishing an international criminal court.[63]

The ILC provisionally adopted a Draft Code of Crimes in 1991[64] and, in its forty-fourth session in 1992, created a working group on an international criminal court. The Working Group produced an extensive report outlining the general bases on which, in its opinion, the establishment of the ICC could proceed.[65]

Not all the ILC's members were pleased with the relatively modest proposals made by the Working Group. But as the group's chair, Abdul Koroma, pointed out, the proposals represented a compromise between those who would have gone much further and those who felt that nothing should be done at all. With the exception of the Court's jurisdiction, which expanded in the 1994 Draft Statute, these proposals (which were themselves largely based on the work of the 1951 and 1953 committees) were substantially adopted in the 1994 Draft Statute issued by the ILC,[66] and many of them found their way into the Rome Statute as well.

RESOLUTION: THE ROAD TO ROME

Following the ILC's report, the U.N. General Assembly granted the ILC a mandate to elaborate a draft statute "as a matter of priority,"[67] although many countries (including the United States) did not support the Draft Code of Crimes.[68] The project gained momentum after the U.N. Security Council created the International Criminal Tribunal for the Former Yugoslavia (ICTY). The adoption of the ICTY's statute suggested not only that a permanent court was needed but also that governments, including the United States, would be willing to support its establishment, at least under some circumstances. The creation of the International Criminal Tribunal for Rwanda (ICTR) shortly thereafter underscored the need for the establishment of an international institution that could address serious violations of international humanitarian law. The problems that the two ad hoc tribunals faced in recruiting top-flight prosecutors and judges, financing their activities, and obtaining custody of suspects—not to mention the allegations of corruption that beset the Rwanda tribunal—did not dampen enthusiasm for the ICC. Rather, they underlined the urgent need for a stable, new, permanent institution that would be ready for any situation.

The ILC considered two draft statutes before finally adopting a sixty-article version in 1994.[69] Deferential to the politics of states and perhaps wary of having its work shelved once again, the ILC took no position on some of the more difficult political questions involved in drafting the Statute (such as the definitions of crimes and the financing of the Court) or took positions deferential to state sovereignty on others (such as jurisdictional regimes and organizational structure).[70]

The basic premise on which the ILC proceeded was that the Court should "complement" national prosecutions, rather than replace them, and that it should try only those accused of the most serious violations of international criminal law in cases in which national trials would not occur or would be ineffective. The ILC did not envisage the Court as an institution that would unify or construct international criminal law and, thus, did not grant the Court any advisory jurisdiction, although there was some discussion among Commission members as to the desirability of doing so.[71]

The ILC envisaged a Court with jurisdiction over both treaty crimes and violations of international humanitarian law. It would act only when cases were submitted to it by States Parties or the U.N. Security Council. It would be in all instances, except for U.N. Security Council referrals, completely dependent on State consent for its operation. Indeed, the proposed State consent regime and system of jurisdictional reservations probably would have completely crippled the proposed Court, except in cases involving affirmative action by the Security Council.

In terms of structure, the ILC contemplated that the Court would have four organs: (1) a Judiciary branch with a pretrial and an appellate division; (2) a Registry; (3) a Procuracy; and (4) a Presidency. The ILC would have permitted the Court's organs, with the exception of the Registry, to function "intermittently." The "permanent" institution desired by human rights advocates and States strongly supporting the establishment of the ICC would be, as conceived by the Commission, only a "stand-by" court in fact.[72]

The ILC's draft statute then returned to the U.N. General Assembly for consideration. The General Assembly established an "Ad Hoc Committee," which met in four weeks of sessions from April to August 1995 and prepared a report that became the basis for the General Assembly to establish a Preparatory Committee to consider the ILC 1994 Draft Statute.[73] The Preparatory Committee, open to all members of the United Nations as well as members of specialized agencies, was charged with "preparing a widely acceptable consolidated text of a convention for an international criminal court as a next step towards consideration by a conference of plenipotentiaries."[74] In 1996 and 1997 the Preparatory Committee held six sessions, each lasting approximately two weeks, and issued a consolidated text of a Draft Statute in April 1998 for the consideration of a Diplomatic Conference later that summer.[75]

The Diplomatic Conference was held in Rome from June 15 to July 17, 1998. The consolidated text that was the starting point of the negotiations was a complex document containing 116 articles, including some 1,300 phrases in brackets. It was extremely difficult to read, let alone understand, and virtually all of the difficult political issues that had been debated for more than two years during the Preparatory Committee meetings leading up to the Rome conference remained unresolved. The Conference was well attended, by both governments and NGOs; and the debates, while often intense, proved extremely fruitful.[76] While a successful conclusion to the Conference was by no means a foregone conclusion, after five weeks of grueling negotiations, a statute was adopted on the last day of the Conference.

The Rome Statute is substantially longer and more complex than any of its predecessor instruments. The 128-article text not only outlines the Court's jurisdiction, but also goes into extensive detail as to the ICC's structure, operations, and functioning. Structurally, the Rome Conference largely adopted the ILC's proposal but added a Pretrial Division and an Assembly of States Parties (for oversight) to the overall structure. It also permits the Prosecutor to bring cases to the Court on his or her own initiative (ex proprio motu), subject to judicial supervision, a provision that was highly controversial and to which the United States was adamantly opposed. Importantly, the Rome Conference rejected the conception of the Court as a "stand-by" institution in favor of a truly permanent structure.[77]

The ILC's 1994 Draft had taken the position that its function was neither to define nor to codify crimes under general international law; rather it viewed the Court's Statute "primarily as an adjectival and procedural instrument."[78] The drafters at Rome took the opposite view and defined the crimes within the Court's jurisdiction. This involved protracted and difficult negotiations between States that wanted broad definitions and States that wanted narrow definitions that would be difficult to apply. The result, as one might imagine, is a compromise text that is not always easy to interpret.[79] The definitions of crimes will be further explicated in an annex to the Statute adopted by Parties to the Treaty (States Parties).[80]

The Statute evidences a constant tension between supranationalism and deference to state sovereignty.[81] It builds on the experience of Nuremberg, Tokyo, and the ICTY and the ICTR. The Court's jurisdiction, at least for the immediate future, is limited to crimes against humanity, genocide, war crimes, and possibly aggression. Until the Statute has been amended to define *aggression*, uses of force that occur outside a state of armed conflict are not criminalized, and thus the Statute, in its current form, prohibits only war crimes, not war itself. The Statute represents a significant improvement over the ILC draft in many respects, particularly institutional structure and jurisdiction. In a significant victory for proponents of a strong and independent Court, it is the Court, not States Parties, that will decide whether cases are admissible, whether the Court has jurisdiction, whether a state's investigation or prosecution is "genuine" in determining complementarity, and whether evidence is admissible or not.[82]

Part 9 of the Statute, on International Cooperation and Judicial Assistance, is the Court's Achilles' heel. Unlike the Statute proposed in 1943 by the London International Assembly, which would have given an ICC its own constabulary, the ICC created in Rome will be completely dependent on states for assistance with respect to the investigation of offenses, the arrest of suspects, the location and procurement of evidence and witnesses, and the enforcement and recognition of its judgments.[83] Both the ILC draft and the Rome Treaty speak in imperatives ("States Parties shall, in accordance with the provisions of this Statute, cooperate fully with the Court in its investigation and prosecution of crimes within the jurisdiction of the Court"[84]). However, because the complementarity principle makes the Court's jurisdiction essentially subordinate to the jurisdiction of national courts, the Court may not issue binding orders to states.[85] This is a serious weakness, and it suggests that while firm notions of state sovereignty may have eroded, the idea is still quite strong.

CONCLUSION

On July 4, 1899, the delegation of the United States invited those in attendance at the First Peace Conference, as well as other eminent personalities, to join a Fourth of July celebration honoring Grotius's memory. The representatives of the twenty-six nations gathered there honored the eminent jurist by laying a commemorative wreath of silver upon his tomb.[86] As Assistant Secretary of State David Hill later wrote:

> The plenipotentiaries of the nineteenth century did homage to the exile of the six-teenth who had taught the world that even in the shock and storm of battle humanity cannot escape the dominion of its own essential laws, and that even independent states are answerable before the bar of human nature for obedience to principles imposed by a Power higher than the prerogatives of princes or the will of nations.[87]

On July 17, 1998, almost one hundred years later, the ICC Statute was signed in Rome. The establishment of the Court raises hopes that the lines between international law, on the one hand, and world order, on the other, are being blurred and that the normative structure being created by international law might influence or even restrain the Hobbesian order established by the politics of states. Indeed, one of the critiques of the ICC is that its reach has exceeded what it realistically should have grasped, although this is a judgment that only history ultimately will be able to make.

Yet if the road to Rome was long and difficult, the journey to the seat of the Court at The Hague[88] may be even more arduous. Sadly, one of the major obstacles to the Court's successful establishment is the refusal of the United States to participate in the creation of this new international institution. There is no doubt that the failure of the United States to join and to support the League of Nations contributed to the ultimate demise of that institution, and one wonders whether the ICC is similarly doomed before it is even established. U.S. participation would mean much to the fledgling Court, both practically (in terms of financing and logistical support) and morally.

As of this writing, ninety-six nations have signed the Rome Treaty, including all fifteen members of the European Union, and States have ratified the Statute.[89] This suggests that the optimism and commitment that propelled the Rome Conference to a successful conclusion continue to prevail. The nations that gathered in Rome in the summer of 1998 bequeathed a precious legacy to the new millennium—one of hope, of commitment, of faith in humanity's soul, and of capacity for goodness. It is encumbent on the leaders of the twenty-first century to ensure the Court's success. Otherwise, this incarnation of the International Criminal Court, like others before it, will recede quietly into the shadowland once again.

NOTES

1. The invitation was communicated through Russia's Foreign Minister, Count Mouravieff. William I. Hull, *The Two Hague Conferences and Their Contributions to International Law* 3 (Boston: Ginn, 1908). Of course, the czar's motives were not completely altruistic. Hull comments not only on the czar's sincerity in wishing for world peace, but also on his desire to "diminish the burden of taxation for military and naval expenditures which presses down with enormously increasing weight upon the shoulders of the people." Hull, *The Two Hague Conferences,* 2.

2. The 1899 Convention for the Peaceful Settlement of International Disputes, with its establishment of a Permanent Court of Arbitration (PCA), is a particularly significant predecessor for the international criminal court (ICC), as others have noted. James Brown Scott, *The Hague Peace Conferences of 1899 and 1907,* Vol. 1 (Baltimore: Johns Hopkins Press, 1909), 254; (Scott, Technical Delegate of the United States to the Second Peace Conference at The Hague, refers to this Convention as the "great and crowning glory of the Conference"). First, the establishment of the PCA suggested that interstate disputes were *justiciable* in some sense of the term, that is, resolvable through recourse to law, and not simply a question of politics. Second, even though the PCA was neither permanent nor a court in the true sense of the term, its establishment signaled a general trend toward international adjudication that the ensuing century brought to fruition. As one scholar recently remarked, international courts are now a familiar feature of the international landscape; John E. Noyes, "From The Hague to Rome: The International Criminal Court in Historical Context," *American Criminal Law Review* 36 (1999): 225.

3. Hull, *The Two Hague Conferences,* 10, 35–36. The Conference also adopted three declarations.

4. Joseph H. Choate, *The Two Hague Conferences* (Princeton, N.J.: Princeton University Press, 1913), ix.

5. Statute, A/Conf. 183/9, July 17, 1998, Annex II.

6. Statute, Annex IV.

7. M. Cherif Bassiouni, "Historical Survey 1919–1998," *The Statute of the ICC: A Documentary History* (Ardsley, N.Y.: Transnational, 1998), 31–32.

8. For a fuller treatment of the Rome Conference and the Statute adopted, see Bassiouni,

"Historical Survey 1919–1998"; Fanny Benedetti and John L. Washburn, "Drafting the International Criminal Court Treaty: Two Years to Rome and an Afterword on the Rome Diplomatic Conference," *Global Governance* 5, no. 1 (1999); Leila Sadat Wexler, "A First Look at the 1998 Rome Statute for a Permanent International Criminal Court: Jurisdiction, Definition of Crimes, Structure and Referrals to the Court," in *International Criminal Law III*, 2d ed., ed. M. Cherif Bassiouni (Ardsley, N.Y.: Transnational, 1998), 254.

9. Leila Sadat Wexler, "The Proposed Permanent International Criminal Court: An Appraisal," *Cornell International Law Journal* 29 (1996): 665, 670–71.

10. By *civil society*, I refer to "uncoerced" networks of human association "formed for the sake of family, faith, interest, and ideology"; Michael Walzer, "The Concept of Civil Society," in *Toward a Global Civil Society*, ed. Dieter Dettke (Providence, R.I.: Bergahn Books, 1995). In adding the term *global*, I adopt the terminology of Richard Falk (and others) who, while recognizing the difficulty of determining the "society" to which one is exactly referring given the weakness of international networks when compared to their national homologues, nevertheless suggests that one can identify "[international] social forces that respond to the patterns of behavior associated with the phenomena of economic globalization." For Falk, "global civil society" refers to the field of action and thought occupied by individual and collective citizen initiatives of a voluntary, nonprofit character both within states and transnationally; Richard Falk, "Global Civil Society: Perspectives, Initiatives, Movements," *Oxford Development Studies* 26 (1998): 99. Richard Falk, "The Nuclear Weapons Advisory Opinion and the New Jurisprudence of Global Civil Society," *Transnational Law and Contemporary Problems* 7 (1997): 333. The given definition of *global civil society* would certainly describe the character of the NGOs in Rome, some of which were large human rights organizations, such as Amnesty International, Human Rights Watch, and Lawyers Committee for Human Rights, others of which were religious organizations (Quaker, Unitarian, and Jewish groups, for example) or academic institutions (The International Law Association, American Branch, for example, which I represented, as chair of its ICC Committee). In addition, many individuals went to Rome not as official "representatives" of governments or NGOs, but out of a sense of deep commitment to the goals the ICC was designed to promote. Benedetti and Washburn, "Drafting the International Criminal Court Treaty," 21–23, 25. The NGO movement was able to amass its strength through the formation of a coalition that originated under the auspices of the World Federalist Movement. The coalition ultimately grew from 30 to 800 NGOs from all over the world. This coalition, the CICC (Coalition for an International Criminal Court), was able to influence the treaty-making process substantially, particularly as it came to form an alliance with the "like-minded group of states."

11. The like-minded group tended to act in concert during the meetings of the Preparatory Committee for the Court and in Rome. Bassiouni, "Historical Survey 1919–1998," 25. The like-minded states became increasingly powerful as the treaty-making continued. Originally, about forty-two states were in the like-minded group, which increased to more than sixty members, including most of the closest allies of the United States. The like-minded group included virtually all the European countries, with the important exception of France. Its success frustrated those opposed to the Court, including the United States. Because the group "was the only one with an operational strategy," it was the moving force behind the conference's successful conclusion. Benedetti and Washburn, "Drafting the International Criminal Court Treaty," 20–21, 30–31.

12. Richard Falk, "The Grotian Moment: Unfulfilled Promise, Harmless Fantasy, Missed Opportunity?" *International Insights* 13, no. 3 (1997). See also Richard Falk, "The Grotian Quest," *International Law: A Contemporary Perspective* 36 (1985).

13. The end of the Cold War also made possible the establishment of the two ad hoc tribunals for the former Yugoslavia and Rwanda, both of which are, in a sense, the practical precedents of the Court.

14. One might also add the Internet, without which the NGO coalition could never have reached the numbers it did, nor could it have disseminated information so quickly.

15. Hugo Grotius, born on April 10, 1583, is considered one of the "founders" of modern international law (David J. Hill, Introduction to *Hugo Grotius, the Rights of War and Peace* [Cambridge, England: 1901], 10), although many of his theories were challenged by other writers after his death. W. S. M. Knight, *The Life and Works of Hugo Grotius* (London: Sweet and Maxwell, 1925), 195–98. His most significant work was *De Jure Belli ac Pacis* (The Rights of War and Peace), which he composed while in exile (from Dutch persecution) in France.

16. Falk, "The Grotian Quest." In his essay on the shadowland, Falk describes the search for institutions that can address current international problems as a "Grotian quest." See also Saul Mendlovitz and Merav Datan, "Judge Weeramantry's Grotian Quest," *Transnational Law and Contemporary Problems* 7 (1997): 401, 402.

17. Richard Falk, "The Grotian Moment," *International Law: A Contemporary Perspective*, eds. Richard Falk, et al. (Boulder, Colo.: Westview, 1985).

18. The push to go forward in Rome, with or without the U.S. government (but with the support of many Americans, either in their private capacities or through NGOs) and other key world players, also suggests that the Rome Conference may not have been just a Grotian moment for the international legal system, but a Constitutional moment as well— an effort by the peoples of the world, as well as, or in spite of, their governments, to construct a new constitutional conception of the international legal order. The strong presence of the NGOs and their transnational lobbying efforts suggested a quiet constitutional revolution of sorts—the idea that the ultimate sovereignty over the world's human beings might lie not in their governments but in their peoples. See, for example, Bruce Ackerman, "Constitutional Politics/Constitutional Law," *Yale Law Journal* 99 (1989): 453. That such a "revolution" would materialize in establishing an ICC is logical—for government leaders who have traumatized their own countries (or their neighbors) are, of course, the most likely defendants before the Court and have the most to gain by opposing it. Other aspects of the "revolutionary" nature of the Rome Conference and Treaty are explored in Leila Sadat Wexler and S. Richard Carden, "The New International Criminal Court: An Uneasy Revolution," *Georgetown Law Journal* 88 (2000): 381.

19. Anthony C. Arend and Robert J. Beck, *International Law and the Use of Force: Beyond the U.N. Charter Paradigm* (New York: Routledge, 1993), 16.

20. (Hague) Convention (No. IV) Respecting the Laws and Customs of War on Land, Oct. 18, 1907, art. 2, 36 Stat. 2277, T.S. No. 539, 1 Bevans 631.

21. (Hague) Convention (No. IV) Respecting, art. 3.

22. (Hague) Convention (No. IV) Respecting, preamble.

23. Hull, *The Two Hague Conferences*, 1 (describing the first quarter century of the nineteenth century).

24. The Commission was established at the plenary session of the Preliminary Peace

Conference in 1919, "Historical Survey of the Question of International Criminal Jurisdiction: Memorandum Submitted by the Secretary General," U.N. Doc. A/CN.4/7/Rev.1, U.N. Sales No. 1949. V.8 (1949), 7.

25. "Commission on the Responsibility of the Authors of the War and on the Enforcement of Penalties: Report presented to the Preliminary Peace Conference," *American Journal of International Law* 14 (1920): 95, 123.

26. "Treaty of Peace between the Allied and Associated Powers and Germany" (June 28, 1919), art. 227, reprinted in 11 *Martens Nouveau Recueil* (Ser. 3) 323 (Fr.). The tribunal was to be international in character, being composed of five judges, one appointed by the United States, Great Britain, France, Italy, and Japan, respectively.

27. Matthew Lippman, "Nuremberg: Forty-five Years Later," *Connecticut Journal of International Law* 7, no. 1 (1991): 10–11. Leila Sadat Wexler, "The Interpretation of the Nuremberg Principles by the French Court of Cassation: From Touvier to Barbie and Back Again," *Columbia Journal of Transnational Law* 32 (1994): 289, 300.

28. Sadat Wexler, "The Proposed Permanent International Criminal Court," 670–71. The idea was again revived after the assassination of King Alexander of Yugoslavia in 1934; and in 1937 a convention was opened for signature on the creation of an international criminal court that would try persons accused of offenses established in the Convention for the Prevention and Punishment of Terrorism. Because the proposed court's subject matter jurisdiction was so limited, and relatively well defined, it avoided many of the objections raised to earlier proposals. Nevertheless, only thirteen nations signed the Convention, and it never entered into force. See "Convention for the Creation of an International Criminal Court," opened for signature, Nov. 16, 1937, *League of Nations O.J. Spec. Supp.* 156 (1938); League of Nations Doc. C.547(I)M.384(I)1937V (never entered into force), reprinted in *International Legislation* 7 (1935–1937): 878, ed. Manley O. Hudson, (1941). "Historical Survey of the Question of International Criminal Jurisdiction: Memorandum Submitted by the Secretary General," U.N. Doc. A/CN.4/7/Rev.1, U.N. Sales No. 1949. V.8 (1949), 16.

29. Sadat Wexler, "The Proposed Permanent International Criminal Court," 671–72. While many scholars suggested that the Court would function more as a common law court than a continental court (i.e., the code need not precede the Court), this conception would ultimately run afoul of three countervailing trends: (1) an increasing awareness of the need for fairness in criminal proceedings; (2) legal positivism as the prevailing conception of legitimate lawmaking; and (3) an additional dimension of the sovereignty concern—that States would be reluctant to surrender sovereignty to the court if the crimes were not clearly defined in advance.

30. Sadat Wexler, "The Proposed Permanent International Criminal Court," 672 (quoting remarks of Sir Graham Bower to the 1926 meeting of the International Law Association). To this, one member retorted, "The honorable gentleman seems to forget that behind the shake hands [*sic*] there are millions of mourning widows and crying orphans." See also Michael Scharf's chapter on justice vs. peace in this volume.

31. See M. Cherif Bassiouni, "From Versailles to Rwanda in Seventy-Five Years: The Need to Establish a Permanent International Criminal Court," *Harvard Human Rights Journal* 10, no. 11 (1997); and Timothy L. H. McCormack, "Selective Reaction to Atrocity: War Crimes and the Development of International Criminal Law," *Albany Law Review* 60 (1997): 681, 684–98.

32. Sadat Wexler, "The Proposed Permanent International Criminal Court," 672–73.

33. "The Agreement for the Prosecution and Punishment of Major War Criminals of the European Axis" (August 8, 1945), Charter of the International Military Tribunal, 8 U.N.T.S. 279, reprinted in *American Journal of International Law* 39 (1945): 257.

34. "The Charter and Judgment of the Nuremberg Tribunal: History and Analysis: Memorandum Submitted by the Secretary General," U.N. Sales No. 1949.V.7 (1949): 3.

35. "The Agreement for the Prosecution and Punishment," art. 1.

36. "The Agreement for the Prosecution and Punishment," 257.

37. Judgment of October 1, 1946, International Military Tribunal Judgment and Sentence," *American Journal of International Law* 41 (1947): 172, 333.

38. Secretary General's Memorandum, 39–40.

39. Secretary General's Memorandum, 39–40.

40. Egon Schwelb, "Crimes Against Humanity," *British Yearbook of International Law* (1946): 178.

41. Claude Lombois, *Droit Pénal International,* 157 (1979) ("ad hoc law").

42. Robert H. Jackson, *The Nuremberg Case* (New York: Cooper Square Publishers, 1971).

43. Ruth Wedgwood, "The Case for a Permanent War Crimes Court," *Christian Science Monitor,* August 16, 1995: 19.

44. The Soviet delegation in particular objected to the creation of an international penal jurisdiction on the grounds that it would violate national sovereignty. Others felt that the organization of an international criminal court was premature, either because there existed no international criminal law or because there existed as yet no international enforcement mechanism. At the insistence of the French delegation in particular and after a compromise proposal made by the U.S. representative, who suggested that the jurisdiction of the proposed international penal tribunal become optional, the provision was restored.

45. "Prevention and Punishment of the Crime of Genocide," G.A. Res. 260B(III), reprinted in *United Nations Resolutions, Series I: Resolutions of the General Assembly* 2, ed. Dusan J. Djonovich (1957), 320.

46. "Prevention and Punishment of the Crime of Genocide," 320.

47. Ricardo J. Alfaro, "Question of International Criminal Jurisdiction," U.N. Doc. No. A/CN.4/15 (1950), reprinted in [1950] *Year Book of the International Law Commission* 2, no. 1, U.N. Doc. A/CN.4/SER.A/1950/Add.1, 17 (supporting the Court's establishment). Emil Sandström, "Question of International Criminal Jurisdiction," U.N. Doc. No. A/CN.4/ 15 (1950), reprinted in *Year Book of the International Law Commission* 2, U.N. Doc. A/ CN.4/SER.A/ 1950/ Add.1, 18 (opposing the Court's establishment).

48. Sadat Wexler, "The Proposed Permanent International Criminal Court," 678.

49. "Report of the International Law Commission Covering the Work of Its Sixth Session," (June 3–July 28, 1954), 9 U.N. GAOR Supp. No. 9, U.N. Doc. A/2693 (1954), reprinted in *Year Book of the International Law Commission* 2, U.N. Doc. A/CN.4/SER.A/ 1954/Add.1, 200.

50. "International Criminal Jurisdiction," G.A. Res. 489 (V), reprinted in 3 *United Nations Resolutions, Series I: Resolutions of the General Assembly* 151 ed. Dusan J. Djonovich, 1957.

51. "Summary Records of the Thirty-Fifth Session," [1983] *Year Book of the International Law Commiss*ion 1, U.N. Doc. A/CN.4/SER.A/1983, 21, paraphrasing Lombois, *Droit Pénal International,* 83 (GAOR 5th Sess., 6th Com., 240th Mtg.).

52. "Report of the Committee on International Criminal Jurisdiction on Its Session Held from 1 to 31 August 1951," U.N. GAOR 7th Sess., Supp. No. 11, U.N. Doc. A/2136 (1952). The Committee was careful to point out that it did not consider its terms of reference to include the issue of the *desirability* of the court's establishment; rather, its task was to elaborate concrete proposals for the consideration of the General Assembly to permit it "to appreciate the full scope of the problems involved" "Report of the Committee on International Criminal Jurisdiction," art. 2, 11. The Committee members also made it clear that no member of the Committee would be committing his government to any of the Committee's decisions by participating in the Committee's deliberations and voting on the draft texts. "Report of the Committee on International Criminal Jurisdiction," art. 12.

53. "Report of the Committee on International Criminal Jurisdiction," art. 3.

54. "Report of the Committee on International Criminal Jurisdiction," art. 3.

55. "Report of the Committee on International Criminal Jurisdiction," art. 25.

56. Sadat Wexler, "The Proposed Permanent International Criminal Court," 679.

57. "Report of the Committee on International Criminal Jurisdiction," art. 27. This declaration could be made either prior to the crime's commission or afterward by special agreement or unilateral declaration; "Report of the Committee on International Criminal Jurisdiction," art. 26. Furthermore, jurisdiction was subject to prior approval by the General Assembly.

58. "Comments Received from Governments Regarding the Report of the Committee on International Criminal Jurisdiction," U.N. GAOR, 7th Sess., Annex 2, Agenda Item 52, 1, U.N. Doc. A/2186 and Add.1 (1952), 16.

59. "International Criminal Jurisdiction," G.A. Res. 687 (VII), reprinted in *United Nations Resolutions, Series I: Resolutions of the General Assembly* 4, ed. Dusan J. Djonovich (1957).

60. "Report of the 1953 Committee on International Criminal Jurisdiction," (July 27–August 20, 1953), U.N. GAOR 9th Sess., Supp. No. 12, U.N. Doc. A/2638 (1954).

61. "Definition of Aggression," G.A. Res. 3314 (XXIX), reprinted in *United Nations Resolutions, Series I: Resolutions of the General Assembly* 13, ed. Dusan J. Djonovich (1974), 342.

62. For an analysis of this phase of the Court's development, see Sadat Wexler, "The Proposed Permanent International Criminal Court," 683–85.

63. The 1989 resolution was introduced by a coalition of sixteen Caribbean and Latin American nations led by Trinidad and Tobago. Their initiative is described in "Summary Records of the Forty-Second Session," *Year Book of the International Law Commission* 1, U.N. Doc. A/CN.4/SER.A/1990, 39, 24. Because they were specifically concerned with the problem of extraditing and prosecuting international narco-terrorists, the resolution specified that the ILC should address the crime of illicit trafficking in narcotic drugs across national frontiers and should presumably discuss the international criminal court (or other trial mechanism) in that context. "International Criminal Responsibility of Individuals and Entities Engaged in Illicit Trafficking in Narcotic Drugs across National Frontiers and Other Transnational Criminal Activities: Establishment of an International Criminal Court with Jurisdiction over Such Crimes," G.A. Res. 44/39, U.N. GAOR 44th Sess., Supp. No. 49, 311, U.N. Doc. A/44/49 (1989).

64. "Report of the International Law Commission Covering the Work of Its Forty-Third Session" (April 29–July 19, 1991), U.N. GAOR Supp. 46, No. 10, U.N. Doc. A/46/10 (1991),

reprinted in *Year Book of the International Law Commission* 2, No. 1, U.N. Doc. A/CN.4/ SER.A/1991/Add.1 (Part 2).

65. Annex, "Report of the Working Group on the Question of an International Criminal Jurisdiction," 58. "Report of the International Law Commission Covering the Work of Its Forty-Fourth Session," (May 4–July 24, 1992), U.N. GAOR Supp. 47, No. 10, U.N. Doc. A/47/10 (1992), reprinted in *Year Book of the International Law Commission* 2, No. 1, U.N. Doc. A/CN.4/SER.A/1992/Add.1 (Part 2).

66. Sadat Wexler, "The Proposed Permanent International Criminal Court," 685.

67. "Report of the International Law Commission on the Work of Its Forty-Second Session," G.A. Res. 47/33, U.N. GAOR 47th Sess., Supp. No. 49, U.N. Doc. A/47/49 (1992), 287.

68. "Comments and Observations on the Draft Code of Crimes Against the Peace and Security of Mankind Adopted on First Reading by the International Law Commission at Its Forty-Third Session," U.N. Doc. A/CN.4/448 and Add.1 (1993).

69. "Report of the International Law Commission on the Work of Its Forty-Sixth Session, Draft Statute of an International Criminal Court," (May 2–July 22, 1994), at p. 51, U.N. GAOR, 49th Sess., Supp. No. 10, U.N. Doc. A/49/10. The ILC also considered Professor M. Cherif Bassiouni's draft statute for the establishment of an international criminal jurisdiction to prosecute violators of the Apartheid Convention in developing its 1993 and 1994 drafts. Bassiouni, "Historical Survey 1919–1998," 15–16.

70. There is no doubt, however, that the ILC's draft provided a thoughtful and useful place to start—indeed, as Bassiouni notes, there are many aspects that merit "high praise." Bassiouni, "Historical Survey 1919–1998," 17. See also Sadat Wexler, "The Proposed Permanent International Criminal Court."

71. Sadat Wexler, "The Proposed Permanent International Criminal Court," 687–707.

72. Daniel H. Derby, "An International Criminal Court for the Future," *Transnational Law and Contemporary Problems* 5 (1995): 307, 311.

73. On the 1995 Ad Hoc Committee, see Bassiouni, "Historical Survey 1919–1998," 18–19. The Ad Hoc Committee served to bridge the gap between the theory of the Statute as prepared by the ILC and many of the practical and political problems that governments had with the Statute. Additionally, most of the Preparatory Committee delegates had been present during the meetings of the Ad Hoc Committee, meaning that they were already familiar with the text and with the difficult issues they would face in preparing the work of the Diplomatic Conference. Bassiouni, "Historical Survey 1919–1998," 20.

74. "Establishment of an International Criminal Court," G.A. Res. 50/46, U.N. GAOR, 50th Sess., U.N. Doc. A/RES/50/46 (1995).

75. For an excellent analysis of the Preparatory Committee's work, see Bassiouni, "Historical Survey 1919–1998," 21–25.

76. Sadat Wexler, "A First Look at the 1998 Rome Statute," 655–57.

77. The Statute provides that the judges are all to be elected as full-time members of the Court (although there is a provision permitting the Presidency to reduce their terms as the workload so warrants) and that the Prosecutor, Deputy Prosecutors, and Registrar shall all serve on a full-time basis. Statute, A/Conf. 183/9, July 17, 1998, Annex II., arts. 35(1), 35(3), 42(2), 43(5). Sadat Wexler, "A First Look at the 1998 Rome Statute," 668–69.

78. "Report of the International Law Commission," 71.

79. For a preliminary analysis of the definition sections of the Rome Statute, see Sadat Wexler, "A First Look at the 1998 Rome Statute," 659–68.

80. Statute, A/Conf. 183/9, July 17, 1998, Annex II, art. 9.

81. Sadat Wexler and Carden, "The New International Criminal Court: An Uneasy Revolution."

82. Sadat Wexler, "A First Look at the 1998 Rome Statute," 656–57.

83. Sadat Wexler and Carden, "The New International Criminal Court."

84. Statute, A/Conf. 183/9, July 17, 1998, Annex II, art. 86.

85. Unlike the ICTY, for example, which did so in the *Blaskic* case, *Prosecutor v. Tihomir Blaskic*, International Criminal Tribunal for the Former Yugoslavia (Appeals Chamber, October 29, 1997).

86. The wreath bore the following inscription: "To the memory of Hugo Grotius in Reverence and Gratitude from the United States of America on the Occasion of the International Peace Conference at The Hague, July 4, 1899." Hill, Introduction to *Hugo Grotius, the Rights of War and Peace*, 16.

87. Hill, Introduction to *Hugo Grotius, the Rights of War and Peace*, 16.

88. Statute, A/Conf. 183/9, July 17, 1998, Annex II., art. 3(1).

89. See "Rome Statute Signature and Ratification Chart." http://www.igc.apc.org/icc/rome/html/ratify.htm (February 27, 2000).

3

Lessons from the International Criminal Tribunals

Richard J. Goldstone and Gary Jonathan Bass

The most important lessons from a century's worth of efforts at international justice revolve around the difficulty of bringing power and justice together. The creation in 1993 of the International Criminal Tribunal for the Former Yugoslavia (ICTY) was a first: the first truly international war crimes court in modern history. "It is a breakthrough," said Boutros Boutros-Ghali, then the U.N. Secretary General. "For the first time, a tribunal is created by the international community and not by the country that won the war."[1]

The major previous efforts to punish war criminals had been far more narrow in their scope. Nuremberg, the most famous example, was created by the victorious Allies with the specific purpose of bringing judgment on their wartime Nazi foes. The Tokyo tribunal did much the same in Japan. In a less well known but important effort after World War I, the Allies tried to bring to book German and Turkish war criminals—their enemies in war. But unlike all these tribunals, the new ICTY in The Hague would not be subject to the same accusations of victors' justice.[2]

But this moral strength could also be a practical weakness. While the Allies in World Wars I and II had sat in judgment because of the morally arbitrary fact of having won a war, their wartime anger and bitterness could as a matter of crude politics be translated into a resolute desire to punish the war criminals, to translate chance into right. Not so for the ICTY. None of the great powers in 1993 were seriously committed to the punishment of ex-Yugoslav war criminals. The punishment of Axis war criminals was a matter of the first order for the Allies; the punishment of ex-Yugoslav war criminals weighed heavily on Bosnian minds, but not on those of American and European diplomats. So the Hague tribunal was more pure than its predecessors, but also far weaker.

The creation of a permanent International Criminal Court (ICC) is a further step down the road from partiality to impartiality. But it risks being even more practically handicapped than The Hague and its sister tribunal for Rwanda in Arusha, Tanzania. The ICTY has struggled with funding, with hostility from members of the U.N. Security Council, with staffing, and above all with arrests. It has always enjoyed the support of the Islamic world; and in the year or so prior to this writing, it has profited greatly from the support of the United States and Great Britain, two of the most powerful countries on earth. But the ICC, of course, is already out of favor with the United States, the sole superpower. There is a risk that the ICC will be created in a weakened condition and that power and justice will not be able to be brought together.

What has the world learned from the two ad hoc war crimes tribunals for ex-Yugoslavia and Rwanda? There is no end of answers, but this chapter will focus on four main historical lessons—not because they are the only ones, but because they are the ones most likely to be useful to those considering the prospects for the ICC.

First, the difficulties of creating ad hoc tribunals are so great that they can make the timely delivery of justice all but impossible. Second, tribunals can play an important role simply by establishing the truth about atrocities. Third, the judicial operations of the two current ad hoc tribunals have been obviously fair, undermining the concerns of critics of an ICC that it would be a Court out of control. And fourth, renegade regimes must not be allowed to defy a legitimately created international tribunal; when they do, the tribunal risks becoming a token gesture, not a genuine step toward some kind of international justice.

TIMELY JUSTICE

One of the most obvious signs of the initial weakness of the world's response to the wars in the former Yugoslavia was the amount of time it took to create The Hague Tribunal. As early as 1991, when the Serb-dominated Yugoslav National Army besieged Vukovar and Dubrovnik in Croatia, it was clear that these wars would be waged in a criminal fashion. Warren Zimmermann, the last U.S. ambassador to Yugoslavia, later wrote that such sieges were "the first major war crimes in Yugoslavia since World War II."[3] Among human rights activists, at least, the massacre of perhaps two hundred Croats from a Vukovar hospital became a symbol of such brutality.

But the world response was little and late. U.S. and Western European leaders concentrated on avoiding military intervention and only looked to institutions of international justice as a halfway measure. The Serb extremist campaign of "ethnic cleansing" started in Bosnia in April 1992, but it was not until October 1992—after Roy Gutman's July 1992 reports in *Newsday* about Serb-run concentration camps, and the nightmarish ITN television images of the Omarska concentration camp in August 1992—that the United Nations took the first small step toward bringing war criminals to book: setting up a commission of experts to look into evidence of war crimes. This commission, the object of U.N. bureaucratic neglect and obstruction from some Western European states, was not able to speed up the process of seeking justice.

On February 22, 1993, the U.N. Security Council finally approved the creation of the ICTY. It took three months to create a statute for the tribunal. But even the nominal creation of the court did not mean much. The General Assembly had to pick eleven judges from a short list drawn up by the Security Council, taking into account the representation of the various legal and cultural traditions across the planet. This panel, instead of starting its real business of handing down rulings, had to busy itself with setting up basic rules of procedure and even finding office space in The Hague. Indeed, they could not have handed down any verdicts for the simple reason that there was still no prosecutor to bring cases.

The selection of a prosecutor became a political football in the U.N. Security Council. Playing out different and often sharply divergent views on how the world community ought to deal with the Balkan wars (and some other rivalries that had nothing to do with Bosnia), the Security Council debate was distinctly politicized. The council considered candidates from Britain, Canada, the United States, Argentina, Kenya, and India before finally settling on a Venezuelan. But he did not want the job and resigned in February 1994 before starting work. In August 1994, Richard Goldstone—an author of this chapter—finally took office. The prosecutor's office still had to assemble a competent international staff. By then, the tribunal had spent an astonishing fifteen months without a prosecutor. It was over two years since the discovery of concentration camps in Prijedor.

Such delays are not just undignified; they are damaging. It is more difficult for a tribunal to have a deterrent effect if that tribunal is being created in the middle of a conflict. And the formidable operational challenge of finding witnesses and gathering forensic evidence only gets harder as time goes by. Most important of all, such delays are deeply unfair to the victims of war crimes: the world promises some kind of redress and then loses attention. (The same criticism can be leveled against the slowness of the North Atlantic Treaty Organization [NATO] to arrest war crimes suspects after the Dayton Accords.) The Security Council demonstrated that it is not a body well suited for promptly setting up ad hoc institutions of international justice. A permanent court, by definition, only has to be created once.

A HISTORICAL RECORD

The denial of atrocity is closely linked to the committing of atrocity. As their followers killed, the leaders of the Hutu génocidaires and the Bosnian Serb nationalists denied that they were doing any such thing. After a war, distorted memories can lay the groundwork for a fresh outbreak of violence.

It is for this reason that a thorough debunking has long been seen as one of the most important functions of a war crimes tribunal. In December 1919, Ernest Pollock, the British solicitor general after World War I, argued that compiling charges against German war crimes suspects, even if the suspects could not be tried, would create "for all time a record of German brutality."[4] Robert Jackson, the U.S. Supreme Court justice who served as the U.S. chief prosecutor at Nuremberg, wanted the evidence prepared for the trials to stand as a massive documentary record of Nazi criminality. So did John Maynard Keynes, then working as a British official. Henry Stimson, Franklin Roosevelt's secretary of war and the prime mover behind the idea of Nuremberg, wanted the trials "to make a full and public record of the whole evil system of Nazism, viz: as a gigantic conspiracy to violate the rules of war for the purpose of getting an advantage over their enemies which would permit them to rule the world by a system of terrorism."[5]

This record was a clear success of Nuremberg. The sheer quantity of information is staggering. The files on the Nazi SS alone filled six freight cars. Jackson later told President Harry Truman that the documentary record he had assembled amounted to over five million pages.[6] Afterward, Nuremberg published eleven volumes of documents and twenty-two volumes of the proceedings, at around five hundred pages per volume. There are also many important records in the U.S. National Archives.[7] Alan Bullock, a prominent historian of the Nazi era, recalled reading all those published volumes:

> And I became intensely excited about them because—you can argue whichever way you want about whether it's justice or not—but from the point of view of the historian the Nuremberg trials were an absolutely unqualified wonder. I mean, the greatest coup in history for historians. The capture of the records of the most powerful state in the world immediately after the event![8]

Attending the Eichmann trial in Jerusalem in 1961, Hannah Arendt wrote, "Even today, eighteen years after the war, our knowledge of the immense archival material of the Nazi regime rests to a large extent on the selection made for prosecution."[9] In turn, this impartial record has encouraged postwar Germany—or at least the Federal Republic—to confront its past honestly. These efforts have helped build a powerful German culture of remembering and atoning, thereby laying some of Germany's old ghosts to rest.[10]

Such projects do not always work out as well. After World War I, some British officials had hoped that war crimes trials in Ottoman Turkey would help drive home to Turks the magnitude of the Young Turk regime's crimes against Armenians and (of particular interest to the British) Britons. When the trials fell apart, and without access to the Ottoman archives, the hopes for compiling a historical record were quashed. To this day, the Turkish government—a successor of the regime of Atatürk, not of the Young Turks at all—goes to considerable lengths to deny the persecution of the Armenians. Each year from 1984 to 1990, Turkey successfully lobbied to stop the U.S. Senate from adopting a resolution to name April 24—the day Armenians say the genocide started—as a national day of remembrance of human cruelty and of the slaughter of the Armenians.[11] One cannot imagine Germany doing anything remotely like this, and Nuremberg is part of the reason.

The logistical difficulties are daunting. Even in the best of circumstances, it is hard to prevent war criminals from destroying the evidence. Between the Allies' acceptance of Japan's surrender and the signing of that surrender, Japanese militarists burned records of the secret police and the military, transcripts of imperial conferences, cabinet deliberations, and records on prisoners of war and on campaigns in China.[12] Before Japan surrendered, some Japanese officers killed witnesses of war crimes. And by the end of August 1945, over a thousand Japanese officers had committed suicide.[13]

But the fact that it is hard to gather a definitive historical account does not mean that it is not worth doing so. The absence of a well-established historical record facilitates denial that atrocities ever happened. For instance, Radovan Karadzic denied that there were executions at Srebrenica in July 1995.[14] And many Bosnian Serbs do not believe that Ratko Mladic was involved in mass executions at Srebrenica—despite the facts that he was filmed separating Muslim men from women and that mass graves have been exhumed.[15] Already a fringe in Europe claims that the horrific August 1992 ITN television footage of emaciated Bosnian Muslim prisoners at a Bosnian Serb–run concentration camp was faked.[16] As time goes on, that fringe may grow.

The two international criminal tribunals (ICTs) have already started to fight such historical fictions. The testimony of Drazen Erdemovic, who participated in the Bosnian Serb Army's executions at Srebrenica, helped pinpoint the sites of mass graves. And the trials in Arusha have assembled a picture of a planned and systematic genocide, not a haphazard outburst of violence, as some would believe. Tribunals can play an important role in fighting forgetting.

FAIRNESS

Critics of the ICC have worried that a permanent international tribunal might be uncontrollable. But it is by now clear that the ICTs have been strictly managed by the rules of precedent and procedure, in much the same way that domestic courts in stable liberal countries regulate their own powers and conduct.

If anything, the ICTs have been legalistic to a fault. They have not delivered shotgun justice, as Nuremberg and Tokyo were sometimes accused of having done. Quite the opposite—fhe ICTs have gone through the frustrations and the delays that come with the genuine exercise of due process. Judges take issue with the chief prosecutor; rules of evidence are strictly maintained; precedent is given its due homage. This legalism is often terrifically frustrating to prosecutors. For instance, Dusan Tadic was acquitted on a number of counts because two judges felt that the conflict in northwest Bosnia had not been international in character when Tadic committed his crimes at the Omarska concentration camp, and thus the Geneva Conventions could not apply. And in November 1999, the appeals court for the Arusha Tribunal ordered that Jean-Bosco Barayagwiza, who had been indicted for genocide and crimes against humanity, be set free. The court, to the dismay of the Rwandan government and tribunal prosecutors, noted that Barayagwiza had been detained in Cameroon without being charged and then had spent too much time in custody in Arusha awaiting trial.

To be sure, the two tribunals have handed down a number of remarkable verdicts. Jean Kambanda, a former prime minister of Rwanda, pleaded guilty to the charge of genocide before the Arusha tribunal. Jean-Paul Akayesu, who had been mayor of Taba, was convicted of genocide in September 1998—the first such international conviction ever. On top of that, the court ruled that rape and sexual violence may be acts of genocide if committed with genocidal intent. These are a series of legal milestones.

But the most remarkable accomplishment of the two courts are the more quotidian operations. The uprooting of corruption and incompetence at the Arusha tribunal was a vital step if such courts are not to fall into disregard. The most important legal achievement is the quiet operation of due process: ordinary law in extraordinary circumstances.

RENEGADE REGIMES MUST NOT BE ALLOWED TO DEFY AN INTERNATIONAL TRIBUNAL

Even after the creation of the ICTY, Balkan states have found it easy enough to snub the tribunal. There is no shortage of examples. Croatia resisted the efforts of Judge Louise Arbour, the chief prosecutor of the former Yugoslavia and the Rwanda tribunals, to subpoena Croatian records pertinent to the trial of Tihomir Blaskic, a Bosnian Croat military leader. From the signing of the Dayton Accords in December 1995 until finally capitulating in October 1997, Croatia snubbed international efforts to bring Croat war crimes suspects to book in The Hague. One indicted Croat was arrested by Bosnian Croats on separate murders of Croats but acquitted of those particular charges and then freed—to the anger of American, Bosnian, and tribunal officials, who said this was a violation of Dayton.[17] Despite repeated formal complaints from the tribunal to the U.N. Security Council, Yugoslavia still has not surrendered three of its officers known to be on Yugoslav soil. And Ratko Mladic, twice indicted by the Hague tribunal for genocide and crimes against humanity, has been seen in rump Yugoslavia. Now that NATO has become more vigorous in arresting war crimes suspects in Bosnia, Yugoslavia is becoming a haven for U.N.-indicted war criminals.

Such defiance has shown no signs of evaporating. Under three specific Security Council resolutions, the Hague tribunal has jurisdiction over the 1998 war crimes in Kosovo—a province of Serbia, and therefore clearly under the tribunal's mandate to pursue war crimes committed in the territory of the former Yugoslavia since 1991. But Kosovo became another opportunity for Yugoslav noncompliance. The Yugoslav justice minister and foreign minister have both publicly denied the Hague tribunal's jurisdiction in Kosovo. Judge Arbour wrote a letter to Slobodan Milosevic, the Yugoslav president, requesting access to Kosovo for on-site investigations of the kind indispensable to the tribunal's work. But much of Arbour's team were denied visas, and Arbour herself was granted only a seven-day, single-entry visa and a warning that she had no right to go to Kosovo. Arbour did not go to Yugoslavia. Milosevic's disregard for the tribunal was again brought before the Security Council. In January 1999, after the Racak massacre, Arbour tried once again to gain access to Kosovo and was turned back at the border. Milosevic's intransigence on the tribunal's jurisdiction in Kosovo has proved to be of a piece with his massive campaign of "ethnic cleansing" there since the start of NATO bombing of Yugoslavia in March 1999.

Such heel-dragging and outright obstruction must not be allowed to become a feature of the ICC's proceedings. Croatian and Serbian noncompliance has seriously undermined the credibility and the effectiveness of the Hague tribunal. One should not assume that an ICC will have it any easier. To the contrary, in the case of the former Yugoslavia, at least the major Western powers have made a serious commitment to building a sturdy peace in Bosnia. The same would not be true if an ICC were seeking justice in, say, Cambodia or Uganda. The Balkans are now a Western concern; and even so, Yugoslavia and Croatia have managed to get away with stiffing the tribunal. Those countries that voted in Rome for the creation of the ICC should not treat their vote as a mere token.

Even if the great powers are inconsistent in their interest in the international rule of law, they should at least be sensible to a more pragmatic argument. When a minor country like Yugoslavia defies the tribunal, it is the problem not just of a small and rather weak U.N. institution. It is a direct challenge to the authority of the Security Council that unanimously voted for the creation of the tribunal in The Hague. Tolerating such snubs can only encourage more of them, if not from Milosevic or Franjo Tudjman, then from other pariah leaders. If the world now commits to an ICC, then it must realize that challenges to that Court are also a challenge to the authority of the world community.

CONCLUSION

This chapter has laid out four broad lessons that have been painfully learned by the experiences with the ICTs and with prior tribunals in this century. To reiterate, first, this chapter has argued that the problems and delays inherent in setting up ad hoc tribunals in time of crisis are so daunting that they overwhelm the timely pursuit of justice. Second, this chapter has pointed to the important role tribunals can play just by establishing an unimpeachable record of past crimes. Third, the argument by critics of an ICC that such a Court might be out of control is undermined by the experience of the jurisprudence of the Arusha and Hague tribunals. These tribunals have been fair, suggesting that an ICC could be so, too. Fourth, this chapter has warned that renegade states should not be allowed to snub legitimate and fair international tribunals.

The hope is that an ICC will be a step forward. By having a court already set up, the world can make the timely delivery of justice more likely. By relying on the fairness of the ad hoc tribunals, an ICC can establish its own legitimacy as a responsible instrument of justice. The danger, of course, is that the ICC will face many of the same problems with enforcement and resources that have plagued ICTs.

For all the difficulty of aligning justice with power, for all the setbacks and reversals and half-steps, one can still discern signs of progress. The notion of international justice is increasingly on the lips of diplomats and policy makers, spoken with a seriousness that would have been inconceivable during the Cold War.

Practice has a way of lagging behind norms, so one should not get carried away. Power and justice are still uneasy partners. But there are signs of a nascent consensus that the most gross violations of human rights can no longer be cloaked by the claims of state sovereignty. Since Nuremberg's successful indictment of crimes against humanity, the world has seen the emergence of an international jurisdiction to try the most egregious crimes. This universal jurisdiction is reflected in a whole series of international conventions that take a stand against the worst kinds of brutality: the Genocide Convention of 1948, the Torture Convention, the Apartheid Convention, and the "grave breach" provisions of the Geneva Conventions. Many States have stepped in to put teeth to these norms, as when Israel put Adolf Eichmann on trial or, more recently, when a number of Bosnian Serbs were put before national courts in Germany, Denmark, and Switzerland. The creation of the two ad hoc international tribunals for the former Yugoslavia and Rwanda is an important step along the way, as was the British apprehension of Augusto Pinochet for the human rights abuses of his regime in Chile after the ouster of Allende. Also important is NATO's new policy of more vigorous pursuit of indicted war criminals in Bosnia, from the first NATO arrest raid in July 1997 to the December

1998 arrest of General Radislav Krstic, one of the senior Bosnian Serb officers indicted for the 1995 slaughter at Srebrenica. It has become a commonplace that crimes against humanity are a universal concern, both legally and practically. Under the growing new consensus, there is a recognition that tolerating such atrocities diminishes and threatens everyone.

NOTES

1. Stanley Meisler, "U.N. Names South African Judge as Balkans War Crimes Prosecutor," *Los Angeles Times*, December 25, 1993, A5.

2. Montgomery Belgion, *Epitaph on Nuremberg: A Letter Intended to Have Been Sent to a Friend Temporarily Abroad* (London: Falcon Press, 1946); Wilbourn E. Benton and Georg Grimm, eds., *Nuremberg: German Views of the War Crimes Trials* (Dallas, Tex.: Southern Methodist University Press, 1955); and Richard H. Minear, *Victors' Justice: The Tokyo War Crimes Trial* (Princeton, N.J.: Princeton University Press, 1971).

3. Warren Zimmermann, *Origins of a Catastrophe: Yugoslavia and Its Destroyers—America's Last Ambassador Tells What Happened and Why* (New York: Times Books, 1996), 158.

4. Anglo-French conference, London, December 13, 1919, 11 A.M., in *Documents on British Foreign Policy 1919–1939: Volume II: 1919*, ed. E. L. Woodward and Rohan Butler, first series (London: His Majesty's Stationery Office, 1948), 758.

5. Henry L. Stimson, in reference to the Nuremberg trials, *Henry L. Stimson Diaries*, vol. 49, November 19, 1944, Yale University Library, 35.

6. Eugene Davidson, *The Trial of the Germans: An Account of the Twenty-Two Defendants before the International Military Tribunal at Nuremberg* (Columbia: University of Missouri Press, 1997), 33–34.

7. National Archives II, College Park, Md., World War II war crimes records (Nuremberg), R.G. 238.

8. Ron Rosenbaum, *Explaining Hitler: The Search for the Origins of His Evil* (New York: Random House, 1998), 81.

9. Hannah Arendt, *Eichmann in Jerusalem: A Report on the Banality of Evil* (London: Penguin, 1994), 231.

10. Charles S. Maier, *The Unmasterable Past: History, Holocaust, and German National Identity* (Cambridge, Mass.: Harvard University Press, 1988).

11. Edward Alexander, *A Crime of Vengeance: An Armenian Struggle for Justice* (New York: Free Press, 1991), 4–5.

12. Arnold C. Brackman, *The Other Nuremberg: The Untold Story of the Tokyo War Crimes Trials* (New York: William Morrow, 1987), 40.

13. Brackman, *The Other Nuremberg*, 44.

14. Pazit Ravina, "Atrocities, What Atrocities?," *Times* (London), February 11, 1996.

15. David Rohde, *Endgame: The Betrayal and Fall of Srebrenica, Europe's Worst Massacre since World War II* (New York: Farrar, Straus & Giroux, 1997), 387, 391.

16. Luke Harding, "A shot that's still ringing," *Guardian* (London), March 12, 1997, T2.

17. *New York Times*, December 8, 1995, A18. Peter Galbraith, U.S. ambassador to Croatia, pointed out that Ivica Rajic was freed in Mostar, outside of Croatia, and that Rajic was a renegade.

4

The Statute of the ICC: Past, Present, and Future

Bartram S. Brown

On July 17, 1998, at the end of a marathon, five-week, diplomatic conference in Rome, 120 states voted to approve the text of a treaty[1] to create a permanent International Criminal Court (ICC). The United States, historically a crusader for international human rights and the rule of law, was isolated as one of only seven countries voting against the text of that treaty, known as the Rome Statute. The United States has stressed that it will neither sign nor ratify the Statute in its present form and has even suggested that U.S. policy may go beyond mere nonparticipation to one of "actively opposing" the ICC. At least ninety-six countries have already signed the Rome Statute, and when sixty of them have ratified it, the ICC will officially come into being. U.S. opposition to this important new institution is a disturbing development.

ICC negotiations began in earnest when the U.N. General Assembly in late 1995 created a Preparatory Committee on the Establishment of an International Criminal Court (PrepCom).[2] A series of six PrepCom sessions held between 1996 and 1998 resolved a number of technical questions, but many difficult issues remained unresolved. Therefore, the General Assembly decided to hold a Diplomatic Conference in Rome in June and July of 1998. The objective was to reach agreement on the final text of a treaty, the Rome ICC Statute, that would create the last great international organization of the twentieth century.

The next section of this essay, which reviews the history of the Rome Diplomatic Conference, draws heavily on the experience of the author who participated in that Conference as a legal adviser to the Republic of Trinidad and Tobago. This is followed by a section that examines the principal features of the Rome Statute, including the crimes it would place within the ICC's jurisdiction, the composition and administration of the Court, and the process for bringing a case to trial before the ICC. The conclusion briefly considers some of the principal U.S. objections to the Statute and the possibility that continuing negotiations at the United Nations might help to meet some of these objections.

ROME CONFERENCE DYNAMICS

Delegations from 162 different countries participated in the Rome Conference, and the negotiations were long and intense. Not only did the Conference last five weeks, but it involved simultaneous negotiations at different sites and on many different levels.

No real negotiation could occur in the formal and largely ceremonial "Plenary Sessions" held for the first three days of the Conference (when speeches were made by all states) or on the last day (when the results of the negotiations were formally ratified). The highest decision-making body of the Conference was the "Committee of the Whole," but real negotiations had to be conducted in smaller sessions that focused on one set of issues at a time. Thus the next level of negotiations was conducted in "working groups." These were in turn broken down into even smaller groups, called "informals," to discuss subsets of specific issues.

Unlike the more formal sessions, the informals were often held in small rooms that could not accommodate every delegation. Simultaneous translation sometimes was available when important issues were first being discussed. But the nitty-gritty guts of the negotiations were largely conducted in English, a tremendous advantage for delegates from English-speaking states.

For five weeks, all these levels of negotiations were held simultaneously on different sets of issues, making it impossible for any one delegate to attend more than a fraction of the sessions. The United States sent a large and extremely talented delegation to the Conference, as did other diplomatic powerhouses like France and the United Kingdom (U.K.). Sometimes, especially toward the end of the Conference, the negotiations would continue until after midnight. This placed an even greater strain on the smaller delegations.

Nongovernmental organizations (NGOs) helped many smaller delegations compensate for their size and generally had an impact on the Rome Conference that far exceeded their formal status. NGOs were symbolic representatives of international civil society, strongly supporting the creation of an ICC. They lacked the rights and privileges of a state; they had no vote and were excluded from even observing the key informal negotiations. The United Nations provided just one meeting room for the 137 NGOs officially represented at the conference. It quickly became one of the busiest centers of activity. NGOs offered delegates access to an impressive body of technical expertise. NGOs' papers on the major issues were distributed widely, and their experts were only too happy to consult with national delegates. NGO representatives followed the negotiations very carefully and maximized their effectiveness through the NGO Coalition for an ICC (CICC).[3] NGO expertise leveled the playing field by making it possible for even the smallest delegations to follow and to participate in shaping many complex and technical issues.

Throughout the Conference, the U.S. delegation offered itself as the voice of "realism," insisting time and again that good intentions could only take the ICC so far. The United States saw a number of hidden perils in the text of the Draft Statute, fearing that the ICC might unfairly charge U.S. soldiers and that a Prosecutor able to initiate investigations would be dangerous. The United States believed that states should be able to choose from among a short list of crimes when accepting the jurisdiction of the ICC and that the ICC's authority should be based on state consent instead of on notions of "universal" or "automatic" jurisdiction. Another concern was that the notion of "war crimes" was too broad and might be stretched to include acts inadvertently committed by U.S. troops during humanitarian missions abroad. The United States wanted to require U.N. Security Council authorization for every ICC prosecution, which would alleviate many other substantive concerns by granting each of the five permanent members of the Council, including the United States, a veto.

The requirement of Security Council consent was completely unacceptable to the so-called "like-minded" states, a broad coalition of those favoring a strong and independent ICC. The United Kingdom had joined the like-minded group by agreeing during the December 1997 PrepCom to accept a key compromise formulated by Singapore. The "Singapore compromise" transformed the requirement that the Security Council approve every ICC investigation into the option for a Security Council decision to delay ICC investigations or prosecutions. The United Kingdom became the first of the Council's five permanent members to agree that its veto privilege would not be extended to all ICC prosecutions. Some delegates believed that, in insisting on a veto, the United States was clinging to both great power privilege and Cold War paranoia.

The mood of the delegates and observers shifted significantly during the Conference. At the beginning, there was a strong sense that the Conference was about to do something of truly historic proportions. This euphoric mood was periodically replaced by pessimistic portents of gloom, the feeling that perhaps the world was not yet ready for a truly effective ICC.

The like-minded states were especially eager for U.S. support, realizing that an ICC would be much more effective with the backing of the world's preeminent power. Yet the U.S. delegation, apparently under very restrictive instructions from Washington, failed to show flexibility or to accept compromise on key issues. Four weeks into the Conference, some delegates began to wonder if the United States were really "negotiating" at all, and many began to contemplate the possibility of proceeding without U.S. support.

According to general U.N. practice and to the specific rules of the Rome Conference, the goal of the Committee of the Whole was to achieve consensus on all substantive issues.[4] Should all feasible efforts to reach agreement fail, a "Bureau" composed of the officers of that Committee[5] would recommend a course of action. The Bureau could put any contested matters to a vote with decisions to be taken by a three-fifths majority of the representatives present and voting. A skilled Bureau is often essential to success at a diplomatic conference, but in Rome the Bureau was destined to play a greater role than usual.

With less than two weeks to go, Philippe Kirsch, the chairman of the Committee of the Whole, took the initiative in trying to break the logjam. He attempted to narrow the disagreement on key issues by distributing a Discussion Paper[6] that reduced the number of alternative formulations on each issue. National delegation comments on the Paper's alternatives set the tone for developments during the final week of the Conference.

Ambassador David Scheffer, the head of the U.S. delegation, forcefully restated the U.S. positions. The United States rejected all proposals for automatic jurisdiction over core crimes, preferring to require state consent to ICC jurisdiction over each crime (with the exception of genocide). Scheffer also stressed that the prior consent of the state of nationality of the accused should be required if that state were not a party to the Statute. He did suggest, however, that the United States might compromise on the role of the Security Council.[7] If the Conference would accommodate U.S. concerns on the other key issues, Scheffer said he might be in a position to recommend signing the Statute.[8]

For almost two days, each delegation reacted to the Bureau Discussion Paper. A "virtual vote"[9] recording these public statements was compiled by the NGO CICC. The results were summarized and widely distributed within the Conference. They revealed that on many critical issues, such as automatic jurisdiction over core crimes, the state consent required for jurisdiction, the power of the Prosecutor to initiate cases, and the role of the Security Council, the positions of the United States were very much in the minority. This information bypassed the diplomatic niceties of the consensus procedure, weakening the negotiating position of the United States, just as an "actual vote" might have done. The majority began to gain a sense of its strength.

With time beginning to run out, Kirsch and the Bureau formulated a "Bureau Proposal"[10] that went further than the earlier Discussion Paper in attempting to narrow the options. The proposal attempted to obtain broader consensus by limiting the ICC's jurisdiction and independence. Many delegates were shocked that the draft failed to endorse automatic ICC jurisdiction over core crimes, a Prosecutor with independent authority to initiate cases, or other elements that had just been supported by large majorities. National comments were compiled into a second virtual vote, confirming the results of the week before.[11] As the last week of the Conference began, Kirsch made a bold decision. The Bureau would formulate one last compromise proposal: a package-deal version of the entire ICC Statute, which would be presented to the Committee of the Whole for a single up-or-down vote.

NGOs were publicly supporting a strong ICC, helping shape the Rome dynamic. The International Committee of the Red Cross expressed concern that if the ICC did not have automatic jurisdiction, it "would be a retrograde step for international law and would severely limit the court's effectiveness."[12] The president of the American Bar Association endorsed an independent prosecutor and universal jurisdiction, and he advised governments to move forward with or without the United States.[13] Some observers were quick to blame the United States for the lack of consensus,[14] even though other important states such as France, China, and India remained opposed to the majority's like-minded vision of the ICC.

The Bureau consulted with delegates from many different countries and caucuses, all of whom were apprehensive about a compromise package. The like-minded states were concerned that the Bureau's ultimate proposal might place too many limits on the ICC's jurisdiction. They knew, based on the national responses to the Bureau's Discussion Paper, that most states at the Conference supported the "like-minded" position on the critical issues.

India began to formulate a set of amendments that it wanted the nonaligned countries to support. India's amendments called for aggression to be included as a crime, for the use of nuclear weapons to be specified as a war crime,[15] and for the deletion of all references to the Security Council.[16]

The Bureau Proposal[17] was distributed after midnight on July 16, just before the last day of the Conference. The proposal attempted to accommodate the positions and the concerns of the United States while still creating an independent and effective ICC. To a large extent it followed the "like-minded" blueprint, but there were a number of wrinkles and exceptions. For example, the crimes within the ICC's jurisdiction included not only genocide, crimes against humanity, and war crimes, but also aggression. However, aggression was left to be defined by the State Parties at a later date. Nuclear, chemical, and biological weapons were all omitted from the list of weapons the use of which constitute a war crime. ICC jurisdiction required the consent of either the territorial state or the state of nationality of the accused. The ICC Prosecutor could initiate investigations or prosecutions on his or her own authority.

On the penultimate day of the Conference, the U.S. delegation proposed an amendment incorporating a radical new way to address continuing U.S. concerns about jurisdiction and state consent.[18] This proposal seemed to represent an offer of real compromise by the United States, but it raised new and difficult issues when the time for substantive negotiations already had passed. Had this same proposal been offered earlier in the Conference, it conceivably might have provided the basis for a grand compromise on jurisdiction and state consent.

The vote on the Chairman's compromise was held at 10 P.M. on July 17. Both the United States and India proposed their amendments, hoping to undo the "package" offered by the Chairman. Norway moved that "no action" be taken on India's amendment, and the motion was approved by a vote of 114 for to 16 against, with 20 abstentions. When the U.S. amendment was offered, a similar "no action" motion was passed, with 113 votes for, 17 against, and 25 abstentions.

The Committee of the Whole adopted the proposed Draft Statute by consensus at about 10:30 P.M., and the Assembly erupted into spontaneous jubilation and applause. The U.S. delegates did not join the celebration. The head of the U.S. delegation called for a nonrecorded vote on the Statute in the final Plenary Session. That vote was 120 states for, 7 against, with 21 abstentions. While the votes of individual states were not officially listed, it appears that the United States and its close ally Israel were joined by states such as China, Libya, Iraq, and Yemen in opposing the treaty.[19] The United States had suffered a diplomatic defeat of epic proportions.

THE ROME STATUTE

The Rome Statute is a treaty. When ratified by sixty states it will create a permanent International Criminal Court based at The Hague, Netherlands. The institution's goal will be to help ensure that individuals who commit the most serious of international crimes will be punished. As a criminal court that tries individuals, it will be fundamentally different from the International Court of Justice, which can only decide disputes between states. The ICC will initially have eighteen full-time judges divided into separate chambers dealing with trials, pre-trial matters, and appeals. Their number and status may be adjusted later according to the caseload.

The stated goal of the Statute is to permit the exercise of international jurisdiction only to the extent necessary to prevent impunity for those committing the crimes within its jurisdiction. This is to be accomplished through a system of "complementary" jurisdiction, according to which the ICC will be barred from investigating or prosecuting cases that have been pursued in good faith by any state.

The states ratifying the Statute will invest the ICC with its basic jurisdiction over crimes committed on their territory or by their nationals. Except for when ICC action is triggered by the U.N. Security Council, either the territorial state or the state of nationality of the accused must consent to ICC prosecution. State consent is provided either by having joined the Court or by accepting its jurisdiction for a particular situation.

Basic principles of criminal law and of international human rights law require the careful definition of crimes and other aspects of due process. Due in no small part to the vigorous efforts of the United States, these principles are strongly reflected in the ICC Statute. The Statute is characterized throughout by its careful concern with matters such as the definition of crimes, respect for the rights of the accused, and the selection of qualified judges and prosecutors. As a safeguard against abuses, the Statute provides for the use of a Pre-Trial Chamber of judges to oversee the Prosecutor's discretionary decisions. A three-judge Trial Chamber will hear the evidence in each case and will convict only if those judges find that guilt has been proven beyond a reasonable doubt. The decisions of both the Pre-Trial Chamber and the Trial Chamber are subject to appeal to an Appeals Chamber of five judges.

States will need to cooperate both in creating the ICC and in helping it to function effectively. Those ratifying the Statute accept the obligation to cooperate with the ICC by executing its arrest warrants and complying with requests for evidence and other assistance. States that decline to ratify will not be required to cooperate, but they may choose to do so. Individuals convicted by the ICC will be sentenced to terms of imprisonment to be served on the territory of States that agree to accept them for this purpose.

Crimes within the Jurisdiction of the ICC

Under the Rome Statute, the ICC will have jurisdiction over the three core crimes of genocide, crimes against humanity, and a carefully negotiated (and thereby limited) list of the most serious war crimes. Even though each of the core crimes had been established under international law since the 1940s, it was difficult to reach consensus on definitions for purposes of the ICC Statute. This difficulty resulted in a narrowing of the definitions. In most cases the definitions in the Statute are narrower than the crimes' definition under general international law. The Statute contains a "savings clause" stating that its definitions of crimes are without prejudice to the rules of general international law.[20] The political compromises of the ICC Conference could not make legal anything that was previously illegal.

The crime of aggression also is listed within the ICC's jurisdiction if the Statute can be amended to define this crime and the conditions for its prosecution. A two-thirds majority of States Parties would be required to define and to establish ICC jurisdiction over the crime of aggression.[21] Only if the amendment has been ratified by a supermajority of seven-eighths of the States Parties can it bind a State Party that has not accepted the change.[22] This may never happen because the definition of *aggression* has long been a subject of controversy among states. The Statute provides that its provisions concerning aggression "shall be consistent with the relevant provisions of the Charter of the United Nations,"[23] meaning that it will recognize the special role of the Security Council in determining whether an act of aggression has occurred.

Genocide

There was little controversy concerning the crime of genocide. In 1948, only a few years after the Nazi Holocaust ended, the U.N. General Assembly adopted the text of the Genocide Convention. That text enshrined a new international consensus defining and condemning the crime of genocide, and it anticipated the possibility that those charged with genocide might be tried by "such international penal tribunal as may have jurisdiction." [24] Since then, 127 states have become parties to the Convention and another 42 have signed it. In deference to this unusually broad support, the ICC Statute incorporates verbatim the Convention's definition of *genocide*.[25] According to this definition, genocide occurs when killing or other listed forms of mistreatment are "committed with intent to destroy, in whole or in part, a national, ethnical, racial, or religious group, as such."[26]

War Crimes

The term *war crimes* refers to a broad category of acts prohibited during armed conflict that have, over a period of time, come to be recognized under international law as criminal. They present definitional problems not raised by the very narrow and specific concept of genocide. Many war crimes are defined by treaty. The most important of these are the Geneva Conventions of 1949[27] and the 1907 Hague Convention (IV) Respecting the Laws and Customs of War and Its Regulations.[28] However, some war crimes are outlawed principally by unwritten customary international law rather than by treaty. In some cases, even where there is a treaty prohibiting a specific war crime, the treaty's effectiveness is limited by the fact that many states have failed to sign or ratify it.

Because there are so many different war crimes, recognized to varying degrees by treaties and by customary international law, there were many disagreements concerning which of these crimes should be subject to prosecution under the Statute. The final, four-part list of these war crimes represents a compromise, and it is far from all-inclusive. This list includes the most fundamental war crimes, such as the killing, torture, or mistreatment of civilians or prisoners of war (POWs); intentional attacks on civilian objects; and the bombardment of undefended towns, dwellings, or buildings that are not military objectives. It also includes intentional attacks on those involved in humanitarian assistance or peacekeeping missions in accordance with the U.N. Charter and even the destruction of enemy property not required by the necessities of war. As noted earlier, the use of chemical or biological weapons, which have been comprehensively banned by international treaty, is notably missing from the Statute's list of war crimes.

There was considerable debate in Rome about what general limitations, if any, should apply. The Statute clarifies that the ICC has jurisdiction regarding war crimes in particular when "committed as part of a plan or policy or as part of the large scale commission of such crimes."[29] A widespread or systematic range of illegal activity has always been an essential element in defining crimes against humanity but had never before been viewed as an element in the definition of war crimes.

The limitation originated with the U.S. government, which was concerned that if civilians inadvertently were killed in the course of a peacekeeping mission abroad, U.S. troops might be exposed to ICC jurisdiction. The original U.S. proposal would have strictly limited the ICC's jurisdiction over war crimes to those that were part of a policy or that were committed on a large scale. As adopted in the form proposed by the Bureau, the Statute makes these crimes the focus while leaving the ICC with the flexibility to prosecute other war crimes in appropriate cases. This illustrates the struggle of the Conference, and of the Bureau, to balance the minimum jurisdictional requirements of an effective ICC with U.S. concern that such a court might investigate war crimes after every U.S. military mission.

Another issue discussed at great length concerned jurisdiction over war crimes, particularly those committed during the course of internal armed conflicts (versus international conflicts, involving two or more countries). India and China, fearing intrusion into their internal affairs, wanted the ICC to address only international conflicts. But because so many war crimes today occur in civil wars, the United States and other nations considered it vital to maintain some ICC jurisdiction over internal conflicts.

As it stands, the Statute covers certain acts, such as the use of prohibited weapons and the starvation of civilians, only when committed in international armed conflict. Some crimes committed in internal conflicts fall under ICC jurisdiction only when committed during a "protracted" armed conflict between governmental authorities and organized armed groups or between such groups.[30] This demonstrates how the jurisdiction of the ICC has been subjected to limitations beyond those required by customary international law (although the Statute is progressive in specifically addressing crimes of gender violence whether committed in internal or international armed conflict[31]).

Ultimately, the Statute does authorize the prosecution of a broad range of war crimes even if committed during internal conflict.[32] These include mistreating noncombatants; rape and sexual crimes; conscripting children under the age of fifteen into the military; and intentionally directing attacks against civilians, nonmilitary objectives, or those involved in humanitarian assistance or peacekeeping missions in accordance with the U.N. Charter. The Statute makes clear that the

ICC's jurisdiction regarding internal armed conflict does not apply to "internal disturbances and tensions," such as riots, or to isolated and sporadic acts of violence[33]—a restriction arguably implicit in the very notion of war crimes.

Crimes against Humanity

The Statute recognizes the jurisdiction of the ICC over crimes against humanity when any one of a long list of prohibited acts[34] is committed "as part of a widespread or systematic attack directed against any civilian population."[35] It is also part of the definition of *crimes against humanity* that the act must have been committed with knowledge that it forms part of a widespread or systematic attack against civilians.

The Charter of the Nuremberg Tribunal was the first multilateral legal instrument[36] that expressly provided for the prosecution of crimes against humanity as an offense separate from war crimes.[37] The legal concept emerged in large part to remedy the argument that international law did not apply to criminal acts directed by a government against its own civilian population.[38] Extending international law so far into what was considered a sovereign sphere of activity is only justified when certain conditions have been satisfied. Formulating these core conditions has been the central challenge in the definition of crimes against humanity.[39]

The United Nations has adopted or considered multiple definitions of crimes against humanity, including a General Assembly resolution endorsing the standards of the Nuremberg Charter,[40] the International Law Commission (ILC) Draft Code of Crimes against the Peace and Security of Mankind,[41] and the Statutes of the International Criminal Tribunal for Former Yugoslavia (ICTY) and International Criminal Tribunal for Rwanda (ICTR). In spite of the confusing diversity of these formulations, the negotiations leading to the ICC Statute produced consensus on a narrowly defined core concept of crimes against humanity to be applied by the ICC.

The consensus reflects the concern of some states that ICC jurisdiction over these crimes should not intrude too far into their internal affairs. Not all widespread and systematic atrocities against civilians will qualify. In a major limitation on the ICC's jurisdiction, crimes against humanity can be found only where conduct involves the multiple commissions of the listed atrocities. These must be committed against civilians pursuant to or in furtherance of the policy of a state or other de facto political organization to commit such atrocities.[42] While this high jurisdictional threshold goes well beyond the requirements of general international law, it still defines crimes against humanity broadly enough to cover the pattern of such crimes seen recently in, for example, Chile, Cambodia, Bosnia, Kosovo, and Rwanda.

Composition and Administration of the Court

The ICC's success will depend on its ability to decide cases fairly. The Court will therefore need highly qualified Judges and Prosecutors. The Judges are to be chosen from among persons of high moral character, impartiality, and integrity who possess qualifications required for appointment to their highest national judicial offices. All must be nationals of a State Party and fluent in either French or English, the working languages of the ICC. Each nominee must have established competence and experience in criminal law and procedure or in relevant areas of international law such as international humanitarian law and the law of human rights.

Other matters to be taken into account in selecting the Judges include the need for the representation of the principal legal systems of the world, equitable geographical representation, a fair representation of male and female Judges, and the need for expertise on specific issues such as violence against women and children. No two Judges may be nationals of the same state.[43]

States Parties will nominate candidates for election to the ICC, although the Assembly of States Parties may create an Advisory Committee on Nominations. Those nominated will be either experts in criminal law and procedure or experts in international law. At least half of the selected Judges will be criminal law and procedure experts. Judges will be elected by the Assembly of States Parties. The secret ballot election will require a two-thirds majority of States Parties voting and present.[44]

The Statute provides for an ICC originally composed of eighteen Judges, who are to serve a single nine-year term. There was considerable debate in Rome on these basic structural issues, and flexibility was written into the Statute. Thus, the requirement that all Judges be full-time members of the Court may be relaxed, based on the Court's workload.[45] If the workload becomes too burdensome, the total number of Judges may be increased by the States Parties.[46]

The Judges are then to elect a President and two Vice Presidents.[47] The 18 Judges will be assigned to an Appeals Division of five Judges (including the President), a Trial Division of no fewer than six Judges, and a Pre-Trial Division of no fewer than six Judges.[48] The Trial and Pre-Trial Divisions are to be composed predominantly of Judges with criminal trial experience. Judges are not to engage in any activity likely to affect confidence in their independence[49] or to participate in any case in which their impartiality might be questioned on any ground. Either the Prosecutor or the person being investigated or prosecuted may request the disqualification of a Judge on this ground.[50]

The head Prosecutor and one or more Deputy Prosecutors will be elected by an absolute majority of the Assembly of States Parties to a single nine-year term in office. They must have extensive criminal trial experience.[51] Members of the Office of the Prosecutor are not to seek or to act on instructions from any external source. The ICC's principal administrative officer will be a Registrar elected to a five-year term by an absolute majority vote of the Judges.[52]

A Judge, the Prosecutor, or the Registrar may be removed from office for serious misconduct or for a serious breach of his or her duties under the Statute. The removal of a Judge will require a two-thirds vote of the Assembly of States Parties on a recommendation adopted by two-thirds of the other Judges. The Prosecutor may be removed by an absolute majority of States Parties, and a majority of the Judges can remove the Registrar.[53]

The Statute establishes an Assembly of States Parties as the plenary organ to provide management oversight to the other organs of the Court, to decide the budget, and to decide whether to alter the number of Judges. Assembly decisions on substantive matters will require a two-thirds majority of the States present and voting.[54] Amendments may not be adopted until seven years after the Statute enters into force. The Assembly will decide by majority vote whether to consider proposed amendments. It may deal with the proposal itself, or it may convene a Review Conference for that purpose. Amendments can be adopted by a two-thirds vote of all the States Parties but shall not come into effect for all States Parties until ratified by seven-eighths of them. A special rule applies to modifications affecting the list of crimes or their definitions. These amendments do not bind a State Party who has not ratified them, and the nationals of such a State Party are not subject to prosecution under the amendment.[55]

STEPS IN BRINGING A CASE TO THE ICC

The various steps in bringing a case to the ICC, as discussed in the next section, are summarized in the appendix in this volume.

Ratification of the ICC Statute

The ICC will not come into existence until sixty states have signed and ratified the Statute.[56] Nearly two years after the conclusion of the Rome Conference, ninety-six states had signed the Statute, and ten had completed the process of ratification.

Ratifying the Statute entails accepting binding obligations, including cooperating with the ICC in the investigation and the prosecution of crimes within its jurisdiction[57] and ensuring that there are procedures available under national law for all forms of cooperation specified under the Statute.[58] Most states will need to adopt implementing legislation or to make other adjustments in their national law before ratifying. This process could take years, even after the political decision to ratify the Statute has been made.

Preconditions to the Exercise of the ICC's Jurisdiction

Before the ICC can act on a case, its jurisdiction must be accepted by either the territorial state where the crimes allegedly have been committed or by the state of the nationality of the accused. Any state that becomes a Party to the Statute automatically accepts the jurisdiction of the ICC. Other states may also accept that jurisdiction by declaration. No such consent is required, however, for cases based on a referral by the Security Council, as discussed later.[59]

Initiation of Investigations and Prosecutions

There are three ways in which ICC investigations or prosecutions can be triggered. Any State Party to the Statute can refer to the Prosecutor for investigation of a situation in which crimes within the Court's jurisdiction appear to have been committed.[60] The Security Council also has the authority to refer such a situation to the Prosecutor.

The ICC Prosecutor also may initiate an investigation proprio motu (on her own authority) on the basis of information on crimes within the jurisdiction of the Court and for this purpose may seek additional information from any reliable source, including states, international organizations, and NGOs.[61] Many supporters of a strong ICC believed that it was essential to incorporate this third possibility into the Statute. They feared that, for political reasons, States Parties and the Security Council sometimes might hesitate to initiate investigations. Allowing the Prosecutor to seek information from NGOs also opens up the process for participation by these important private actors.

Investigations initiated solely on the Prosecutor's authority are subject to early review by the Pre-Trial Chamber. If the Prosecutor concludes that there is a reasonable basis for proceeding with such an investigation, he must request the Pre-Trial Chamber to authorize it. Authorization is given only if the Pre-Trial Chamber decides by a majority vote of its three Judges[62] both that there is a reasonable basis to proceed and that the case appears to fall within the jurisdiction of the ICC.[63] The Statute recognizes the interest of victims in this process by allowing them to submit their views and information to the Pre-Trial Chamber.

Admissibility, Complementarity, and ICC Deferral to National Courts

One of the most sensitive issues in the negotiation of the ICC Statute was the relationship between the jurisdiction of the ICC and that of national courts. The ICC was created to complement, not to displace, the criminal jurisdiction of states. Under the principle known as "complementarity,"[64] the ICC is to function as a jurisdictional "safety net" only when there is no alternative forum to prosecute those linked to serious international crimes.

The Rome Statute expressly limits the jurisdiction of the ICC to cases where no state with jurisdiction has investigated or prosecuted the case.[65] Any state with jurisdiction can assert a superior right to deal with a case simply by investigating and/or prosecuting it. When this happens, the ICC must defer to national proceedings even if the state determines that no prosecution is warranted. The only exception is where the state concerned "is unwilling or unable genuinely to carry out the investigation or prosecution."

In order to preserve the jurisdiction of states and to limit the ICC's right to intrude on that jurisdiction, the Statute sets out in clear and narrow terms the standard of what constitutes the "unwillingness" or "inability" of a state to carry out a genuine prosecution. The ICC may find unwillingness only where the national proceedings or the decision not to prosecute were made for the purpose of shielding the person from criminal responsibility; where there has been an unjustified delay in the proceedings inconsistent with an intent to bring the suspect to justice; or where the proceedings were, or are not, independent or impartial and are conducted in a manner inconsistent with an intent to bring the suspect to justice.[66]

In determining if a state is unable to carry out a genuine prosecution, the Court will consider whether "due to a total or substantial collapse or unavailability of its national judicial system, the state is unable to obtain the accused or the necessary evidence and testimony or otherwise unable to carry out its proceedings."[67]

The principle of ICC deferral to national criminal proceedings is embodied in an elaborate set of procedural requirements limiting the ICC Prosecutor's authority to proceed with a case. Article 19 contained such procedures prior to the Rome Conference, but the United States sought additional provisions to strengthen complementarity. The resulting Article 18 is intended to make it easier for any state that has investigated or is investigating a case to challenge at the very outset any ICC investigation of that case. The ICC Prosecutor must notify all states with jurisdiction about any investigations commenced, except those based on a Security Council referral.[68] After receiving this notice, states have one month to notify the Prosecutor of their own investigation of the persons concerned. The ICC Prosecutor must defer to any state's investigations, even that of a nonparty state, unless a Pre-Trial Chamber decides to authorize the investigation. Under Article 17, the Pre-Trial Chamber can do so only if two out of three Judges find that the state concerned is unwilling or unable to carry out a proper investigation. Should the Pre-Trial Chamber make such a determination, the state involved may appeal the decision to the Appeals Chamber on an expedited basis, where a majority of five Judges will decide the matter.

The Prosecutor's deferral to a state investigation is open to review if there is a significant change in circumstances affecting that state's unwillingness or inability to prosecute.[69] In such a case the Prosecutor may reapply to a Pre-Trial Chamber for authorization to conduct an investigation.

Pending a ruling on admissibility, or even when an ICC investigation has been deferred under Article 18, the Prosecutor may ask the Pre-Trial Chamber to authorize steps for the preservation of evidence. This is envisioned only in exceptional cases where there is a unique opportunity to obtain important evidence or where there is a significant risk that such evidence may not be subsequently available.[70]

In addition to the procedures under Article 18, another complete procedure for challenges to the jurisdiction of the Court or to the admissibility of a case is set out in Article 19 (the initial compromise reached prior to Rome). These two Articles exemplify the multiple procedural safeguards provided for within the Statute.

For each case, the ICC must satisfy itself that all applicable jurisdictional requirements have been met. Challenges to ICC's jurisdiction may be formulated by an accused, by a state with jurisdiction on the ground that it is investigating or prosecuting the case or has already done so, or by the territorial state or the state of nationality of the accused.[71] States are required to raise their challenges at the earliest possible opportunity, and, as a general rule, a state or an individual may raise such a challenge only once.[72]

The Pre-Trial Chamber is to rule on these challenges when no charges have yet been confirmed. After this stage, the Trial Chamber will rule on them. All such rulings are subject to appeal. Once an ICC trial has begun, the admissibility of that case can only be challenged on the grounds that the person accused has already been tried for the conduct in question.[73]

Possible Deferral of a Case Pursuant to Decision of the Security Council

Under Chapter VII of the United Nations Charter, the Security Council may decide what measures are necessary to maintain international peace and security. Although it was accepted during the Rome negotiations that nothing in the ICC Statute should undermine this fundamental role, there was disagreement regarding the degree of control the Security Council should have over the ICC.

The United States argued that the Security Council's authorization should be required for every ICC prosecution. Under this scenario any one of the Security Council's five permanent members, through the use of the veto, could have prevented an ICC prosecution. Other states felt that the ICC's independence and effectiveness would be severely compromised if every investigation required prior approval of the Security Council, which is a political body in which each permanent member wields a veto.

The Statute, as adopted in Rome, balances respect for the Security Council's role with the need to maintain the independence of the ICC.[74] It allows the Security Council to suspend any ICC investigation or prosecution for a (renewable) period of twelve months by passing a resolution to that effect under Chapter VII of the U.N. Charter. A single veto can prevent the suspension or renewal.[75]

Investigation/Evaluation by the Prosecutor

After the referral of a situation by a State Party or by the Security Council, the Prosecutor must make a preliminary decision as to whether to proceed with a full investigation. Unless he finds that there is insufficient evidence that a crime has been committed, that the potential case would be inadmissible, or that an investigation would not be in the interests of justice, he is to initiate a full investigation.[76] If the Prosecutor decides not to proceed, he informs both the Pre-Trial Chamber and the referring entity, which may request that the Pre-Trial Chamber review the decision.[77]

Once an investigation has begun, the Prosecutor is to collect evidence, including testimony from victims, witnesses and potential suspects, and may seek the cooperation of states and NGOs.[78] The Pre-Trial Chamber may authorize any orders or warrants requested by the Prosecutor for purposes of the investigation.[79] Where an arrest warrant has been issued, the accused is to appear before the Pre-Trial Chamber, which will then make a decision concerning the person's release or pre-trial detention.[80]

The Pre-Trial Chamber must hold a hearing on the confirmation of the charges. Within a reasonable time before that hearing, the accused is to receive a copy of the charges and a description of the Prosecutor's evidence. At the hearing, the Prosecutor must support each charge with sufficient evidence to establish grounds for the case, and the person accused may object to the charges, challenge the evidence presented by the Prosecutor, and present his or her own evidence. Based on this hearing, the Pre-Trial Chamber will decide whether to confirm or to dismiss each charge. Once charges are confirmed, the case will be referred to a Trial Chamber.[81]

Trial, Appeal, and Penalties

The Statute provides for trial by a three-Judge Trial Chamber that is entirely separate from the Pre-Trial Chamber. The trial is to be held in the presence of the accused, consistent with all the rights of the accused recognized by international human rights law.[82] These include the presumption of innocence, the right to a public hearing, the right to counsel, the right to a speedy trial, and the right to compel the attendance of witnesses on the same terms as the prosecution. The trial procedures set out in the Statute are to be supplemented by Rules of Procedure and Evidence to be adopted by a two-thirds majority of the Assembly of States Parties.[83]

The Statute provides for some important innovations. The first of these is the possibility of special measures for the protection of victims and witnesses whose fear of retribution, public humiliation, or other harm may make it difficult for them to participate in the proceedings.[84] Such measures have proved essential to the work of the recent ad hoc international tribunals. The Statute also provides that in making its decision in a case, the Court may order appropriate reparations to the victims of a person convicted.[85]

The onus is on the Prosecutor to prove the guilt of the accused beyond a reasonable doubt.[86] The decisions of the Trial Chamber can be made by a majority of the three Judges.[87] The ICC appeals process differs from that in the United States because in the ICC, both a conviction and an acquittal are subject to appeal. This reflects the practice of most civil law systems, such as those of U.S. allies in Europe. Thus, any decision of the ICC Trial Chamber may be appealed to a five-Judge Appeals Chamber. The Appeals Chamber can reverse or amend decisions or sentences of the Trial Chamber, or it can order a new trial before a different Trial Chamber.[88]

Those convicted may be sentenced to imprisonment of up to thirty years or, when appropriate, to a term of life imprisonment. A fine or a forfeiture of assets or proceeds derived from the crime may also be imposed.[89] The Court may order assets to be transferred to a Trust Fund for the benefit of crime victims and their families.[90]

A convicted criminal will be sent for imprisonment to a state designated by the Court from a list of those agreeing to accept sentenced criminals.[91] This imprisonment will be subject to the supervision of the ICC, and the conditions of imprisonment must meet widely accepted international treaty standards governing the treatment of prisoners.[92]

International Cooperation and Judicial Assistance

Under the ICC Statute, the States Parties agree to assist the Court in its investigation and prosecution of crimes within its jurisdiction.[93] This requires them to comply with the ICC's requests to arrest suspects, to transfer people to the Court, and to produce evidence. As a general principle, the ICC Statute accommodates the requested state's national procedures (including judicial, legal, and administrative practices). These are to be taken into account by the ICC in formulating requests for state cooperation.[94] However, the States Parties have agreed to ensure that necessary procedures will be available under their law.[95] In considering

ICC requests for cooperation, national courts are not to relitigate issues of admissibility that the Court has already decided.[96]

A State Party that denies an ICC request for cooperation must notify the ICC of the reasons for that denial. If the assistance requested is prohibited by the State's law on the basis of an existing fundamental legal principle of general application, the ICC must modify the request as necessary.[97]

If a requested State Party determines that disclosure of the information requested would prejudice its national security interests, a special regime applies. If the state refuses to provide the evidence requested, it must provide specific reasons for its decision unless they, too, would compromise its national security.[98] If the ICC determines that a State Party's refusal to cooperate violates the Statute, the Court may refer the matter to the Assembly of States Parties or to the U.N. Security Council (if the case is one based on a Security Council referral).[99] The Statute does not specify what sanctions, if any, might be imposed on states for noncompliance.

Financing

The ICC is to be financed primarily through contributions from States Parties.[100] Assessments are to be based, with appropriate adjustments, on the scale of assessments used for the United Nations regular budget.[101] During the Rome negotiations, the U.S. government argued strongly that nonparties should not be forced to finance the ICC via their contributions to the U.N. budget. The Statute seeks to accommodate this concern by noting that the ICC may receive funds provided by the United Nations "in particular in relation to expenses incurred due to referrals by the Security Council."[102] Thus where the Security Council makes use of the ICC, the Statute anticipates that the United Nations may wish to contribute to the special expenses incurred.

The ICC may also receive and utilize voluntary contributions from governments, international organizations, individuals, corporations, and other entities, based on criteria to be adopted by the Assembly of States Parties.[103]

CONCLUSION

When the Rome Conference adopted the Statute, it also established a follow-on PrepCom.[104] The PrepCom is to lay the foundation for the eventual functioning of the Court. It will prepare proposals for the Court's establishment and finalize the draft texts of the rules of procedures and evidence and of the elements of crimes.

Participation in the PrepCom is open to the United States as a signatory to the Final Act of the Conference.[105] The U.S. government has been actively participating in the PrepCom sessions, despite insisting that it cannot sign the Rome Statute without some type of policy changes—if not to the Statute itself then to the rules of evidence and procedure or to the elements of crimes.[106]

The United States remains extremely concerned about precluding ICC prosecution of U.S. officials and military personnel and has proposed exempting from ICC jurisdiction individuals who a state acknowledges were acting as agents of that state. The United States could thereby ensure that Americans conceiving or executing U.S. policy never would be subject to an ICC. Many ICC signatories are certain to view this as opening an enormous loophole because someone such as Slobodan Milosevic could easily ensure that his actions would be acknowledged as official acts.

Other U.S. concerns at the post-Rome PrepCom include returning to the original Geneva Convention language the crime of transferring populations,[107] shaping the process of defining the crime of aggression, and clarifying the details of the Assembly of States Parties' control over the prosecutor. The United States also is committed to changing the regime governing amendments to the Statute. If a State Party declines to ratify an amendment relative to a new crime, the ICC cannot prosecute that State's nationals for that crime.[108] Nonparty states will not have this option. The U.S. government, which presumably expects to remain a nonparty for the foreseeable future, rejects this privilege.

While the United States has now focused on its most important objectives, some of its goals appear to require fundamental modifications of the Statute's intent, if not its language. Such changes will not be easy to achieve. The function of the PrepCom is to help bring the Court of the Rome Statute into being, not to modify its agreed tenets.

The United States has stressed the benefits of U.S. support for the ICC. As Ambassador David Scheffer notes, "A lot of governments recognize that if the United States can be brought on board, the treaty, in a pragmatic sense, can be greatly strengthened . . . because we can bring our resources, our enforcement capabilities, our diplomatic skills, and so much of what we provide to the ad hoc tribunals."[109] The support of the Security Council, of which the United States is a key member, also will be important because it will eliminate the need for state consent and it will permit involvement of the Security Council in enforcing orders of the Court.

Although the participation of the United States is much to be desired, it is not absolutely essential to the success of the ICC. Even active U.S. opposition probably could not prevent the Statute from achieving its next milestone: the sixty ratifications needed to bring the ICC into existence. Washington may be able to resolve some of its concerns by continuing a constructive dialogue within the context of the PrepCom. Yet it will be impossible to provide an absolute guarantee that U.S. nationals would never be prosecuted without U.S. consent and to simultaneously create an independent and effective ICC.

NOTES

1. Rome Statute of the International Criminal Court ("Statute"), U.N. Doc. A/CONF.183/9 (reissued for technical reasons), July 17, 1998.

2. U.N.G.A. Res. 50/46, U.N. Doc. A/RES/50/46, December 11, 1995.

3. In a remarkable feat of coordination, the CICC organized experts from a variety of fiercely independent NGOs into teams focused on specific subject areas.

4. *Rules of Procedure for the United Nations Diplomatic Conference of Plenipotentiaries on the Establishment of an International Criminal Court,* U.N. Doc. A/Conf.183/6, June 23, 1998 (*"Rome Conference Rules"*), Rule 52(d).

5. The Bureau of the Committee of the Whole was composed of the chairman, Mr. Philippe Kirsch (Canada); three vice presidents, Ms. Silvia Fernandez de Gurmendi (Argentina), Mr. Constantin Virgil Ivan (Romania), and Mr. Phakiso Mochochoko (Lesotho); and the Raporteur, Mr. Yasumasa Nagamine (Japan). Final Act of the United Nations Diplomatic Conference of Plenipotentiaries on the Establishment of an International Criminal Court, done at Rome on July 17, 1998 (U.N. Doc. A/Conf.183/10, para. 19).

6. U.N. Doc. A/Conf. 183/C.1/L.53 of July 6, 1998.

7. Unattributed, "U.S. Lays Down its Cards," *Terra Viva,* July 10, 1998.

8. See Lawrence Weschler, chapter 5 this volume, for a fuller discussion of the statement.

9. According to the NGO count, 76 percent of delegations rejected the high threshold for war crimes proposed by the United States; 73 percent supported automatic jurisdiction over core crimes; 76 percent supported empowering the Prosecutor to initiate cases on his or her own authority; 79 percent supported the Korean formulation requiring only limited state consent to jurisdiction (the basis of what is now Article 12); and 81 percent opposed requiring Security Council approval for each ICC investigation. The United States was among the 75 percent who favored ICC jurisdiction over internal as well as international armed conflict. "The Numbers: NGO Coalition Special Report on Country Positions," *CICC Monitor* (July 10, 1998): 1.

10. U.N. Doc. A/Conf. 183/C.1/L.59 of July 10, 1998.

11. "The Virtual Vote," *CICC Monitor* 23 (July 15, 1998): 1.

12. *International Committee of the Red Cross: Concerns on Jurisdiction of the International Criminal Court Relating to the Bureau Proposal* (A/Conf.183/C.1/L.59) (Information Conveyed by New Zealand), U.N. Doc. A/Conf. 183/INF/9, July 13, 1998.

13. "Build a Strong Court, and Hope the U.S. Will Follow, Says ABA President," *On the Record,* July 14, 1998, 1.

14. Unattributed, "Activists: U.S. Making a Mockery of ICC," *Terra Viva,* July 13, 1998, 3.

15. Many developing states objected to the Statute's perceived discrimination against "poor countries' weapons of mass destruction" by criminalizing chemical and biological weapons while ignoring nuclear arms.

16. The Council is seen by many developing states as a bastion of Western and great power privilege because of its composition and veto voting procedure.

17. The Draft Statute proposed by the Bureau, which was eventually adopted as the Rome Statute, first appeared as U.N. Doc. A/Conf. 183/C.1/L.76 of July 16, 1998.

18. The amendment would have offered nonparty states limited protection from the

jurisdiction of the ICC by requiring their consent to "jurisdiction over acts committed [on their] territory . . . or committed by [their] officials or agents . . . in the course of official duties and acknowledged by the State as such." U.N. Doc. A/Conf. 183/C.1/L.90 of July 16, 1998, art. 7 (1). It was designed to alleviate the concern that U.S. political leaders and military personnel could be tried for carrying out U.S. policy.

19. Because the final vote was registered by a nonrecorded electronic vote, there is no official record of national voting. One measure of U.S. isolation is that not all countries voting "no" acknowledged their vote. Major newspapers and other media sources offered varying reports. It is undisputed that the United States, Israel, and China voted "no". See, e.g., *New York Times*, July 20, 1998, A15; and *Sun* (Baltimore), July 26, 1998, 4C (both naming Libya, Iraq, Qatar, and Yemen as "no" votes); *Los Angeles Times*, July 22, 1998, (naming seven states in addition to the United States, i.e., Iraq, Libya, China, Indonesia, Turkey, Mexico, and Israel); *Independent* (London), July 22, 1998, 3 (including India and Algeria); *Herald* (Glasgow), July 25, 1998, 15 (includes Sudan among "no" votes). However, it appears that Israel may well join the Court now that its main concerns (about the Statute's language regarding treatment of people in occupied territories) have been satisfied.

20. Statute, art. 10.

21. Statute, art. 121(3).

22. Statute, art. 121(4).

23. Statute, art. 5(2).

24. Convention on the Prevention and Punishment of the Crime of Genocide, 78 U.N.T.S. 277, December 9, 1948 "Genocide Convention."

25. While the ICC Statute restates the Genocide Convention's definition of *genocide*, it does not incorporate the list of punishable acts from that convention, which includes conspiracy to commit genocide, direct and public incitement to commit genocide, attempt to commit genocide, and complicity in genocide.

26. Statute, art. 6.

27. Convention for the Amelioration of the Condition of the Wounded and Sick in Armed Forces in the Field, August 12, 1949, 75 U.N.T.S. 31; Geneva Convention for the Amelioration of the Condition of Wounded, Sick, and Shipwrecked Members of Armed Forces at Sea, August 12, 1949, 75 U.N.T.S. 85; Geneva Convention Relative to the Treatment of Prisoners of War, August 12, 1949, 75 U.N.T.S. 135; and Geneva Convention Relative to the Protection of Civilian Persons in Time of War, August 12, 1949, 75 U.N.T.S. 287.

28. Carnegie Endowment for International Peace, *The Hague Conventions and Declarations of 1899 and 1907* (New York: Oxford University Press, 1915), 100.

29. Statute, art. 8(1).

30. Statute, art. 8(2)(f), par. 2 (e).

31. See Statute, art. 8(2)(b)(xxii) and art. 8(2)(e)(vi).

32. The complete list of war crimes applicable to internal armed conflict appears in art. 8(2)(c) and art. 8(2)(e).

33. Statute, art. 8(2)(d) and art. 8(2)(f).

34. The list includes murder; extermination; enslavement; deportation or forcible transfer of population; imprisonment or other severe deprivation of physical liberty in violation of fundamental rules of international law; torture, rape, sexual slavery, enforced prostitution, forced pregnancy, enforced sterilization, or any other form of sexual violence of compa-

rable gravity; persecution against any identifiable group or collectivity on political, racial, national, ethnic, cultural, religious, gender, or other grounds that are universally recognized as impermissible under international law, in connection with any of the other prohibited acts referred to in the definition of crimes against humanity or any crime within the jurisdiction of the Court; enforced disappearance of persons; the crime of apartheid; or other inhumane acts of a similar character intentionally causing great suffering, or serious injury to body or to mental or physical health. Statute, art. 7(1).

35. Statute, art. 7(1).

36. "Crimes against humanity" had earlier been mentioned in a diplomatic note when France, Great Britain, and Russia denounced the 1915 massacre of Armenians in Turkey as "crimes against humanity and civilization for which all members of the Turkish Government will be held responsible together with its agents implicated in the massacres." M. Cherif Bassiouni and Peter Manikas, *The Law of the International Criminal Tribunal for the Former Yugoslavia* (Irvington-on-Hudson, N.Y.: Transnational 1996), 589, quoting Yougindra Kushalani, *The Dignity and Honour of Women as Basic and Fundamental Human Rights* (The Hague: Martinus Nijhoff, 1982): 14.

37. Article 6 of the Nuremberg Charter lists crimes against humanity as one of the three categories of crimes within the jurisdiction of the Nuremberg Tribunal: "(c) CRIMES AGAINST HUMANITY: namely, murder, extermination, enslavement, deportation, and other inhumane acts committed against any civilian population, before or during the war, or persecutions on political, racial, or religious grounds in execution of or in connection with any crime within the jurisdiction of the Tribunal, whether or not in violation of the domestic law of the country where perpetrated." Charter of the International Military Tribunal, *annexed to* The Agreement for the Prosecution and Punishment of the Major War Criminals of the European Axis, August 8, 1945, art. 6, 59 Stat. 1544, 82 U.N.T.S. 279, art. 6(c).

38. Bassiouni and Manikas, *The Law of the International Criminal Tribunal for the Former Yugoslavia*, 540.

39. The Legal Committee of the United Nations War Crimes Committee explained the basis for international intervention this way:

Isolated offences did not fall within the notion of crimes against humanity. As a rule systematic mass action, particularly if it was authoritative, was necessary to transform a common crime, punishable only under municipal law, which thus became also the concern of international law. Only crimes which either by their magnitude and savagery or by their large number or by the fact that a similar pattern was applied at different times and places endangered the international community or shocked the conscience of mankind, warranted intervention by States other than that on whose territory the crimes had been committed, or whose subjects had become their victims. *History of the United Nations War Crimes Commission and the Development of the Laws of War: Compiled by the United Nations War Crimes Commission, London* (1948), 179.

40. *Affirmation of the Principles of International Law Recognized by the Charter of the Nuremberg Tribunal*, U.N.G.A. Res. 95 (1), U.N. GAOR, 1st Sess., Part II, at 188, U.N. Doc. A/64/Add.1 (1946), December 11, 1946.

41. Report of the International Law Commission on the work of its Forty-Third Session, April 29–July 19, 1991, U.N. GAOR, 46th Sess., Supp. No. 10, at 70, 147, U.N. Doc. A/46/10 (1993), at 265.

42. Statute, art. 7(2)(a).
43. Statute, art. 36.
44. Statute, art. 36.
45. Statute, art. 35(1) and (2).
46. Statute, art. 36(2).
47. Statute, art. 38(1).
48. Statute, art. 39.
49. Statute, art. 40.
50. Statute, art. 41.
51. Statute, art. 42.
52. Statute, art. 43.
53. Statute, art. 46.
54. Statute, art. 112.
55. Statute, art. 121.
56. Statute, art. 126(1).
57. Statute, art. 86.
58. Statute, art. 88.
59. Statute, art. 12.
60. Statute, art. 13(a), art. 13(b), and art. 14. See also Robinson Everett's discussion, chap. 8, in this volume.
61. Statute, art. 15 (1) and art. 15(2).
62. Some critics have argued that the Statute's Article 39(2)(b)(iii) makes it possible for a single Judge of the Pre-Trial Chamber to override complementarity. In fact, Article 57(2)(a) makes it clear that the relevant rulings "must be concurred in by a majority of its judges." The Article goes on to distinguish "other cases" in which a single Judge of the Pre-Trial Chamber could act.
63. Statute, art. 15(3) and art. 15(4).
64. The Rome Statute first introduces this concept in its Preamble when it emphasizes "that the International Criminal Court established under this Statute shall be complementary to national criminal jurisdictions." Preamble, par. 10.
65. Statute, art. 17(1).
66. Statute, art. 17(2).
67. Statute, art. 17(3).
68. Due to the special authority of the Security Council under Chapter VII of the U.N. Charter, a different regime applies to situations referred to the ICC Prosecutor by the Security Council.
69. Statute, art. 18(3).
70. Statute, art. 18(6).
71. Statute, art. 19 (1) and art. 19(2).
72. Statute, art. 19(4). But if the Pre-Trial Chamber rejected a State's preliminary challenge to admissibility under Article 18, this does not preclude a later challenge under Article 19(2) "on the grounds of additional significant facts or significant change of circumstances." Statute, art. 18(7).
73. Statute, art. 19(4).
74. Additional issues relating to balancing the pursuit of justice with maintenance of peace are discussed in Michael Scharf's chapter (chap. 11, this volume).

75. Statute, art. 16.
76. Statute, art. 53(1).
77. Statute, art. 53(2) and art. 53(3).
78. Statute, art. 54.
79. Statute, art. 56, art. 57, and art. 58.
80. Statute, art. 60.
81. Statute, art. 61.
82. This list of internationally recognized fair trial rights was originally formulated in Article 14 of the International Covenant on Civil and Political Rights, to which the United States is a party. The list is reproduced in full in Article 67 of the Statute.
83. Statute, art. 51.
84. Statute, art. 68.
85. Statute, art. 75(2).
86. Statute, art. 66.
87. Statute, art. 74.
88. Statute, art. 83(1) and art. 83(2).
89. Statute, art. 77.
90. Statute, art. 79.
91. Statute, art. 103.
92. Statute, art. 106.
93. Statute, art. 86.
94. See Statute, art. 89(1), art. 91(2)(c), art. 91(4), art. 93(1), and art. 99(1).
95. Statute, art. 88.
96. See Statute, art. 89(2), art. 90(2), art. 95, and art. 99(4).
97. Statute, art. 93(b) and art. 93 (3).
98. Statute, art. 72(1) and art. 72 (b).
99. Statute, art. 72(7)(ii) and art. 87(7).
100. Statute, art. 115(1).
101. Statute, art. 117.
102. Statute, art. 115(b).
103. Statute, art. 116.
104. Final Act of the United Nations Diplomatic Conference of Plenipotentiaries on the Establishment of an International Criminal Court ("Final Act"), done at Rome on July 17, 1998 (U.N. Doc. A/Conf. 183/10*), Annex F, par. 1. The Final Act merely certifies which states and observers participated in the conference and acknowledges the final result. Signing it does not entail any treaty obligation and is not to be confused with signing or ratifying the Rome Statute.
105. Final Act, Annex F, par. 2.
106. Barbara Crossette, "Tying Down Gulliver with Those Pesky Treaties," *New York Times*, August 8, 1999, Section 4, p. 3, Column 1. See also David Scheffer's comments in chapter 6 of this volume.
107. Significant progress on this point was made. See Edith M. Lederer, "Compromise Reached on War Tribunal," *Associated Press*, December 18, 1999.
108. Statute, art. 121(5).
109. Crossette, "Tying Down Gulliver."

5

Exceptional Cases in Rome: The United States and the Struggle for an ICC

Lawrence Weschler

PRELUDE: "THE MOTHER OF ALL MOTHERBOARDS"

"This is easily the most complex international negotiation I have ever been involved in," Philippe Kirsch, the chairman of the International Conference aimed at promulgating an international criminal court (ICC), commented one afternoon during a rare break in the proceedings. The chief legal adviser to the Canadian Foreign Ministry, the youthful-seeming Kirsch could claim an improbably vast experience chairing such convocations (in recent years, he'd spearheaded, among others, conferences on maritime terrorism; the safety and deportment of U.N. workers in the field; refinements of various International Red Cross protocols; and, most recently, nuclear terrorism). As it happened, he wasn't even supposed to be anywhere near this particular process, having been dragooned into his current role, on an emergency basis, when the highly regarded Dutch legal adviser Adriaan Bos, who'd been chairing the painstaking four-year-long preparatory committee (PrepCom) process leading up to the Rome meeting, fell gravely ill a mere three weeks before the opening of the final convocation. "We have representatives here from one hundred sixty-two countries," Kirsch continued, "confronting, many of them for the first time, a draft document of over two hundred pages, consisting of one hundred twenty articles, and containing thirteen hundred brackets, that is to say, thirteen hundred issues which the six Preparatory Conferences couldn't resolve, leaving multiple options to be tackled one by one by everybody gathered here—the thirteen hundred hardest issues.

"There's the simple linguistic complexity of the undertaking." (Earlier, the head of the drafting committee had related to me a confounding moment when the Chinese delegate had suddenly started objecting to the eventual Court's seat being in The Hague—although, as it turned out, it wasn't The Hague that was bothering him; rather, "it was the shockingly inappropriate reference to—how shall I put it?—the Court's derriere.") "There's the way we have to interweave all sorts of different legal procedural traditions," Kirsch went on, "for instance, the Napoleonic civil law tradition on the one hand and the Anglo-Saxon common law tradition on the other. The one enshrines an activist investigating judge as the finder of fact; the other favors an adversarial procedure, defense versus prosecution before a studiously impartial judge. The one allows trials in absentia; the other finds such trials utterly abhorrent. And so forth. And that's not even getting into, say, traditions of Islamic law. How does all that get channeled into a single statute?

"And precisely what law is the eventual Court supposed to be enforcing—the Geneva Conventions, the Hague law, the Genocide Treaty, the Crimes against Humanity jurisprudence flowing out of the Nuremberg Tribunal? Not everyone subscribes to all of those standards, and in any case, much of this body of law exists in so-called 'customary' form, which is to say the degree to which it is actually observed is subject to evolving customary practice, which is in constant flux. This Statute, on the other hand, has to be precise, every detail spelled out, all the ambiguities clarified. For example, the law of war with regard to international conflict is considerably more developed than that applying to internal conflicts, even though most conflict nowadays comes in the latter form. There are some countries here that don't want the Tribunal having any say over internal conflicts, while others are pushing for a fairly stiff internal conflict regime. Some countries insist on the death penalty, while others insist that they will walk out if the death penalty is included. Some countries want the Tribunal to be as much under the [U.N.] Security Council's control as possible—several of the Permanent Five, for example. Others—India, Pakistan—insist on its being completely free of any Security Council role." (There had been a marvelous moment in the Committee of the Whole just that morning when the Indian and the Pakistani delegates had taken to lavishly praising each other for taking precisely that stand. Translation: they both wanted to be entirely free to enter into savage war, no holds barred, with one another, at any moment, without having to worry about their case getting referred to the Tribunal by any meddlesome Security Council.)

"And it goes on and on," Kirsch continued. "How will the judges be chosen? Who will pay for the entire operation? With everything to be resolved in just five weeks. Some countries want the use or even the threat of using nuclear weapons included as a war crime—India, again, for instance. Others, such as the United States, would storm out of the conference were that to happen. Trinidad and Tobago started this whole recent phase of negotiations back in 1989 by reviving a long-dormant proposal for a permanent International Criminal Court—only what they wanted it to address was drug crimes, and they still want that. Others want it to cover the crime of aggression, which nobody at the U.N. has been able to define in fifty years. Others want to include terrorism—but how do you define that?

"Some favor a strong, robust Court; others say they do but clearly don't; while others say they don't and mean it. It often depends on who happens to be in power back home at the moment: a fledgling democracy that a few years ago might have been a dictatorship, or the other way around; a country just coming out of a civil war or just about to go into one. They all look at matters differently, and differently than they might have a few years ago or might a few years from now. It's incredibly dispersed."

"Like a 3-D chess game," one of Kirsch's lieutenants interjected, "being played on a rotating board."

"On a rotating fluid board," elaborated another.

"And on top of everything else," Kirsch resumed, "this Conference is transpiring under a truly unprecedented degree of public scrutiny. The NGOs [nongovernmental organizations] are here in force, incredibly well disciplined and coordinated. They've got representatives monitoring all the working groups and even inside the Committee of the Whole." (The General Assembly had passed a special measure earlier in the year that allowed NGOs unprecedented access into the Committee of the Whole, at which point the press had been allowed in as well.) "Everything is happening in full view. Nothing happens without everybody knowing about it instantaneously. It's really altogether unique."

"People compare it to the land-mines process," Alan Kessel, the acting head of the Canadian delegation, interjected, referring to the international campaign that had culminated the previous year in Ottawa with a comprehensive land mine ban (which the United States, up till then, had pointedly declined to sign onto). "Some of the NGO people sometimes say, 'Well, we can do it like the land mines.' But land mines was . . . I mean, by the end, that was a simple on-off switch. Either you were for it or you were against it. This, by contrast, is like a great big motherboard. You touch a switch here and five lights blink off over there. You attend to one of those, and sixteen flash on over here. This conference has to be the Mother of all Motherboards!"

Double Vision

There were times, sitting on the margins of the Committee of the Whole in Rome, gazing out over the hall and squinting one's eyes in a particular way, that one could momentarily envision the hundreds of delegates and experts gathered there—the blue–black Africans, the turbaned Iranians, the Brits in their Savile Row finery and the Russians in theirs, the Chinese and the Japanese and the Indians, the Americans toting their ever-present satchels and briefcases—as a vast convocation of the Family of Man, all gathered together in that one place at last, finally and once and for all, to face down the greatest scandal of the twentieth century, the galling impunity with which millions and indeed hundreds of millions of victims had been hounded to their deaths, and to proclaim, on the cusp of the new millennium, in the firmest possible voice, "Never Again!"—to proclaim it and mean it and make it so: that never again would victims be permitted to sink like that into oblivion, and never again would their tormentors be permitted to harbor such blithe confidence regarding their own indubitable inviability.

It was possible, squinting one's eyes one way, to see it like that. But then, if you squinted them another way or if you cocked your ear such that you were actually listening to some of the speeches, suddenly the same convergence of delegates could transmogrify from stand-ins for the Family of Man to the representatives of 162 separate and distinct states, each one zealously husbanding its own righteous sovereignty, each one all for lavishing such vigilance on the other guy but damned if it was going to subject itself or its compatriots to any such intrusive oversight. In fairness, not all of them felt that way and certainly not all the time; but these were, after all, diplomats first and foremost, whose overriding brief, here as anywhere else (as one of the NGO representatives observed dispiritedly from the margins), was "to protect sovereignty, reduce costs, and dodge obligations."

I mentioned that double vision one afternoon to a young lawyer on an important Southern Hemisphere delegation, a veteran of the PrepCom process and one of the most energetic presences in the working-group trenches; and he noted that many of the delegates experienced themselves in a similarly doubled light. "Especially among some of the younger, middle- and lower-ranking delegates," he said, "many of whom start out as the representative of Country X to the ICC Diplomatic Conference but slowly find their allegiances shifting, so that they become rather the delegate of the ICC Conference back to their foreign ministry, and presently, even, a sort of secret agent, burrowing toward a successful outcome. 'My minister says this,' they'll tell you, 'but I think if you propose it this other way, he won't notice, and we can still accomplish the same purpose'—that sort of thing."

I was struck by the similarity of that sort of drama to accounts I'd read of the American Constitutional Convention of 1787–88, and indeed I often had the sense of being witness to a parallel sort of historic undertaking. Just as back then, fiercely independent states were being enjoined to surrender part of their precious sovereignty to an as yet inchoate united entity and were doing so at best grudgingly (insisting on the primacy of "state's rights" to the very end—an insistence that could arise out of an honest concern for the more authentic, responsive kind of governance available at the more localized level but that could just as easily arise out of more perverse imperatives, such as the desire to preserve the institution of slavery). So the nation-states gathered in Rome seemed driven by a similar amalgam of authentic and then more suspect misgivings.

THE ROME PROCESS

Conference Dynamics

For the first three weeks of the Conference, Chairman Kirsch and his multinational associates in the Conference's executive Bureau maintained an almost studied aloofness, allowing the delegates to flounder in the complexities of the evolving document. Although many of the delegates were veterans of the PrepCom process, many more were encountering the Draft Statute for the first time (many of the smaller countries simply hadn't been able to afford to send delegations to the earlier meetings), and there was a cliff-steep learning curve. In addition, the Rome meeting had elicited the attendance of higher-ranking delegates; and as one of the PrepCom veterans noted wryly, "Such types aren't generally prone to humility. They are incapable, for instance, of saying, 'I don't understand this provision. Could you explain it to me?' Instead they launch into a long flowery statement detailing their own manifest misunderstanding of the matter, all so as to provoke you, at the very end, into responding with the simple clarification they'd been trying to elicit all along. But it can take forever." The various working groups were plowing through the myriad brackets all the while, struggling toward occasional consensus and moving on. But the tough questions—the independence of the Court and its Prosecutor, the oversight role of the U.N. Security Council, the sort of jurisdiction that the Court would be able to extend over precisely what sort of law—remained scarily unresolved, and time seemed to be fast running out.

At the beginning of the fourth week of a five-week Conference, expertly gauging the growing sense of anxiety in the hall, Kirsch launched a series of calibrated interventions—working drafts on major issues in which he attempted to narrow the contours of the sprawling debate, bracketing out extreme positions that weren't any longer likely to elicit consensus, narrowing the options on any given contentious matter to three or four options, floating various compromises, narrowing the options still further. It was remarkable to watch the way he seemed to amass authority—stature he'd doubtless be needing to spend later on—simply by being the one who was at last moving the process demonstrably forward.

By the middle of the fourth week, a range of possible outcomes was beginning to arc into view. One afternoon around that time, I worried out a sort of flow chart with a Latin American delegate. There seemed at that point to be basically three possible outcomes: On the one extreme, the Conference could completely collapse by the end of the next week, the delegates storming home in unbridgeable anger. At the other extreme, they might emerge with a truly robust Court—"Not just a court," in the words of the Canadian Foreign Minister Lloyd Axworthy, "but a court worthy of the name"—a court with powerful jurisdiction over clean, clear law, a strong mandate, and the wherewithal to carry it out. Wasn't going to happen, was the simple verdict of my Latin American friend—no way.

Between the two extremes were middle possibilities: One branch debouched in a sort of crippled court, a Potemkin court, a court in name only; something that would look for all the world like a full-fledged court, but whose tendons—as to jurisdiction, independence, authority—would have been surgically severed from the outset. It would be an excuse court: a court to which the Great Powers could refer intractable problems as if they were actually doing something, confident that nothing would actually get done. The other branch led toward a fledgling court, a baby court, a court whose powers and prospects, at the outset at any rate, would be highly circumscribed but that still had the capacity to grow. "Something like your own Supreme Court in the original Constitution," my Latin American friend volunteered. "I mean, if you look at the Constitution itself, the Supreme Court at the outset really had very little authority, it was very weak. For instance, the Constitution itself doesn't grant it the right of judicial review—the power, that is, to rule on the constitutionality of the acts of other branches or of the sovereign states. That was a power it only grabbed for itself, fifteen years later, with Justice Marshall's ruling in *Marbury vs. Madison*. And maybe one could imagine a similar development here. A baby court now that gradually gains the confidence of the world community through its baby steps and then, at some moment of crisis in the future, under appropriate leadership . . . On the other hand, that presupposes that it's given room to grow." This raised the alternatives of a baby in a spacious crib, as it were, or a baby in a tight-fitting lead box. "Imagine, for instance," my Latin American friend ventured, "if the U.S. Constitution had specifically forbidden the possibility of judicial review." The baby in the lead box. "On the other hand," he smiled conspiratorially, "maybe it would be possible to build some hidden trapdoors into that lead box."

America's Bottom Line

One afternoon, one of the most canny thinkers in the hall, a leading Asian delegate, was parsing some of the 3-D game's more intricate strategic considerations for me: "The thing is," he explained, "you want to create a court that the parties that might need it would still be willing to sign on to. I mean, face it, we're not going to need to be investigating Sweden. So, the treaty needs to be 'weak' enough, unthreatening enough, to have its jurisdiction accepted without being so weak and so unthreatening that it would thereafter prove useless. It's one of our many paradoxes."

And yet, paradoxically, those last few weeks, the biggest challenge facing the process no longer seemed to be coming from such neo-renegade states. Rather, it was being presented, with growing insistence, by the United States, whose position was truly paradoxical.

The United States had been one of the principal moving forces behind the Nuremberg Tribunal and more recently was a leading sponsor of the ad hoc tribunals on Rwanda and the former Yugoslavia (dozens of lawyers from the Justice Department, the Pentagon, and other government agencies had been seconded to serve stints in the Prosecutor's office in The Hague, and several of those were now serving on the U.S. delegation in Rome as well). Secretary of State Madeleine Albright—herself a childhood witness to the Holocaust in Europe—had played a strong role in fostering the ad hoc tribunals during her time as Ambassador to the United Nations. She had made the apprehension and prosecution of accused war criminals one of the rhetorical touchstones of her tenure at State. In addition, on several occasions across the preceding years, President Bill Clinton had issued forceful calls for a permanent war crimes tribunal, most recently in March 1998 when he addressed genocide survivors and government officials in Kigali, Rwanda.

The U.S. delegation—forty strong, and easily the best prepared and most professionally disciplined at the Conference—was spearheaded by David Scheffer, Albright's ambassador-at-large for war crimes issues, who had clearly been consumed by the subject for some time. Over lunch one afternoon, on the rooftop cafeteria atop the Conference proceedings, he became quite emotional, describing a trip he had taken to Rwanda in December 1997, accompanying Secretary Albright: the horrors he had witnessed, the terrible testimonies he had heard. He grew silent for a moment, gazing out toward the Coliseum, before continuing: "I have this recurrent dream in which I walk into a small hut. The place is a bloody mess, terrible carnage, victims barely hanging on, and I stagger out, shouting, 'Get a doctor! Get a doctor!' and I become more and more enraged because no one's reacting fast enough." He went on, passionately invoking the importance of what was going on down below us and insisting on the necessity of its successful outcome.

And yet, as the Conference lumbered toward its climax, the U.S. delegation seemed increasingly gripped by a single overriding concern. Senator Jesse Helms, the Republican head of the Foreign Relations Committee, had already let it be known that any treaty emerging from Rome that left open even the slightest possibility of any Americans ever, under any circumstance, being subjected to judgment or even oversight by the Court would be "dead on arrival" at his committee. The Pentagon was known to be advancing a similarly absolutist line. The State Department, sugarcoating the message only slightly, regularly pointed out how, in Scheffer's words, "The American armed forces have a unique peacekeeping role, posted to hot spots all around the world. Representing the world's sole remaining superpower, American soldiers on such missions stand to be uniquely subject to frivolous, nuisance accusations by parties of all sorts. And we simply cannot be expected to expose our people to those sorts of risks. We are dead serious about this. It is an absolute bottom line with us."

Originally the U.S. team thought it had addressed this concern with a simple provision mandating that the Court only be allowed to take up cases specifically referred to it by the Security Council—where the United States has a veto (as do Britain, France, China, and Russia). In effect, the Americans seemed to be favoring a permanent version of the current ad hoc tribunals, the authority of which would all flow from the Security Council but without the cumbersome necessity of having to repeatedly start all over again (statutes, staffing, financing). The rest of the Permanent Five also tended to favor such an approach for obvious reasons of self-interest but also out of concern over the Security Council's own paramount mission, enshrined in Chapter VII of the U.N. Charter—the securing and maintenance of world peace.

The Role of the Security Council

The entire Rome Conference was transpiring under the motto "Peace and Justice," but, as proponents of the Security Council's primacy liked to point out, there would come times when the two might not necessarily coincide, at least not simultaneously. In order to secure peace, the Security Council might need to negotiate with technically indictable war criminals and might even need to extend pledges of full amnesty to them in the context of final peace agreements. At such moments, it couldn't very well have an unguided Prosecutor careering about, upending the most delicate of negotiations. Therefore, if the Security Council was "seized" with an issue—as the term of art has it—it needed to be able to forestall, even if only temporarily, any such Court interference.

Opponents of this line—many of the countries that didn't happen to have such veto power, and the preponderance of the NGO observers—liked to cite a Papal remark to the effect that "If you want peace, seek justice," further pointing out that as often as not, historically, a Security Council "seized" with an issue was a Security Council seized *up* and paralyzed. The veto-encumbered Security Council was the very institution, after all, that for fifty years after Nuremberg had proved incapable of mounting trials in the cases of Idi Amin, Pol Pot, or Saddam Hussein (at the time of his genocidal Anfal campaign against his own Kurdish population). Most of the time over the past fifty years, war criminals have had sheltering patrons among the Permanent Five—Pol Pot, for instance, had the Chinese; the Argentine generals had the Americans (just as, more recently, U.S. Ambassador Bill Richardson had actively shielded the Congo's Laurent Kabila from the full force of Security Council oversight into the ghastly massacres involved in the campaign leading up to his installation). In this context, the Yugoslav and the Rwandan ad hoc tribunals had been historic flukes (in both instances, the product, as much as anything else, of Security Council embarrassment over its failure to take any more concerted action to stop the violence itself). "If we're going to have gone to all this trouble," my Latin American friend commented, "only to have ended up with a slightly more streamlined version of the very failed system we gathered here in the first place to overcome, it will hardly have been worth the bother."

As it happened, it was Lionel Ye, a lanky and self-effacing, young government attorney out of Singapore, generally regarded as a master of the 3-D game, who came up with a possible route out of the impasse through the simple expedient of turning the conundrum on its head. Instead of requiring Permanent Five unanimity to launch a Court investigation, why not require Permanent Five unanimity in order to block one? More specifically, why not establish a regime where a simple majority vote of the Security Council could at any time forestall any further Court action on a given case for a renewable period of up to twelve months (though any single Permanent Five veto could derail the stalling effort). After all, Ye pointed out, if a majority of the Security Council, including all five Permanent Five members, agreed on the peacekeeping necessity of temporarily blocking Court action, there'd likely be something to it.

The Permanent Five were understandably dubious about the so-called Singapore Proposal. But in what may have been the single most important development during the PrepCom process, in December 1997, Great Britain, under fresh New Labour auspices (with its highly vaunted new "ethical foreign policy"), swung around behind the Singapore Proposal. In so doing, Britain became the first and only Permanent Five member to join what was becoming known as the "like-minded" group—a loose coalition of some sixty countries (including, among others, Australia, New Zealand, Canada, most other European countries, except France, and most of the newly democratizing countries in Latin America and sub-Saharan Africa) favoring a more robust Court.

State Referrals and the Independent Prosecutor

To suggest that the Security Council could block certain Court initiatives was likewise to acknowledge that one might want to include other ways, besides Security Council referral, of instigating such cases in the first place. And indeed two further such procedures had been broached during the PrepCom process.

The first would allow so-called State referrals, such that any State Party to the Treaty (any State that had both signed and ratified the Treaty) could on its own and by itself refer a complaint to the Court. Some argued that that ought to be enough: if not a single one of the sixty countries that were going to have to ratify the treaty before it went into effect was willing to lodge a complaint—singling out, say, Hussein's Anfal campaign against the Kurds—then how much merit was such a complaint going to be likely to have?

The NGOs were supporting State-referral; however, from bitter experience over the past several years, they had come to feel that in fact it would not be enough. As it happened, Human Rights Watch (HRW) had recently spent several years shopping around the very case of Hussein's Anfal campaign, trying to find a country willing to lodge a formal complaint against Iraq with the International Court of Justice (ICJ) in The Hague (the ICJ lacks the authority to hear criminal cases against individuals but is still empowered to adjudicate certain sorts of claims against entire countries). Despite the widespread publicity and documentation regarding Iraq's manifest depredations (including the indiscriminate use of poison gas), HRW was unable to find a single state willing to pursue the matter. (Most fretted over issues of trade—if not now, in the future—or of retaliation, and even some of the Nordic European states in the end backed off, citing domestic political complications.)

For that reason, the "soft coalition" of the NGOs and the like-minded group were additionally advocating an independent Prosecutor—a Prosecutor's office, empowered to evaluate complaints from any source (nonparty states, Party States, NGOs, news reports, the petitions of individual victims) and to launch investigations or prosecutions on its own (subject, granted, to majority Security Council postponement). Only an office thus empowered, it was argued, would be able to respond to the worst crimes in real time, as they were happening, efficiently and free of political coercion.

Nonsense, countered that proposal's adamant opponents (the United States chief among them). "For one thing," Scheffer suggested to me, "such a prosecutor would be inundated with complaints from Day One. His fax machine would be permanently jammed up. With no filter between him and the world, and no possible way of responding to all the complaints, his selection process would of necessity take on a political tinge. Why did he choose to pursue one matter and not another? Each time he passed on a given matter, he'd lose that much more of his desperately needed authority."

The proponents of an independent Prosecutor argued that such dilemmas were no different than those faced by any other prosecutor anywhere in the world—all of whom face decisions like that every day.

"But those prosecutors exist in a framework of accountability," Scheffer pointed out, when I rehearsed that argument for him. "States are accountable to their polities; the members of the Security Council are accountable to theirs. There are checks and balances. But who would this independent Prosecutor be accountable to?" Scheffer himself didn't specifically raise the specter, but others did: What would prevent such an independent Prosecutor from ballooning into a sort of global

Kenneth Starr—if not worse. This office, after all, stood to become, as it were, the judicial branch of a world government that lacked an effective, functioning, democratically chosen legislative or executive branch to check and oversee it— an untethered international Kenneth Starr, floating free.

The proponents of an independent Prosecutor, for their part, scoffed at the notion. For one thing, the Prosecutor, like every member of the Court, would be answerable to an Assembly of States Parties and removable at any time for cause. Certainly at the outset, his budget would be minuscule and he'd be utterly dependent on the good will and cooperation of states (for instance, he'd have no police or enforcement resources of his own). He'd continually be having to demonstrate his upstanding character and evident fairness because, from the outset, what authority he'd be able to muster would be largely moral. Beyond that, with regard to any specific case, the way the statute was evolving, he'd have to present his evidence and justifications every step of the way before a supervising panel of judges: he wouldn't even be able to launch an investigation without their authorization.

None of this assuaged the U.S. delegation, which remained fixated on the prospect of that lone American marine—a peacekeeper stationed, say, in Somalia— getting nabbed on some capricious charge and inexorably dragged into the maw of the machine, his fate at the mercy, as it was sometimes phrased, of some Bangladeshi or Iranian judge.

"What is the United States talking about?" an exasperated like-minded diplomat virtually sputtered at me one evening over drinks. "This Prosecutor is going to have a lot more important things to worry about than some poor marine in Mogadishu."

Earlier I'd tried a similar argument on one of those incredibly competent and respected mid-level delegates—in this case, a Pentagon lawyer attached to the U.S. delegation: "Surely the Prosecutor is going to have a lot more important things . . . ," I said. "Not necessarily," he countered, recalling some recent proceedings at the International Criminal Tribunal for the former Yugoslavia (ICTY) where, "At a certain point, word came down from the Prosecutor that they really had to find more Croats to indict. There were too many Serbs getting indicted, it was too unbalanced. The Prosecutor had to be able to project the appearance of fairness.

"And I can almost guarantee you," he continued, "that a similar thing will happen one day up ahead. Say, it's something like the end of Desert Storm, and the Prosecutor has been able to round up and indict dozens of Iraqis. You just watch: the Iraqi government will be lodging all sorts of trumped-up, phony complaints about Americans; and the Prosecutor will come under terrific pressure to indict a few of them as well, just to demonstrate his fairness."

I subsequently related the Pentagon lawyer's scenario to my like-minded friend, at which point he immediately shot back, "But that's what complementarity is for!"

The Principle of Complementarity

Complementarity was perhaps the keystone of the entire Draft Statute, and one would have thought it would have gone a long way toward answering U.S. concerns. For central to the entire enterprise was the notion that national judicial systems would be taking precedence over international ones, and specifically over this Court. That is to say that if a state could show that it was itself already dealing with any given complaint in good faith—investigating and if necessary prosecuting—then those national efforts would automatically trump the ICC's. "In fact," the like-minded diplomat continued, "in the best of all possible worlds, one day in the future, the International Court will have no cases whatsoever. Under the pressure of its oversight, all national judicial systems will be dealing in good faith with their own war criminals, at the local level. That would obviously be a better system, and getting to such a point is one of the goals of the entire exercise. In the meantime, democracies like the United States, with highly developed systems of military as well as civilian justice, would invariably be able to shield their own nationals by invoking complementarity." (To further buttress this doctrine of complementarity, the United States had demanded an entire Statute section requiring the Prosecutor to notify any investigative target's home state at the outset of its investigation, so that the home state could apply to the Court on complementarity grounds from the very start.)

As it happened, Conference participants were being afforded a high-profile object lesson in the proper workings of a complementarity regime during the very weeks of their deliberations. Earlier that year (1998), a U.S. marine jet flying too low on training maneuvers in the Italian Alps had tragically sheared the cables on a ski lift, an accident that claimed twenty lives. The plane's crew had initially been charged with manslaughter in Italian courts. But from the moment that U.S. military prosecutors filed court-martial charges against two of those officers (at the same time clearing two others)—as it happened in the very middle of the fourth week of the Conference—the Italian prosecutor dropped all his charges, exactly as he was required to do in keeping with the complementarity provisions in the bilateral "Status of Forces Agreement" governing the presence of U.S. forces in Italy.

"And on top of that," my like-minded drinking companion was continuing, "the Americans have the protection of the chapeau"—the preamble, as it were, of the section defining what sorts of crimes could come under the prosecutor's scrutiny. War crimes were to come under the Court's jurisdiction "in particular when committed as part of a plan or a policy or as part of a large-scale commission of such crimes." Crimes against humanity would need to be part of a "widespread or systematic" attack directed against civilians in order for the Court to be able to assert jurisdiction. The Americans would have preferred "widespread *and* systematic," but still the former wording would likewise have seemed to radically narrow the exposure of any single or group of marine peacekeepers who wandered down the wrong alleyway in Mogadishu.

The Americans, however, were not satisfied. As far as they were concerned, there still remained a chance, however slim, that Americans could find themselves exposed on the wrong side of the line. And, as Scheffer insisted to me one afternoon in the halls, almost jabbing his finger into my chest with his intensity, "The exposure of American troops is really serious business, and bland assurances about the unlikelihood of any given outcome simply don't move the mail back where I come from."

The Requirement of State Consent

Which may be why the American delegation chose to make its stiffest stand on the question of jurisdiction itself.

The legal issue involved went something like this: Suppose the Prosecutor had reason to launch an investigation or a prosecution regarding a particular case, either on her own or because she had had the case referred to her by a State Party or an NGO. What conditions, particularly with regard to states that had not yet chosen to join onto the treaty, would have to be met for the Prosecutor to be able to move forward?

The Germans favored giving the Prosecutor the widest possible latitude in this regard, which is to say universal jurisdiction. They pointed out, for instance, that according to the Geneva Conventions, every signatory (for all intents and purposes, all the countries of the world) not only had the right but also the obligation to pursue war criminals from any countries anywhere—and failing anything else, to deliver them up for trial in their own courts. (Granted, in practice, most countries had thus far failed to enact the necessary enabling legislation, but according to their signatures on the Conventions, as well as on the Genocide Treaty, they had acknowledged such universal jurisdiction over war crimes.) All that was being asked here was that states together transfer the rights granted to each one of them separately to the Court they were founding in concert. The Germans did not need to point out that the doctrine of universal jurisdiction had been a cornerstone rationale at the Nuremberg Tribunals—the crimes of which the defendants there had been accused were universal in nature, as hence was the Tribunal's jurisdiction; otherwise all that could have been possible there would have been so-called "victor's justice" (which the Americans have always insisted was not what they were perpetrating). If such a principle was good enough for the Germans at Nuremberg, the Germans in Rome seemed to be saying, it ought to be good enough for everybody else now.

This viewpoint, however, so rattled international lawyers affiliated with several of the delegations—not just the Americans—that by the middle of the fourth week, Kirsch's Bureau had already shaved it from its list of four possible remaining options regarding jurisdiction. The broadest of these, the so-called Korean Plan, stipulated that in order for the Prosecutor to claim jurisdiction over any given case, at least one of the following four states would have to be a party to the Treaty (or at any rate accept the jurisdiction of the Court in that particular case):

- The state where the crime took place
- The state of nationality of the accused
- The state that had custody of the accused
- The state of nationality of the victim

A narrower second option mandated that the state in which the crime took place would have to be a State Party. A yet narrower third option stipulated that both that state and the state having custody would have to be States Parties. Finally, a fourth option would limit the Court's jurisdiction exclusively to accused who were themselves nationals of States Parties.

Guess which one the United States was favoring.

The Soundings Proceed Apace

Kirsch was inviting all the delegations to stand up and, as briefly as possible, to indicate how they were tending with regard to each of the contentious issues highlighted in his paper, including the issue of jurisdiction. In effect, he was conducting a poll without having to have recourse to any actual vote ("the dreaded *v*-word," as he'd characterized that prospect for me during our conversation), the polarizing consequences of which could have blown the Conference apart at any moment. (He was trying to nudge the process along through a sequence of grudging consensual concessions, culminating only at the very end with a single up-or-down vote.) So, one by one the delegates were rising to lay out their preferences.

It was vaguely unsettling, once again—this tug of war between the claims of humanity and those of sovereignty, especially if, squinting your eyes, you momentarily chose to visualize the proceedings from the point of view of a victim, or a victim's survivor, who might one day be seeking recourse before this Court. For it is, of course, of the essence of genocide itself that it denies the essential humanity of its victims: they are not humans like the rest of us; they are vermin, swine, subbeings worthy solely of extermination. Granted, here the question wasn't so much one of humanity as one of standing: myriad seemingly arbitrary hoops through which an eventual victim would someday have to jump before being deemed worthy of recognition by this Court (whether his violator was or was not a national of a State Party; whether the war in which the violations took place had or had not been international in scope; and so forth). But in the end it came down to the same thing: victims whose core humanity had already been trampled on in the crime itself facing a good chance of seeing their humanity denied all over again by an abstruse legal process in which, clearly, some stood to be counted as more fully human than others.

Having said that, it was striking how many countries were still coming out in favor of the broadest possible remaining jurisdictional option, and—my canny Asian informant's paradox notwithstanding—how many of these included countries only recently, if ever so precariously, emerged from their own totalitarian or genocidal sieges. Many of the Latin American delegates, for example, were lawyers whose own attempts to settle accounts with their countries' earlier military rulers had been stymied by amnesties those militaries had been able to wrest, on leave-taking, from their still timorous civilian successors. The president of Korea, whose country was offering that broadest remaining jurisdictional scheme, had himself been a longtime prisoner of one such regime—as had the president of South Africa been of another. The pattern recurred throughout the hall. The delegate from Sierra Leone, whose country at that very moment was being ravaged by renegade bands of recently dislodged coup plotters, got up and delivered a riveting plea for the most robust possible Court. Afterward, he commented to me, "For many of the delegates here, these pages are just so much text. For me, they are like a mirror of my life. This article here," he said, flipping through the Draft Statute, "this is my uncle; this one here, my late wife; this one here, my niece. This is not just paper for me."

On the other hand, there were others—India, Pakistan, most of the Middle Eastern delegations—who were decidedly more suspicious of the Court. ("I had the chief of the Iranian delegation in here a few minutes ago," the head of the drafting committee told me at one point, "and believe me, he's just as spooked at the prospect of having one of his people dragged before an American judge as the Americans are the other way around.")

Kirsch's sounding continued apace—several delegations going for the Korean option, others going for the second or the third—until eventually David Scheffer got up to deliver the U.S. response. On several issues (the degree of coverage of crimes committed in internal wars, for example), the United States was notably expansive. (Scheffer indicated, for the first time, that under certain conditions the United States might even be willing to entertain something like the Singapore compromise.) But when it came to the question of jurisdiction, Scheffer was adamant: the United States was insisting on the fourth option (that the court be denied jurisdiction over the nationals of any country that had not signed the treaty). Not only, he said, would the United States refuse to sign any treaty that dealt with jurisdiction in any other manner, but it "would have to actively oppose" any resultant Court—whatever that meant. On the other hand, Scheffer concluded, if this and all "the other approaches I have described emerge as an acceptable package for the Statute, then the United States delegation could seriously consider favorably recommending to the U.S. government that it sign the ICC Treaty at an appropriate moment in the future." Scheffer's address sent a chill through the auditorium: Defy us and we'll kill the baby; accede to our terms and, well, we're not sure; we'll see.

More startling yet was the seeming ineffectiveness of the American stand: it didn't seem to be changing anybody's mind. A few minutes after Scheffer's presentation, tiny Botswana got up and spoke of "the breathtaking arrogance" of the American position. And, ironically, it was precisely the sort of line represented by Jesse Helms back in Washington that so seemed to be undermining U.S. authority there in Rome (as it had, last year, during the land mines negotiations in Ottawa). "The U.S. struts around like it owns this place," one NGO observer pointed out. "It doesn't own this place: it owes this place." Indeed, the fact that the United States was still well over a billion dollars in arrears in its debt to the United Nations was having a direct impact on the efficient operation of the Conference itself: there was a distinct shortage of interpreters on site; documents had to be sent back to Geneva for overnight translation; inadequate photocopying facilities caused backups.

America's U.N. debt, furthermore, had had a direct impact on many of the countries it was now trying to influence. Samoa's representative commented to me, "The Fijians have peacekeepers scattered all over the world, too, and you don't see them worrying about their boys' exposure before this Court. What they do worry about is how, thanks to the U.S. debt, the U.N. has fallen behind in paying the salaries of those peacekeepers, leaving Fiji itself to have to pick up the tab, which, I assure you, it can afford far less than the U.S." America's implicit threat not to help finance the Court unless it got its way thus tended to get discounted by delegates dubious that it ever would even if it did.

By the same token, many delegates discounted the likelihood of the United States ever ratifying the treaty no matter what. "David Scheffer could draft the entire document, every single word of it," David Matas, a lawyer with the Canadian delegation, commented toward week's end, "and the Senate would never ratify it. It took America forty years to ratify the Genocide Convention. The United States still hasn't even ratified the Convention on the Rights of the Child. There are only two countries in the entire world that have failed to do so—the United States and Somalia—and Somalia, at least, has an excuse: they don't have a government. So, one has to wonder, why even bother trying to meet such demands?"

Beyond that, the logic of the U.S. position seemed all twisted in knots: still obsessed over this question of the status of its own soldiers in the field, the United States was saying that it would only endorse a Treaty that included an explicit provision guaranteeing that the resultant Court would hold no purchase on the nationals of countries that hadn't signed onto the treaty. So, in other words, the United States appeared to be signaling the fact that it had no intention of signing onto the Treaty—or, at any rate, of ever ratifying it. (Surely, Helms would be able to shoot down any treaty whose only conceivable, if ever so remote, threat to American soldiers would come if the Senate ratified the plan.) And meanwhile, in the words of Kak-Soo Shih, the exasperated head of the Korean delegation, "In order to protect against this less-than-one-percent chance of an American peacekeeper's becoming exposed, the U.S. would cut off Court access to well over ninety percent of the cases it would otherwise need to be pursuing. Because what tyrant in his right mind would sign such a treaty? What applies to America also applies to Hussein; and simply by not signing, he could buy himself a pass."

"No, no, NO!" Scheffer insisted, when I brought this argument back to him. "Hussein would still be vulnerable to a Security Council referral under Chapter VII, by virtue of Iraq's being a signatory to the U.N. Charter."

Except, as my like-minded drinking companion subsequently pointed out, bringing the argument full circle, that was the very channel that, thanks to the blocking vetoes and with the sole exceptions of Yugoslavia and Rwanda, had failed to work every other time in the past.

Scheffer was unswayed. Furthermore, he pointed out, the U.S. position was grounded both in common sense and in all prior international law, as codified in the Vienna Convention on Treaties, which stipulates that no state can be held to the provisions of a treaty it has not itself ratified. It would be patently unacceptable for Americans to be held to account before a court and under laws they had themselves not democratically endorsed by way of the actions of their legislative representatives.

But that, too, was nonsense, another Canadian lawyer delegate pointed out to me. "Americans are subjected to courts and laws they didn't vote for all the time. You think an American can come to Canada—or a Canadian go to the U.S., for that matter—break some local ordinance, and then claim, 'Well, I didn't have any say in passing that ordinance, or voting for this judge, so it doesn't apply to me.'" (For that matter, as Michael Posner, the head of the New York–based Lawyers Committee for Human Rights, reminded me, since 1994 the United States has had implementing legislation related to the Torture Convention on its books that allows an American court to go after a visitor from another country for acts of torture he committed in that other country, with penalties ranging from twenty years all the way through death.) "As for American military men on official business," the Canadian lawyer continued, "again, it's a moot point, at least as regards this Court, thanks to the complementarity provisions."

The Option of Opting Out

For his part, though still unswayed regarding the basic argument, Scheffer, too, hoped the matter might prove moot. As he pointed out, the U.S. delegation was still trying to craft a treaty that the country would one day be able to sign onto, which is where a second jurisdictional issue came into play: the so-called opt-out clause. The United States, along with several other important countries (notably including France, which was just as concerned about the status of its Foreign Legionnaires in the field), was supporting language that would make Court jurisdiction automatic for any State ratifying the Treaty as regards the crime of genocide. However, at the time of ratifying, States would have the right to opt out of coverage on war crimes and crimes against humanity, as applied to themselves or to their own nationals. Obviously, the United States had no plans for committing genocide anytime soon, and such a clause would provide yet another way of shielding American forces from the Court's scrutiny.

But the arguments here were virtually identical to those regarding the status of nonstate parties. What would prevent Saddam Hussein from opting out as well? For that matter, why would anybody opt in? And to what kind of crazy Swiss-cheese jurisdictional regime would such a scheme lead? William Pace, the head coordinator of the NGO coalition, parsed the matter in terms of numbers: "Having trouble holding the line with a forum in which five countries, including the U.S., could veto Court initiatives, the U.S. now wants in effect to extend veto power to one hundred eighty-five nations, such that in the end the only forum that would really retain the ability to launch Court action would once again be the one with five vetoes."

THE ENDGAME

The United States Digs In

"Look," an increasingly grim and embattled Scheffer was almost shouting at me by the end of the fourth week, "The U.S. is not Andorra!" He immediately caught himself up short. "That's off the record!" What, I asked—official State Department policy has it that the U.S. is Andorra? Laughing, he continued, "No" (by which I inferred that the comment was no longer off the record), "but the point is that the world—I mean, people in there, some of the people in there—have yet to grasp that the challenges of the post–Cold War world are so complex that, in some instances, the requirements of those few countries that are still in a position to actually do something by way of accomplishing various humane objectives simply have got to be accommodated. And you can't approach this on the model of the equality of all states. You have to think in terms of the inequality of some states. There have been times, there will come others, when the U.S. as the sole remaining superpower, the indispensable power, has been and will be in a position to confront butchery head-on, or anyway to anchor a multilateral intervention along such lines. But in order for that to be able to happen, American interests are going to have to be protected and American soldiers shielded. Otherwise it's going to get that much more difficult, if not impossible, to argue for such humanitarian deployments in the future. Is that really what people here want?"

A few minutes later, Charles Brown, the official spokesman of the U.S. delegation, who'd been listening in on my conversation with Scheffer, pulled me aside. "We're coming to the endgame now," he suggested, "and basically, we're facing three possible outcomes: a Court the U.S. is going to be able to be part of; a Court the U.S. can't yet be part of but could still support—cooperating behind the scenes, assisting in detentions, sharing intelligence, and providing other sorts of background support—and which it might one day still be able to be part of; or a Court the U.S. will find it impossible to work with and may yet have to actively oppose.

"And, frankly, I don't see how this Court is going to be able to flourish without at least the tacit support of the United States." He pointed to' my notepad. "Remember that flow chart you were showing me the other day? The baby in the nurturing crib or the baby in the lead box. It seems to me there's a third possibility: a baby alone, unprotected, in the middle of a vast, open field."

Choosing Sides

"It's as if we're being forced to choose," Kak-Soo Shih, the Korean delegate, sighed disconsolately late Friday of the fourth week. "A Court crippled by American requirements with regard to state consent, or a Court crippled by lack of American participation."

"The Court could definitely live without U.S. participation," insisted an NGO representative at their news conference that same afternoon. "If all the like-minded sign on, that's virtually all of Europe, with the exception of France. That's Canada, Australia, much of Africa and Latin America, all sorts of other countries—there's funding there, support resources, a definite start. And the U.S. in fact would still be pivotally involved through its Security Council referral role. The U.S. claims it wants a weak treaty which could be strengthened later on. But that's being disingenuous: For one thing, the U.S. itself, anxious at the prospect of the process spinning out of control later on, has placed incredibly high thresholds on amending the treaty—in some instances, seven-eighths of States Parties would have to ratify any changes, not just vote for them at the Assembly of States Parties but get their legislatures to ratify them back home. Almost impossible.

"But in any case," he continued, "the main point is a weak treaty won't work. And even more to the point—you've seen the soundings—a majority of those gathered here are calling for a strong treaty. It's a scandal that two of the major democracies—France and America—are the main ones standing against such an outcome."

Hans-Peter Kaul, the head of the German delegation and one of the most pas-

sionate proponents of a strong Court, was meanwhile addressing a news conference of his own: "We desperately, desperately, desperately want the U.S. on board.
We are not sure the Court will even be workable without the U.S. We are willing
to walk the extra mile, beyond the extra mile, to meet U.S. concerns. So the problem is not on our side, but on the side of the U.S. Will they be willing to move the
slightest bit in order to meet us?"

"The trick," Chairman Kirsch explained to me, "is to emerge with a strong
Statute with incentives enough that down the line currently reluctant governments
may yet want to join on. Because later on it will be far easier to get governments
to change their minds than it will be to change the statute itself. And, anyway, no
government is going to want to join onto a useless statute."

Honing the Final Treaty

By Monday of the fifth and final week, Kirsch's Bureau was facing challenges on
all sides. The United States was still fuming over state consent. India, dubious
about the entire Treaty, was itching to provoke a conference-busting vote on the
question of the inclusion of nuclear weapons and was lobbying the other members of the Non-Aligned Movement hard in preparation. Mexico was still restive
over the Security Council's referral powers. Thailand and others were still trying
to dilute coverage of internal wars. Faced with all of these challenges, Kirsch was
painstakingly guiding the delegates through a second sounding—narrowing the
options—and then a third, steadily aiming toward a Thursday-night final vote.
Informal meetings were burgeoning off to the side, and the truly hot ticket was
the informal informals. Nobody anymore seemed to be pausing for sleep.

The United States, meanwhile, was stepping up the pressure. Albright and
Defense Secretary William Cohen were known to be phoning their counterparts
all over the world, and President Clinton himself was said to be placing some key
calls. (A high American delegate assured me in that last week that Washington
was now focused on these negotiations, "at the very highest level" and over "the
most specific details.") Some of that pressure was proving remarkably hamfisted.
When Defense Secretary Cohen warned his German counterpart that the treaty as
it was currently evolving might force the Pentagon to reconsider the advisability
of even stationing troops anywhere in Europe, the Germans, far from crumbling
in horror, became righteously indignant and leaked word of the demarche back
into the auditorium in Rome, provoking a brief firestorm of outrage and embarrassed denials. The Latin Americans, for their part, were still smarting over a March
incident in which the Pentagon had convened a meeting of military attachés from
throughout the Western Hemisphere, urging them to pressure their home governments to bend to American treaty demands. Several delegates described for me
their enduring annoyance over the ploy, how it had only been with the greatest

difficulty, over the past decade, that their civilian governments had been succeeding, ever so precariously, in easing their officers back into barracks; and they certainly didn't need any Americans coming around, urging the officers back where they didn't belong.

On Monday night, the Russians hosted an exclusive private dinner, limited to top delegates from the Permanent Five, at which tremendous pressure was brought to bear on renegade Britain. When the NGOs got wind of that meeting the following morning and began worrying over a possible wavering in the British line, they instantaneously swung into a typically impressive lobbying blitz, contacting all their affiliates back in England, who in turn started pulling all the right media and parliamentary levers. New Labour's "ethical foreign policy" had already been taking its share of hits earlier in the month (notably over a scandal involving the sale of arms to the warring parties in Sierra Leone); and faced with such a massive upwelling of vigilance, the Brits in Rome appeared to stiffen their position once again.

The Bureau had been aiming to release its final document—the result of hours of frontroom soundings and backroom recalibrations—by midday Thursday; but midday came and nothing emerged. Sierra Leone was brokering a final compromise on the coverage of internal wars. The French were cutting a last-minute deal with Kirsch on their main concern: a seven-year opt-out clause, inside the treaty itself, limited to war crimes alone. (Since their interventions seldom included carpet aerial-bombing campaigns, it was explained to me, they weren't that worried about the Crimes against Humanity provisions.)

Scheffer and Kirsch held several urgent parlays those last few days; both seemed equally desperate to find some way of bringing the United States under the Treaty tent. "And it was amazing," one of Kirsch's top deputies on the Bureau subsequently recounted for me. "Nothing could assuage them. We figured they'd be trying to negotiate, to wrest concessions from us in exchange for concessions on their part. Frankly, as of that Monday morning, we figured the Independent Prosecutor was toast, that we'd have to give him away in the final crunch negotiation. But they never even brought him up. They seemed completely fixated on that Helms/Pentagon imperative—that there be explicit language in the Treaty guaranteeing that no Americans could ever fall under the Court's sway, even if the only way to accomplish that was going to be by the U.S. not joining the treaty. We talked about complementarity, we offered to strengthen complementarity— for instance, a provision requiring the Prosecutor to attain a unanimous vote of a five-judge panel if he was going to challenge the efficacy of any given country's complementarity efforts. In the unlikely event of their ever getting thus challenged, all they would need was one vote out of five. Not enough. In fairness, they seemed on an incredibly short leash. Clearly, they had their instructions from back home— and very little room to maneuver."

Thursday midday dragged into Thursday evening and then past midnight. Still the Bureau's final draft failed to emerge: in fact it only finally came out Friday at two o'clock in the morning. Kirsch was giving delegates less than twenty-four hours to digest the seventy-odd-page tiny-typed document and consult with their capitals. They'd all reconvene for a final Committee of the Whole session that evening at seven.

The Climactic Session: The Final Vote

"Four words. Four little words," Charles Brown, the spokesman for the U.S. delegation, was almost wailing the next morning. "It's incredible. They're within four words of a draft which, even if we couldn't necessarily join, we would still be able to live with. And they're not going to budge. They're going to stuff them down our throat."

On the question of state consent, the Bureau had ended up splitting the difference, stipulating that the Court could exercise its jurisdiction if "one or more of" the following states were parties to the Statute or had accepted the Court's jurisdiction in a given particular case: (1) the state on the territory of which the crime was alleged to have occurred; (2) the state of which the accused was a national.

The NGOs were none too happy with that compromise, either. "They took the Korean plan, split it in half, and left us with North Korea," the indefatigable and endlessly quotable Richard Dicker of HRS's Rome delegation quipped almost immediately. "By leaving out the state of the victim, and even more crucially the state having custody of the accused, they've spawned a treaty for traveling dictators. Even if France, say, joins the Treaty, the next Mobutu or Baby Doc would still be able to summer blissfully undisturbed on the Riviera and to squirrel away his ill-gotten gains in the local banks."

And that, come to think of it, may have been one of the reasons why the French were so avidly pushing for the compromise. My source in the Bureau, on the other hand, told me that several countries besides France had been expressing profound misgivings about the custody clause. In Africa, for instance, former allies are crossing over into each other's countries all the time, and things could get quite messy.

But it was the Americans who, more than anyone else, were denouncing the "state consent" provision, spooking themselves with sordid scenarios. "What if," Scheffer postulated, "the American army finds itself deployed on the territory of Iraq as part of a U.N. force. Now, Hussein and his nationals are not subject to this treaty because he hasn't signed on. But what if suddenly he pulls a fast one, accuses some of our men of war crimes, and, as head of the territory in question, extends the Court permission to go after them on a one-time basis? And one of the really weird anomalies in all this is that, thanks to the French provision, signatories are able to opt out of such exposure for seven years, but nonsignatories aren't afforded the same option."

"Well," said HRW's Dicker, when I relayed that observation over to him, "maybe then the U.S. had better sign on. For that matter," he continued, "if I were an American GI, I'd much prefer being held in a cell in The Hague to one in Baghdad." The United States was going to have one last opportunity to upend the provision at that evening's final meeting of the Committee of the Whole; and all through the day urgent communiqués were coursing from Washington to capitals throughout the world.

Kirsch brought the meeting to order at 7:15 in the evening on Friday, July 17, 1998, and presented the Draft text as a whole, hoping to fend off amendments of any sort. It was generally conceded that if even one provision were called into question, the whole intricately cantilevered structure could start coming apart.

India rose to propose an amendment, reintroducing the use or even the threat to use nuclear weapons as a war crime. Norway immediately moved to table the motion. (The like-minded had agreed among themselves that Norway would serve this function with every attempted amendment.) Then, in one of the most significant moments at the Conference, Malawi rose to second Norway's motion. In a brief speech of strikingly understated eloquence, Malawi noted that because the Treaty was a package, everyone had given up something and gained something else, that many of the delegates had sympathy for India's position, but that pursuing the matter any further would no longer advance the process and could threaten to blow everything up. As Malawi sat back down, everyone realized that the Non-Aligneds had fractured and that India was not going to be able to rely on their votes to subvert the Conference. Chile rose to give another second to Norway's motion. A vote was taken on the question of whether to take a vote, and India lost overwhelmingly (114 against, 16 for, and 20 abstentions).

Scheffer now rose. He looked ashen. "I deeply regret, Mr. Chairman," he began, "that we face the end of this Conference and the past four years of work with such profound misgivings and objections as we have today." Going on to note how tragically the Statute was creating "a court that we and others warned of in the opening days—strong on paper but weak in reality," he proceeded to lay out the U.S. position one more time before proposing a simple amendment: that the words "one or more of" be stricken from the non-State Party provision, such that both the territory and the nationality would be required.

After Scheffer was seated, Norway immediately rose up to table the motion. Sweden seconded Norway's motion, and Denmark followed suit. A vote was held, and the United States lost in a similarly lopsided vote (113 against, 17 for, and 25 abstentions).

Kirsch looked over at Mexico and Thailand—both had earlier indicated their intention to file amendments, but both now shook their heads: no, they would pass. There were no other amendments. A mood of heady celebration was rising in the hall. In that case, Kirsch announced, gaveling the meeting to a close, they would all reconvene in half an hour upstairs, in the flag-decked ceremonial chamber, for the final plenary session, for speeches and a final vote.

Filing upstairs, several of the longtime NGO activists were discussing Scheffer in remarkably sympathetic terms. Over the years, many had had occasion to work with him, and few doubted the fervency of his commitment and concern. "His instincts were better than his instructions," Dicker surmised. "Would make a good epitaph," someone else observed.

The delegates streamed into the plenary chamber and took their seats amidst the flags. There were broad smiles, fierce hugs, a growing swell of elation. Kirsch handed the gavel to the frail guest by his side—Adriaan Bos, the ailing Dutch legal adviser who had piloted the four-year PrepCom process right up till a few weeks before the opening of the Rome Conference. Bos, beaming, banged the session to order, said a few words, and retired to the side. Kirsch called for a vote. It ended up 120 to 7, with 21 abstentions. Cuba voted for the Statute, as did Russia, Britain, and France. The United States was apparently joined by China, Libya, Iraq, Yemen, Qatar, and Israel in voting against it (at American request, the particulars of the vote itself went officially "nonrecorded"). The hall erupted in applause that grew louder and louder, spilling over into rhythmic stomping and hooting that lasted a good ten minutes, the room becoming positively weightless with the mingled senses of exhaustion and achievement.

"This treaty's flawed," Dicker was saying. "It's badly flawed." He cited another nasty little concession, effected at the last minute—the chemical and biological warfare provisions had been deleted so as to undercut India's argument about these being poor men's nuclear weapons, unfairly singled out. He was quiet for a moment, gazing out over the scene. "But it's not fatally flawed."

Theodor Meron, one of the world's most distinguished academic experts on international humanitarian law, who'd been serving as a citizen-adviser on the U.S. delegation but who now seemed almost visibly to be doffing that official role so as to revert to his private academic persona, walked over and seemed eerily content. "Oh," he said, "these last few hours have been unpleasant, of course. But flipping through the pages of the final document, there's much here that's very good, very strong. The articulation of war crimes: completely solid. And the section on crimes against humanity, which heretofore have existed primarily in the form of precedent and custom, here they're codified, in a remarkably robust form, and in particular without any nexus to war. This was a big fight, unclear in the customary law, but here it's clearly articulated that crimes against humanity can even take place in the absence of outright warfare—a major development, as is the section on noninternational war, the most frequent and bloody kind today. The section on gender crimes—rape, enforced pregnancy, and the like—all rising out of recent developments at the Yugoslav and the Rwanda tribunals, but codified here for the first time. There's excellent due process language, mens rea, all of this reflecting a strong American influence. The requirement for a clear articulation of elements—what exactly, in clean legal language, constitutes the elements of a crime. Command responsibility, superior orders: American fingerprints are all over this document, and with just a few exceptions, America's concerns were largely accommodated."

"We'll see," my contact in the Bureau was now saying. "It will take three or four years for the Treaty to garner the required number of ratifications and then come into force. Maybe things will change in the U.S.—they'll be able to give it a second look. Or else, once the Court is up and running, sure enough, a few of those nuisance complaints will get lodged against American soldiers, and the U.S. will invoke complementarity, and, BOOM, they'll be popped right out of there—and the U.S. will cease feeling so threatened. Or there will come some great crisis, and suddenly the U.S. will want to make use of the Court. Time will tell. In the meantime, the Court will be able to start growing."

Jerry Fowler, one of the NGO lobbyists affiliated with the Lawyers Committee for Human Rights, was taking an even longer view: "We didn't get Korea, but what we got is still important: the territorial requirement. Because one of these days there's going to come a Baghdad Spring, and one of the first things the reformers there will want to do is to sign onto this treaty—as an affirmation of the new order, but also as a protection against backsliding. One by one, countries will go through their Springs, they'll sign on, and the Court's jurisdiction will grow. A hundred years from now—who knows?"

A bit later, Fowler's boss, Michael Posner, was gazing back the other way. "Do you realize how long the world has been straining toward this moment—since after World War I, after World War II. It's extraordinary. Who'd have thought it, even ten years ago, that you could get one hundred twenty countries to vote for holding their militaries personally liable before a Prosecutor with even a limited degree of independent initiative? I mean, it's unprecedented, it's absolutely unprecedented. One day it may even be seen to have been the birth of a new epoch."

CODA: THE FATHER OF ALL EXCEPTIONS

"Today, for the first time in history," Forrest Sawyer, sitting in for Peter Jennings, led off that evening's *ABC World News Tonight*, just a few hours later, New York time, "a Secret Service agent testified before a grand jury as part of a criminal investigation on a sitting U.S. president." That and adjacent stories regarding Kenneth Starr's ongoing pursuit of the Monica Lewinsky scandal took up the next seven minutes of air time. The developments in Rome never even got mentioned.

Nor were they broached on NBC or CBS. And they received not a single column-
inch in the following Monday's *Time* or *Newsweek*. Monica and Kenneth Starr
were everywhere.

It occurred to me how surely the siege by this independent prosecutor must
have been coloring President Clinton's responses to the developments in Rome,
leaving him especially wary at the very moment the toughest decisions were having
to be made.

On the other hand, surely, there was more to it than that. At various times,
there in the halls of Rome, various people would invoke the League of Nations.
"If the U.S. walks out on this court," the Syrian delegate assured me, his eyes
twinkling with grim satisfaction (he was all for it, he couldn't wait), "it will be
like the League of Nations." Perhaps, I remember thinking; but in that case, ought
President Clinton be cast in the role of Woodrow Wilson or in that of Henry Cabot
Lodge? Of course, the answer, in retrospect, is both. With regard to the Court,
Clinton wanted to play both Wilson and Lodge. And not half and half: not a wily
Wilson disguising himself as a grimly realistic Lodge, or visa versa. Rather,
Whitmanesque, Clinton wanted to contain multitudes. He saw no contradiction in
being both Wilson and Lodge, each 100 percent and both simultaneously, which
is to say that he was approaching the ICC in much the same way he'd approached
just about everything else in his presidency—gays in the military, national health
insurance, campaign finance reform, land mines, Bosnia, global warming.

CONCLUSION

Less than a week later, on Thursday, July 23, 1998, back in Washington, D.C.,
David Scheffer was called to appear before Jesse Helms's Senate Foreign Relations Committee. He might have been excused a certain feeling of conceptual
whiplash.

For if, by the end there in Rome, he was being treated as a sort of pariah or
leper, now back in Washington he was being unanimously praised as a kind of
returning hero. Positions that had provoked nary a chord of resonance in the Rome
Conference hall were almost drowned in a rising chorus of defiant triumphalism
on Capitol Hill.

Senators Helms, Rod Grams, Joseph Biden, and Dianne Feinstein each addressed Scheffer in turn, congratulating him on the fortitude of his resolve and
pledging their undying contempt for that monstrosity spawned in Rome. Not one
of them focused on Bosnia or Rwanda or Pol Pot or Idi Amin or the Holocaust or
Nuremberg. (Senator Feinstein did wonder about the possible implications for
Israel.) They all seemed utterly and almost uniquely transfixed by the Treaty's
exposure implications for American troops, vowing to protect them and fight it.
Scheffer indicated that the administration was reviewing its options. For starters,

it would be reexamining the more than one hundred bilateral status-of-forces agreements governing the legal status of American servicemembers just about anywhere they might be posted around the globe, with an eye toward tightening them in such a way as to preclude the possibility of any extradition to the ICC.

At that Senate hearing, it became possible to identify what may have been the true underlying anxiety of the U.S. delegation all along, never broached by any of them back in Rome but veritably palpitating just beneath the surface even there. Helms wasn't afraid to name it outright. The status of individual peacekeepers in some Mogadishu alleyway had never been the real concern. Rather, as Helms picked off the examples defiantly, he was going to be damned if any so-called International Court was ever going to be reviewing the legality of the U.S. invasions of Panama or Grenada or of the bombing of Tripoli and to be holding any American presidents, defense secretaries, or generals to account.

"I've been accused by advocates of this Court of engaging in 'eighteenth-century thinking,'" Chairman Helms concluded his statement. "Well, I find that to be a compliment. It was the eighteenth century that gave us our Constitution and the fundamental protections of our Bill of Rights. I'll gladly stand with James Madison and the rest of our Founding Fathers over that collection of ne'er-do-wells in Rome any day."

At some level, of course, Helms was way off the mark in his choice and characterization of antecedents. James Madison, for one thing, was a Federalist—with Alexander Hamilton, the principal author of *The Federalist Papers*—and as such ranged himself passionately against the nativist states-rightsers of his day and in favor of a wider conception of governance.

But at the same time, it seemed to me that Helms was onto something. "We hold these truths to be self-evident, that all men are created equal, that they are endowed by their Creator with certain unalienable rights," Thomas Jefferson strikingly pitched his Declaration of Independence in an assertion of universal human values, an assertion that, cascading down through the ages, from the Rights of Man (1789) through the Universal Declaration of Human Rights (1948), constitutes one of the principal wellsprings of the law feeding into the ICC.

But at the same time, Jefferson cast those assertions in what was, after all, a declaration of independence, of separateness, of American exceptionalism—stirring, defiant themes that had been very much in evidence there in Rome as well.

Part II

The United States and the ICC

6

The U.S. Perspective on the ICC

David J. Scheffer

The determined and sincere efforts of many governments to establish a permanent International Criminal Court (ICC) deserve our appreciation and recognition. All of us involved in this effort sought to draft a treaty that would lead to the enforcement of international humanitarian law by a judicial institution of impeccable credibility and that would deserve our collective participation and support. We all labored for years to negotiate the complex structure of a Court that would fairly reflect the soundest principles and procedures of criminal law and would stand the test of time in a violent and unpredictable world.

Under the leadership of two leading diplomats of the law, Adriaan Bos of the Netherlands and Philippe Kirsch of Canada, we sought a noble and worthy objective whose time has clearly arrived. That objective is to hold accountable and to bring to justice the perpetrators of the most egregious crimes against humankind: genocide, crimes against humanity, and serious war crimes.

SEEKING A CONSENSUS

A permanent ICC is a bold experiment. At Preparatory Committee (PrepCom) meetings in New York and for five weeks in Rome, we deliberated as to how an ICC could be accomplished in a world comprised of sovereign governments, each with its own penal system but all bound together with the cords of customary international law, reflected both in international treaties and in common practice.

The Treaty negotiated in Rome, which a large number of governments have now signed, has many provisions that the United States supports. However, the United States has reluctantly had to conclude that the Treaty, in its present form, contains flaws that render it unacceptable. Even as we recognize this, we also recognize that the final text represented an effort to promote values that are important to the American people: justice, due process, and respect for the rule of law.

In Rome, it had been the strong hope of the United States, as reflected in President Bill Clinton's long commitment to establish an appropriate international criminal court, that the Conference would achieve a consensus on the resolution adopting the Treaty. The Clinton administration has a record that pointed toward that objective and that has ensured that the U.S. support for the existing tribunals for the former Yugoslavia and Rwanda is second to none. Not only does the United States provide both tribunals with significant financial resources, both assessed and through voluntary contributions, but it also uses its diplomatic resources, makes in-kind contributions of personnel and equipment, offers the tribunals important information, and has even brought U.S. military capabilities to bear to ensure that the tribunals are effective.

Thus, we had hoped in Rome for a consensus that would allow the United States to begin planning the kind of support that the permanent Court will need if it is also to be effective—to sustain a costly investigative capability, to build its infrastructure in The Hague, to achieve custody of indictees, and to work with the U.N. Security Council for enforcement initiatives. So long as the United States is unable to join the Treaty, it would be unrealistic to expect the United States to give the Court that level of support.

We fear that, without the United States, the effectiveness of the permanent ICC will fall far short of its potential. We remember the lessons of the early decades of this century when ambitious international institutions were created that, in part because of the lack of American participation and support, either collapsed or became irrelevant.

THE IRONY OF ROME

All of us in Rome shared a common goal—that an international court should be able to prosecute tyrants who commit mass murder, mass rape, or mass torture against their own citizens, while at the same time not inhibiting states from contributing to efforts to help protect international peace and security. The irony of the Rome outcome on Article 12 is not lost on us. Consider the following: A state not a party to the Treaty launches a campaign of terror against a dissident minority inside its territory. Thousands of innocent civilians are killed. International peace and security are imperiled. The United States participates in a coalition to use military force to intervene and to stop the killing. Unfortunately, in so doing, bombs intended for military targets go astray. A hospital is hit. An apartment building is demolished. Some civilians being used as human shields are mistakenly shot by U.S. troops. The state responsible for the atrocities demands that U.S. officials and commanders be prosecuted by the ICC. The demand is supported by a small group of other states. Under the terms of the Rome Treaty, absent a Security Council referral, the Court could not investigate those responsible for killing thousands; yet U.S. senior officials, commanders, and soldiers could face an international investigation and even prosecution.

The complementarity regime is often offered as the solution to this dilemma. However, complementarity is not the answer, to the extent it involves states investigating the legality of humanitarian interventions or peacekeeping operations that they already regard as valid official actions to enforce international law. The Court could decide that there was no genuine investigation by a two-to-one vote. The United States has other concerns of principle about the relationship between Article 12 and international law. The fundamental concern is that in the absence of a Security Council referral, the Court could assert jurisdiction over nonparty nationals.

Another fundamental concern the United States has about the Rome Treaty is the way amendments to crimes are adopted and applied. In its present form, the amendment process for the addition of new crimes to the jurisdiction of the Court or for revisions to the definitions of existing crimes in the Treaty will create an extraordinary and unacceptable consequence. After the States Parties decide to add a new crime or to change the definition of an existing crime, any State that is a Party to the Treaty can decide to immunize its officials from prosecution for the new or amended crime. Officials of nonparties, however, would be subject to immediate prosecution. For a criminal court, this is an indefensible overreach of jurisdiction.

Likewise, there will be some who regard the idea that States Parties can opt out of prosecution for war crimes for seven years, while nonparties cannot, as an incentive to join the Court. Criminal jurisdiction—individual criminal jurisdiction—should not be played with in this way. The United States has other fundamental concerns, such as the inclusion of an undefined crime of aggression. Aggression carries with it an extremely problematic process of definition. How this issue will be resolved is too unclear for so important an issue.

Having considered the matter with great care, the United States will not sign the Treaty in its present form. Nor is there any prospect of our signing the present Treaty text in the future.

FUTURE POLICY

The Preparatory Commission will consider many important issues, including the elements of crimes and the rules of evidence and procedure. As a signatory of the Final Act in Rome, the United States is entitled to participate in the PrepCom. However, in our view, it is also essential that the PrepCom afford the opportunity for governments to address their more fundamental concerns. While we know the few concerns that we have, we do not presume that we have all the answers. No doubt as we discuss how to build an effective Court, new solutions will emerge. We do know that, when building an international institution that is intended to last for the ages, a solid foundation of support is essential. We would hope that such a process might lead to a Court that would command the broad support and credibility that an ICC requires if it is to succeed.

Our choice of this process is also made with care. We have heard it suggested that the United States should exercise "benign neglect" or that we should wait until the Review Conference seven years after entry into force of the Treaty—a Conference to which the United States, as a nonparty, would not be entitled to fully participate. We have rejected both of these options. Another option would be to oppose the Treaty in a variety of ways. We would prefer, however, a policy of positive and forward-looking engagement in the hope of ensuring a Treaty that will stand for values and goals common to us all.

CONCLUSION

The advantages deriving from strong U.S. support for the ICC should not be sacrificed for a concept of jurisdiction that may not be effective and that even runs the risk of dividing us on an issue—international justice—that will be difficult enough to achieve if we are together. The credibility of the Court will be demonstrated in how it builds its relationships with sovereign governments and in how well it supports, and is supported by, the requirements of international peace and security. The international community's willingness and ability to prevent and, where necessary, to respond effectively to atrocities is of fundamental importance to us all. The opportunity remains for the ICC to achieve its full potential. We hold the stakes for international peace, security, and justice to be too great to accept anything else.

NOTE

This essay is adapted from remarks made before the 6th Committee of the 53rd General Assembly, New York, October 21, 1998.

7

The Constitution and the ICC

Ruth Wedgwood

The United States has worked since 1994 to create a permanent International Criminal Court (ICC) for the prosecution of the most serious crimes of genocide, crimes against humanity, and war crimes in the new and violent civil wars of our time. These conflicts flare when national societies and national criminal processes have both broken down. The U.S. campaign for a standing court has built on the experience gained in prosecuting war crimes in two such ruptured societies—the former Yugoslavia and Rwanda. Ad hoc international tribunals were created for those two conflicts by the U.N. Security Council and have tried and convicted military leaders, politicians, and civilians involved in systematic transgressions of the law of war in those countries' bitter wars. Beginning a tribunal anew each time one is needed exacts an obvious cost, delaying the international response to genocidal violence. In addition, the authority of the Security Council to create additional ad hoc institutions has been questioned by some member states of the United Nations.

The alternative of a permanent criminal court was proposed in a draft of the International Law Commission (ILC) in 1994, approved at the time by a distinguished American lawyer and diplomat, Ambassador Robert Rosenstock.[1] From 1994 until 1998, the ILC draft was debated and changed, culminating in the Rome Statute of 1998.[2] The American delegation to the Rome negotiations, led by Ambassador David Scheffer, was disappointed in some portions of the Rome Statute, but has continued to work on rules of evidence and procedure and on the definitions of crimes and the elements of offenses in the ICC Preparatory Commission (PrepCom). In addition, the United States has called for a "binding formula" to permit signature and ratification of the ICC Statute—a package of further guarantees that would recognize the unique security obligations of the United States. These changes would not require Treaty amendment; rather they could be achieved through binding interpretive statements of the PrepCom and the Assem-

119

bly of States Parties, or through agreements entered into by the Court itself. Among the U.S. objectives are guarantees that the Court will defer to good-faith military judgments, that classified information will be protected against disclosure in the justification of military actions, and that non–party states will not be affected by amendments to the scope of the Treaty, including the crime of "aggression." The package would also make clear that the Court must defer to the Status of Forces Agreements (SOFAs) that protect U.S. soldiers, sailors, airmen, and marines deployed abroad. Where a SOFA is in effect, servicemembers are generally exempted from local arrest for any charge connected to the conduct of their official duties, whether for local trial or for extradition. The U.S. package would clarify that servicemembers abroad are also protected against international warrants.[3] Yet perhaps the most important goal of U.S. policymakers is clarifying the status of nationals of non–party states—states that have not yet consented to the Rome Statute. While the United States remains outside the Treaty, its servicemembers should not be subject to investigation or prosecution by the ICC for carrying out the official acts of their governments, unless a matter is referred to the Court by the U.N. Security Council, where the United States holds a veto.

It is, one hopes, virtually inconceivable that any American will ever be named in a charge by the ICC, even though other countries may try to misuse the Court for nuisance purposes. The twenty-first-century democracy of the United States has never embraced the policies that the ICC is designed to punish—the travesties of ethnic cleansing and genocide committed by autocrats like Slobodan Milosevic and Saddam Hussein and the fratricidal warfare of a land such as Rwanda. U.S. military prosecutors and courts have been able to ferret out, investigate, and appropriately punish individual war crimes that may have been committed. American investigations should thus presumptively be final. Under the Rome Treaty's deferential principle of complementarity, the ICC must abide by the outcome of national decisions on prosecution, except where a national justice system has collapsed or where the proceedings are demonstrably a sham.[4] In addition, the ICC's jurisdiction is reserved for cases of the greatest gravity.[5] The lesson of the Rwanda and the Yugoslav tribunals has been that international courts can only handle a distinctly limited number of violations. Hence it is unlikely that the ICC would ever have occasion to charge an American, unless the Court was misused for political purposes or the Court chose to "criminalize" good-faith differences in military doctrine.

THE ICC AND THE U.S. CONSTITUTION

Alongside these policy questions, an equally important discussion has just begun that must also engage our attention. This concerns the ICC and the American

Constitution. On constitutional grounds, is the United States entitled to say yes to the Treaty, or could the U.S. Constitution remain a hidden obstacle to American membership in the ICC? The consistency of the Court with constitutional fairness is a matter of importance and gravity, and neither critics nor supporters of the ICC have yet summoned adequate attention to this central matter.[6] The question must be decided in accordance with the high principles of American constitutional tradition, not simply as a matter of Supreme Court case law. The Senate has appropriately seen itself as an independent guardian of constitutional values. Even where a court might not intrude, the Senate must act on its own constitutional judgment in deciding whether to give its advice and consent to a treaty.

The ICC is a new creation in international jurisprudence, and thus, one should not expect cut-and-dried precedent on the matter. But the most persuasive answer is that there is no forbidding constitutional obstacle to U.S. participation in the treaty. This conclusion follows from a number of principles.

First, the United States has used its treaty power in the past to participate in other international tribunals that affect the lives and property of Americans.

Second, the ICC is carefully structured with procedural protections that closely follow the guarantees and safeguards of the American Bill of Rights and other liberal constitutional systems.

Third, the offenses within the ICC's jurisdiction would otherwise ordinarily be handled through military courts-martial or through extradition of offenders to the foreign nation where an offense occurred. Thus, the detailed structure of American common law trial procedure would not ordinarily be applicable to these cases in any event.

Fourth, a number of the concerns about the ad hoc tribunals for Rwanda and the former Yugoslavia can be avoided in the ICC by well-crafted rules of procedure and evidence and by prosecutorial policy. The United States is taking an active part in the drafting of those rules and will review the whole package before it considers signature.

Fifth, American military personnel will be protected against local arrest by SOFAs, and hence, in almost all instances, a criminal complaint by the Court would have to be addressed to the president of the United States for execution. The president should condition any transfer of a suspect on appropriate assurances on any outstanding concerns, just as he does in extradition treaties to foreign countries. These principles will be examined in the following sections.

Past Participation in International Courts

Most Americans are familiar in their daily lives with the local court systems of state and federal governments, and a few specialized courts, such as the Court of

Claims or Tax Court. The foreign policy and international economic interests of the United States have also led the president, the Senate, and the Congress to approve participation in a number of international tribunals with quite different procedures. U.S. citizens took part as judges, prosecutors, and defense counsel in the International Military Tribunal for the Far East and in the Nuremberg Tribunal for the trial of war criminals from World War II, where much of the proof was offered by affidavit and the right of cross-examination was limited. Since that time, the United States has joined in establishing tribunals for handling commercial and trade claims arising from foreign policy crises, including the Iran-United States Claims Tribunal established by the Algiers Accord,[7] which has remedied the seizure of U.S. business assets during the Iranian revolution, and the Iraqi Claims Commission established by Security Council Resolution 687,[8] which has used innovative methods of proof for compensation of injuries stemming from the Iraqi invasion of Kuwait. U.S. businesses have also been directly affected by the fact-finding and adjudicative procedures of the North American Free Trade Agreement (NAFTA) and the World Trade Organization (WTO), where the procedures do not duplicate those of an American trial courtroom.

Nor has American participation in international tribunals been limited to civil claims. The International Criminal Tribunal for the former Yugoslavia (ICTY), established by the U.N. Security Council in 1993 and headed by an American as president, Judge Gabrielle Kirk MacDonald, from 1997 to 1999, has noted its authority over all actions occurring in the territory of the former Yugoslavia, including peacekeeping and peace enforcement by the North Atlantic Treaty Organization (NATO). So, too, the International Criminal Tribunal for Rwanda (ICTR) has jurisdiction over all events in Rwanda during 1994. American participation in each of these tribunals was approved by the Congress, with implementing legislation designed to permit the turnover of any defendants found within the United States.[9] The procedure of both these tribunals was carefully negotiated by the United States in the Security Council and set out in each court's detailed statute. The procedures were designed to be acceptable to two legal cultures, civil law and common law, though in fact the rules more closely resemble the adversarial system used in common law countries such as the United States, the United Kingdom, and Canada. Yet, there are some variations from American procedure in the ad hoc tribunals, for example, in the use of a panel of three judges for fact-finding rather than a jury.[10] The choice of fact-finders was in part a reflection of the civil law background of many participating countries. The extraordinary wartime conditions in the former Yugoslavia and Rwanda, where jurors as much as witnesses would be subject to intimidation, also make this a more understandable choice. Indeed, even common law countries such as the United Kingdom have felt the need to use bench trials with fact-finding by judges in situations of violent civil conflict, such as the use of Diplock courts in Northern Ireland.

Procedural Protections

American negotiators at Rome worked hard to ensure that the permanent ICC would follow demanding standards of due process. To that end, any defendant is guaranteed the right to have timely notice of the charges against him,[11] the presumption of innocence,[12] the right against self-incrimination, also forbidding any adverse inference from the exercise of the right to silence,[13] the right to the assistance of counsel[14] and to the assistance of an interpreter,[15] the right to bail,[16] the right to a speedy trial,[17] the right to conduct a defense in person or through the defendant's chosen counsel,[18] the right to cross-examine the witnesses against him and to call witnesses on his own behalf,[19] the right to disclosure of any exculpatory evidence,[20] the right not to bear any burden of proof but rather to require the prosecution to prove guilt "beyond reasonable doubt,"[21] and the right not to be subjected to any form of duress or coercion,[22] or any cruel, inhuman, or degrading punishment.[23] In addition, the ICC Statute even guarantees a form of Miranda warnings[24]—a privilege that has often been criticized in the United States since its enunciation by the Supreme Court in 1966 as offering undue protection of criminal suspects. The Miranda case requires oral notice of rights when a defendant is in custodial interrogation. The ICC statute is even more protective, requiring that the prosecution advise a person of his rights before he is questioned *whenever* there are grounds to believe that he has committed a crime, even in *noncustodial* interrogation—including a warning of the right to remain silent, the right to legal assistance, the right to have counsel appointed if he cannot afford it, and the right to be questioned in the presence of counsel.[25]

The major differences from common law procedure in the ICC are the use of a factfinding panel of three Judges instead of a jury,[26] with a verdict to be rendered by the vote of at least two Judges,[27] and the availability of an appeal by the prosecution from errors of fact, law, and procedure.[28] These, and other variations of procedure, will be discussed later.

Courts-Martial, SOFAs, and Foreign Courts

The central question in assessing any variation from domestic common law trial procedures concerns the correct basis of comparison—"Compared to what?" In ordinary circumstances, crimes committed in a foreign country are tried and prosecuted by foreign courts according to their native procedure. If an American offender is arrested abroad, he can be visited by an American consul in accordance with a long-standing consular agreement,[29] but the trial will be by local procedure and local law. Americans do not have a right to take the Constitution with them into foreign lands as a transnational shield against foreign government action. As John Marshall noted in *The Schooner Exchange v. M'Faddon* (1812), the primary jurisdiction in criminal matters belongs to the country where the crime occurred.[30] When American troops are stationed abroad, this principle still holds true, although SOFAs negotiated by the United States with the host country usually provide that offenses committed as part of official duties are to be tried by the United States as the sending country, whereas any private offenses are left to the host country to try according to local procedures.[31] If an offense committed by a soldier in uniform is so far outside the proper performance of his or her duties as not to truly constitute an official act, any potential claim of American jurisdiction under the SOFA may dissolve or be waived and the soldier remitted to foreign authorities for trial. This was the case in the famous matter of *Wilson v. Girard* heard by the U.S. Supreme Court in 1957:[32] a soldier allegedly beckoned a peasant woman toward his machine gun emplacement on a firing range while she was collecting scrap metal from spent ammunition cartridges; he allegedly shot her in the back with an empty cartridge expelled from a grenade launcher, killing her. The soldier, Girard, was turned over to the Japanese authorities for trial, and his claim that Japanese procedures were unfamiliar and unfair gave no cause for relief because the crime was committed on Japanese soil.[33] So, too, in *Holmes v. Laird* (1972),[34] an American serviceman was held to be liable for trial in German courts on a charge of rape, despite his claim that German procedures differed from U.S. constitutional minima. The U.S. Court of Appeals for the District of Columbia Circuit concluded that an American committing a crime in Germany was subject to "such modes of trial and to such punishment as the laws of that country may prescribe for its own people."[35] Thus, in crimes committed abroad, the basis for comparison of the architecture of trial procedures may be the procedure of the foreign state, not the customary procedure of an American courtroom.

The same is true even where a civilian has returned to the United States after commission of an alleged offense abroad. If an extradition request is made by the foreign country for a serious offense, a federal judge or magistrate, sitting as an extradition magistrate, is directed by a congressionally approved implementing statute[36] to determine whether the surrender may proceed. The judge will ask whether there is an applicable extradition treaty between the United States and the requesting country, whether the charged offense falls within that treaty, whether the conduct would constitute a crime in both countries (important, for example, where an offense might be protected activity within the United States), and whether there is probable cause to believe that the defendant committed the offense.[37] The judge is not entitled to withhold extradition simply because the trial procedures of the requesting country differ in some respects from American trial procedures.[38] In fact, very few of the countries entering into extradition treaties with the United States have trial by jury; many are civil law countries in which the method of proof is less adversarial, with less control by trial lawyers; inquiries are conducted by investigative magistrates and fact-finding by panels of judges. Under the long-standing rule of "non-inquiry," the U.S. decision to enter into an extradition treaty agreement with the country is taken as supposing that the foreign procedure is adequately fair.[39] Of course, the Secretary of State is always able to withhold extradition if conditions in the country have changed or if a particular defendant might be subject to invidious discrimination on grounds of race, religion, or political belief; and some judges have noted that procedures that truly "shock the conscience" may not be immune from scrutiny.[40] But neither fact-finding by a panel of judges nor a limited right of appeal by the prosecutor would seem to fit into that mold. For crimes committed abroad, the relevant standard of comparison is generally foreign criminal procedures, rather than American.

The United States has also adhered to a "universal" basis of jurisdiction for certain kinds of serious offenses. This traditionally applied to sea piracy but was extended at the urging of the United States in the 1970s to terrorist offenses including airplane hijacking,[41] airplane bombings,[42] attacks on internationally protected persons,[43] hostage taking,[44] and torture.[45] Recently, the United States voted in the U.N. General Assembly to approve a treaty on terrorist bombings, applying a modified form of universal jurisdiction.[46] Under universal jurisdiction, any state that encounters an offender may arrest and prosecute him or else must extradite him to another treaty party for trial, even if the state has no direct connection to the offense through the nationality of the offender or the victim or through the place of the offense. Universal jurisdiction amounts to a willingness to have any defendant, including one's own citizens, tried under foreign trial procedures— because the category of offense is so serious as to constitute an offense *hostis humani generis* (an offense against all mankind).

Under the Geneva Conventions of 1949, any country that encounters a person accused of war crimes amounting to a grave breach—including murder or torture of civilians or prisoners of war or systematic rape—may try or otherwise extradite the suspect to another country for trial.[47] Thus, in the absence of a SOFA, a foreign country would be entitled to try any person accused of grave war crimes under its local criminal procedure—no matter where the battle took place or the offense was committed—and in doing so would act in perfect conformity with its treaty obligations and with the jurisdictional rules of private international law.

The case against General Augusto Pinochet brought by Spanish magistrate Baltazar Garzon, seeking extradition of the Chilean general from the United Kingdom to Spain, was also based in part on a theory of universal jurisdiction under the international convention against torture. The British House of Lords found that Spain could try crimes that Pinochet allegedly committed against Chilean citizens as well as Spanish citizens in a Spanish courtroom under Spanish procedures.[48]

The United States has extended the idea of universal jurisdiction from its treaty setting to the enforcement of customary international law and the mandatory norms of international law (called *jus cogens* by lawyers). Thus, when Pol Pot was sighted in the Cambodian jungle in 1997, after many years as a fugitive, the United States approached a number of countries, including Canada, seeking his trial under a theory of universal jurisdiction over customary law violations. Neither the Department of State nor the Department of Justice nor the Congress opposed the case on jurisdictional grounds.

Military standards of courtroom procedure are the second pertinent basis of comparison in assessing the trial of serious war crimes by an international tribunal. Under the procedures of the Uniform Code of Military Justice, a soldier accused of mistreating a civilian or harming a prisoner of war is subject to a general court-martial by a military judge and five members,[49] with a verdict rendered by a two-thirds vote of the members in noncapital cases.[50] The procedures of national courts-martial and military commissions have been used even where an offender was a member of a foreign military; for example, a Swiss military court tried a member of the military forces of the Bosnian Serbs for violations of the laws and customs of war under the Swiss Military Penal Code[51] and a member of the Hutu militia for genocide in Rwanda.[52] There has been the further suggestion that it is the nature of the violation, rather than the identity of the defendant, that may set the outer limit of jurisdiction of a military commission. In World War II, a U.S. military commission sitting on the eighth floor of the Justice Department tried and condemned to death several saboteurs who landed on Long Island and planned to destroy American war facilities, including a defendant who was a naturalized American citizen. This procedure was affirmed by the Supreme Court in *ex parte Quirin*,[53] despite the general rule of *ex parte Milligan*[54] that civilians should ordinarily be tried in available civilian courts.[55]

Thus, when activities have occurred abroad and would otherwise fall within foreign national jurisdiction or when the actors are military, the basis for comparison is not the ordinary trial procedure of a common law court. In addition, the Supreme Court has held in a powerful recent line of cases that the Constitution does not always travel abroad. To be sure, there is important and cherished case law that when the U.S. government is acting directly against U.S. citizens, constitutional standards must be applied. This applies to wiretapping[56] and to the trial of military family dependents for ordinary crimes,[57] and in an unusual decision it was extended even to the trial of some German hijackers, who were tried by a jury composed of fellow Berliners after escaping from East Berlin to West Berlin by airplane.[58] However, where the United States has administered territories historically governed by the civil law system, the constitutional right to jury has not applied.[59] In addition, when the U.S. government is not directing the activities of a foreign government, the application of American domestic constitutional standards may be limited even against an alien who will be tried in an American courtroom. For example, in *United States v. Verdugo-Urquidez* (1990),[60] American officials were preparing for a criminal trial in the United States; a search in Mexico by Mexican officials at the request of the U.S. officials was held not to be subject to the Fourth Amendment warrant requirement. Likewise, in *United States v. Alvarez-Machain* (1992),[61] ordinary criminal extradition procedures and treaty protections against irregular arrest were held not to apply to the abduction of a Mexican doctor to stand trial in the United States on charges of participating in the extraterritorial murder of a Drug Enforcement Administration agent. One need not find these cases to be correctly decided or always attractive in their outcome in order to conclude that the actions of an international organization or an international tribunal, even one in which the United States is a co-equal participant with many other treaty parties, are not necessarily equivalent to the action of the U.S. government itself.[62]

Complementarity

Perhaps the greatest safeguard of constitutional protections is, in practice, the assurance that no American would be tried in front of the ICC unless there were an inconceivable breakdown of the justice system within this country. The guarantee of complementarity in the Rome Treaty requires that the Court defer to U.S. processes of justice in all imaginable circumstances. But in assessing even the theoretical possibility of trial before an international criminal tribunal, the relevant standards for comparison include foreign criminal procedures and military courts-martial, which are the likely alternative venues for crimes committed abroad.

Rules of Procedure and Prosecutorial Policy

To be sure, it is critical to assess the actual performance of international war crimes tribunals, to ensure that their practice measures up to the guarantees made on paper. There is certainly room for some caution in the early performance of the ad hoc tribunals for the former Yugoslavia and Rwanda. The Rwanda tribunal registrar failed to allow defendants to select appointed counsel of their choice, saying that geographical distribution in employment had to be maintained; this ill-founded decision was reversed after widespread criticism.[63] In addition, the prosecutor's office of the Rwanda tribunal allegedly failed to assure a speedy trial to a key defendant, Jean-Bosco Barayagwiza, who was accused of inciting the Rwanda genocide through Goebbels-like broadcasts on Radio Milles Collines; he was detained for twenty-two months before his arraignment in Arusha. The appellate chamber dismissed the case with prejudice, as a sanction against the prosecutor and to ensure that there would be no repetition, although the matter was reopened when new facts came to light.[64] Both tribunals have also suffered occasional ex parte communications between the judges and the prosecutors, an informality that would not be permitted in an American courthouse.

Other potential problems can be addressed in the trial process to ensure fair adjudication. For example, defendants may need access to information that states wish to withhold. The ICC cannot require any state to produce sensitive national security information—a provision on which the United States insisted to protect intelligence sources and methods.[65] A defendant may allege that such information is necessary to his defense, say, to corroborate that he attempted to control the actions of his troops on the battlefield. If evidence were not forthcoming, from a third-party government or even from the defendant's own national government, the trial Judge would have to determine whether an inference in favor of the defendant must be drawn at trial.[66] It also remains important to have frank and critical reporting of problems within any international tribunal in order to guard against practices that might challenge a reputation for fairness; the enthusiasm of some for an international court can never be taken as an excuse for obscuring matters that should be addressed.

Other concerns about the Statute can be met in a variety of ways. Some can be addressed by shaping the Court's rules of evidence and procedure. Where the United States may still have concerns, it can pursue other modalities—a statement of "understandings" made upon signature and ratification of the Treaty, conditions to any cooperation agreement between the Court and the United States,[67] or specific conditions to any transfer of custody, a practice known in bilateral extradition.[68]

To ensure that the content of criminal law is clearly specified—in order to give notice to citizens of what law governs their behavior—the United States has taken part in setting out the "elements" of each crime within the ICC's jurisdiction, as part of the work of the PrepCom. Senior American military lawyers with experience in applying the law of war and conducting courts-martial have had the lead in the American delegation at the PrepCom, and their work should give assurance that the definition of war crimes and other international law standards within the Rome Statute will fit American understandings of humanitarian law and the law of war. The Rome Statute excludes criminal liability for soldiers acting under orders unless the conduct in question was "manifestly unlawful"[69]—an additional safeguard against surprise or unwitting action. The intent requirement in the definition of war crimes provides yet another safeguard, ensuring that there is no surprise about applicable standards.

There may be concern about the adequacy of the conditions of detention and confinement, as measured by the relatively high standards of Western countries. The Rome Treaty says that international standards on the treatment of prisoners must be observed;[70] but in practice, prison conditions vary widely.[71] The United States can seek assurances, in contemplating any particular case, that the ICC prosecutor will recommend that the service of sentence be carried out in a place selected from a list of acceptable states or that she will not oppose a transfer for service of sentence to the United States itself.[72] So, too, to avoid any concern about the limits of double jeopardy as measured by traditional common law standards, the United States can seek the assurance that no appeal will be taken by the prosecutor on any charges on which an initial judgment of acquittal is entered.[73] The finality of acquittals should extend to complementarity as well. With the passage of the 1996 War Crimes Act[74] and the 1997 Genocide Convention Implementation Act[75] by the U.S. Congress, it is hard to imagine any circumstance under which complementarity would fail to shield an American defendant from the jurisdiction of the ICC. But in the traditional relationship between state and federal prosecutions, a case can be tried in federal court after a state court verdict under limited and extraordinary circumstances on the argument that a different sovereign is bringing the case.[76] One does not wish to make the doubtful suggestion that there is such a thing as "international sovereignty," and any acquittal within the American trial court system must be taken as dispositive.[77] This, too, may be clarified by presidential statement on adhesion to the treaty, negotiation of a cooperation agreement, or considering any request for transfer.

There is justified concern about the ad hoc Yugoslav tribunal's permitting the use of an anonymous witness at trial on one occasion, despite the prosecution's rationale that the witness—a rape victim—would otherwise be traumatized and placed in danger of retaliation.[78] The American common law system guaranteeing the right of confrontation has never permitted anonymous witnesses whose identity is concealed from the defendant and his or her lawyer except in affidavits for search warrants and arrest warrants, where there are stringent requirements of informant reliability.[79] The ICC would be well advised to exclude the use of anonymous witnesses in its rules of procedure, except perhaps in the most extraordinary circumstances. If the PrepCom fails to clarify this matter, an American president could again condition a cooperation agreement or transfer on suitable assurances concerning the conduct of the trial.

While U.S. treaty power has traditionally had a broad scope, as Justice Oliver Wendell Holmes ruled in *Missouri v. Holland* (1920),[80] U.S. constitutional tradition respects the prerogatives of the House of Representatives in matters concurrently falling within the legislative power, all the more in matters of criminal law. In 1812, the Supreme Court held that there was no federal common law of crimes, thus recognizing the crucial role of the House in enunciating federal criminal law.[81] The preeminent role of the Congress in addressing questions of substantive criminal law can be recognized in a process of accession to the ICC—asking the House of Representatives and the Senate to approve the definitions of crimes and the elements of the offenses in the legislation that is necessary to implement the ICC treaty within American law. If the Senate is willing to give its advice and consent to the Rome Treaty, the terms of the Treaty should nonetheless be enacted within American statutory law by action of the Congress before an American president deposits an instrument of ratification.

The question remains whether, in theory, the Constitution would allow the exercise of ICC jurisdiction over an American citizen or permanent resident alien for conduct occurring within the United States. Extradition of defendants has been permitted to foreign national legal systems for conduct within the United States undertaken as part of an international conspiracy,[82] and this would plausibly extend to conduct that causes injury in a foreign jurisdiction.[83] Crimes that are subject to universal jurisdiction are thought to have an adverse impact on all states in the world community, regardless of the place of offense, and in theory could be the subject of a request for surrender by a foreign court under a bilateral extradition treaty, as well as by the ICC. Acts by citizens within the United States, however, enjoy the strongest claim to constitutional protection at trial because the United States has direct territorial jurisdiction over the offenses and, in the case of war crimes and genocide, has newly enacted statutory jurisdiction as well.[84] Hence, in any accession to the ICC Treaty, it would be advisable to restate the understanding that cooperation with the tribunal will not extend to acts within the United States that have been investigated and/or adjudicated in good faith by American authorities and that the ICC will not exercise any authority over those completed cases.

CONCLUSION

The guarantees in criminal procedure that were the product of hard-won reform in the Founders' framing of the Bill of Rights and in the twentieth century alike are not now to be lightly tossed aside in a move to internationalism. The United States faces the task of showing that one can create an effective mechanism for prosecuting war crimes, genocide, and crimes against humanity while maintaining the highest standards of fairness. The constitutional arguments that will surround the debate over the ICC have a special weight in American culture, for the Constitution is the center of American political philosophy. Though other countries may amend their constitutions to conform to the ICC's structure, the challenge in this country will be to debate whether fair interpretation of the American Constitution as it stands permits participation in the Court. The United States does not often amend its constitution, and should not. At the same time, Americans are a people who went to war more than once in the twentieth century to defeat criminal regimes that trammel human rights. The constitutional question of the ICC deserves address without rhetoric or polemics and in a manner that takes account of its serious moral purpose.

NOTES

1. See Report of the International Law Commission on the Work of Its 46th Session, May 2–July 22, 1994, U.N.G.A., 49th Sess., Supp. No. 10, A/49/10, 1994.

2. Rome Statute of the International Criminal Court, July 17, 1998, U.N. Doc. A/Conf. 183/9, art. 17, reprinted in *International Legal Materials* 33 (1998): 999.

3. Statute, art. 98(2).

4. Statute, art. 17.

5. Statute, art. 17(1).

6. See, e.g., U.S. Senate Committee on Foreign Relations, *Is a U.N. International Criminal Court Consistent with the U.S. National Interest?*: *Hearing before the Subcommittee on International Operations of the Committee on Foreign Relations,* 105th Cong., 2d sess., July 23, 1998, S. Hrg. 105–724, *available at* <http://www.access.gpo.gov/congress/senate>; American Bar Association Task Force on an International Criminal Court and New York State Bar Association, Joint Report on "Establishment of an International Criminal Court," Benjamin R. Civiletti, Chairperson, August 1992, in *International Lawyer* 27 (Spring 1993): 257; and "Report of the Judicial Conference of the United States on the Feasibility of and the Relationship to the Federal Judiciary of an International Criminal Court," reprinted in *International Criminal Court* (September 1991), "Report of the Committee on Foreign Relations," U.S. Senate, S. Rept. 103–71, 103d Cong., 2d sess., *available in* Lexis-Nexus.

7. Algiers Accords, United States-Iran, January 19, 1981, *International Legal Materials* 20 (1981): 223. See *Dames and Moore v. Regan,* 453 U.S. 654 (1981).

8. U.N.S.C. Res. 687 (1991), reprinted in *International Legal Materials* 30 (1991): 847.

9. See *Judicial Assistance to the International Tribunal for Yugoslavia and to the International Tribunal for Rwanda,* Public Law 104–106 [S.1124], 110 Stat. 486 (1996), codified at 18 U.S.C. 3181 *note* (applying the extradition procedures of 18 U.S.C. 3181 et seq. for "the surrender of persons, including United States citizens," to this ad hoc war crimes tribunal).

10. "Statute of the International Criminal Tribunal for Former Yugoslavia," art. 11 and 12, U.N. Doc. S/25704, Annex (1993), reprinted in *International Legal Materials* 32 (1993): 1192; "Statute of the International Criminal Tribunal for Rwanda," art. 10 and 11, S.C. Res. 955, Annex (November 8, 1994), reprinted in *International Legal Materials* 33 (1994): 1602.

11. Statute, art. 60(1).

12. Statute, art. 66(1) and art. 66(2).

13. Statute, art. 55(1).

14. Statute, art. 67(1) (b).

15. Statute, art. 55(2) (c) and art. 67(1) (f).

16. Statute, art. 58(1) and art. 60(2).

17. Statute, art. 67(1) (c).

18. Statute, art. 67(1) (d).

19. Statute, art. 67(e).

20. Statute, art. 55(1).

21. Statute, art. 66(3).

22. Statute, art. 55(1) (b).

23. Statute, art. 55(1) (b).

24. *Miranda v. Arizona,* 384 U.S. 436 (1966).

25. Statute, art. 55(2) (a)–(d).

26. Statute, art. 34, art. 39(2) (b) (ii), and art. 74. It is interesting that in one of the

earliest proposals for a permanent international criminal court, there was a provision for jury trial. See "Revised Draft Statute for an International Criminal Court," Annex to the Report of the 1953 Committee on International Criminal Jurisdiction on Its Session held from July 27–August 20, 1953, U.N.G.A., 9th Sess., Supp. No. 12, A/2645, 1954, reprinted in *The Statute of the International Criminal Court: A Documentary History,* ed. M. Cherif Bassiouni (Ardsley, N.Y.: Transnational, 1998), 749, 754 (Article 37: "Trial shall be without jury, except where otherwise provided in the instrument by which jurisdiction has been conferred upon the Court").

27. Statute, art. 74(3); compare *Johnson v. Louisiana,* 406 U.S. 356 (1972) (states may authorize non-unanimous jury verdicts in other than capital cases).

28. Statute, art. 81(1) (a).

29. See Vienna Convention on Consular Relations, April 24, 1963, 21 U.S.T. 77, 596 U.N.T.S. 261.

30. *The Schooner Exchange v. M'Faddon,* 11 U.S. (7 Cranch) 116, 136 (1812); accord *Wilson v. Girard,* 354 U.S. 524, 529 (1957) ("A sovereign nation has exclusive jurisdiction to punish offenses against its laws committed within its borders, unless it expressly or impliedly consents to surrender its jurisdiction").

31. See, e.g., NATO Status of Forces Agreement, June 19, 1951, 4 U.S.T. 1792, T.I.A.S. No. 2846; *Manual for Courts-Martial United States* (1995 ed.), Rule 201(d), *Discussion* ("Under international law, a friendly foreign nation has jurisdiction to punish offenses committed within its borders by members of a visiting force, unless [it] expressly or implicitly consents to relinquish its jurisdiction to the visiting sovereign. The procedures and standards for determining which nation will exercise jurisdiction are normally established by treaty").

32. *Wilson v. Girard,* 524.

33. *The Schooner Exchange v. M'Faddon,* 116, 136; accord *Wilson v. Girard,* 547–48 (though Japan had no trial by jury, "[p]ursuant to the Administrative Agreement under the Japanese Treaty, Girard will be guaranteed a prompt trial, the right to have representation by counsel satisfactory to him, full information as to all charges against him, the right to confront all witnesses, the right to have his witnesses compelled to attend court, the right to have a competent interpreter, the right of communication with United States authorities, and the presence of a United States representative as an official observer at the trial"); see also *Holmes v. Laird,* 459 F.2d 1211, 1219 n. 58 (D.C. Cir. 1972) ("notwithstanding the serviceman's specific claim that the absence" of full American constitutional procedures "would deprive him of a fair trial in the Japanese courts," *Wilson v. Girard* found "'no constitutional or statutory barrier' to the surrender").

34. *Holmes v. Laird,* 1211.

35. *Holmes v. Laird,* 1218.

36. See 18 U.S.C. 3181 *et seq.*

37. Because the Secretary of State may still decline extradition, it has been held that the judge's action is not "final" in a constitutional sense and hence is rendered as an Article I magistrate, rather than an Article III court. See in re Metzger, 46 U.S. (5 How.) 176, 191 (1847); *United States v. Mackin,* 668 F.2d 122, 125–30 (2d Cir. 1981); *United States v. Doherty,* 786 F.2d 491, 499 n.10 (2d Cir. 1986).

38. The Supreme Court noted in *Neely v. Henkel,* 180 U.S. 109, 122 (1901), that the trial procedures of the Bill of Rights "have no relation to crimes committed *without* the jurisdiction of the United States against the laws of a foreign country" (emphasis added).

See also *Charlton v. Kelly*, 229 U.S. 447 (1913) (upholding the extradition of an American citizen to Italy for trial on a charge of murder).

39. See *Gallina v. Fraser*, 278 F.2d 77, 78 (2d Cir.), cert. denied, 364 U.S. 851 (1960) (American courts will not "inquire into the procedures which await the [defendant] upon extradition"); accord *Sindona v. Grant*, 619 F.2d 167, 174 (2d Cir. 1980), and *Peroff v. Hylton*, 542 F.2d 1247, 1249 (4th Cir. 1976), cert. denied, 429 U.S. 1062 (1977).

40. See *Gallina v. Fraser*, 79; *Sindona v. Grant*, supra note 38, 175; in re Burt, 737 F.2d 1477, 1487 (7th Cir. 1984).

41. Convention for the Suppression of Unlawful Seizure of Aircraft, done at The Hague, December 16, 1970, entered into force October 14, 1971, 22 U.S.T. 1641, T.I.A.S. No. 7192, 860 U.N.T.S. 105.

42. Convention for the Suppression of Unlawful Acts against the Safety of Civil Aviation (Montreal Convention), September 23, 1971, 24 U.S.T. 564; T.I.A.S. No. 7570, 974 U.N.T.S. 177.

43. Convention on the Prevention and Punishment of Crimes against Internationally Protected Persons, Including Diplomatic Agents, December 14, 1973, 28 U.S.T. 1955, T.I.A.S. No. 8532, 1035 U.N.T.S. 167.

44. International Convention against the Taking of Hostages, adopted December 17, 1979, G.A. Res. 34/146, 34 U.N. GAOR Annex, U.N. Doc. A/34/819, at 5 (1979), T.I.A.S. No. 11081; reprinted in *American Journal of International Law* 74 (1980): 2770.

45. International Convention against Torture and Other Cruel, Inhuman, or Degrading Treatment or Punishment, December 10, 1984, G.A. Res. 39/46, U.N. GAOR, 39th Sess., Supp. No. 51, U.N. Doc. A/39/51 (1984), S. Treaty Doc. No. 100–20 (1988), 1465 U.N.T.S. 85; reprinted in *International Legal Materials* 23 (1984): 1027; as modified, *International Legal Materials* 24 (1985): 535.

46. International Convention for the Suppression of Terrorist Bombings, G.A. Res. 52/164 (December 15, 1997).

47. See, e.g., Convention Relative to the Treatment of Prisoners of War [Geneva III], August 12, 1949, arts. 129 and 130, 6 U.S.T. 316, T.I.A.S. No. 3364, 75 U.N.T.S. 135; Convention Relative to the Protection of Civilian Persons in Time of War [Geneva IV], August 12, 1949, arts. 146 and 147, 6 U.S.T. 3516, T.I.A.S. No. 3365, 75 U.N.T.S. 287.

48. Judgments—*Regina v. Bartle and the Commissioner of Police for the Metropolis and Others, ex parte Pinochet* (on appeal from a Divisional Court of the Queen's Bench Division), House of Lords, March 24, 1999; reprinted in *International Legal Materials* 38 (1999): 581.

49. *Manual for Courts-Martial, United States* (1998 ed.), Rules 201(f) (1) (B) and 501. Compare U.S. Constitution, Amendment V ("No person shall be held to answer for a capital, or otherwise infamous crime, unless on presentment of indictment of a Grand Jury, *except in cases arising in the land or naval forces*, or in the Militia, when in actual service, in time of War or public danger"—emphasis added); U.S. Constitution, art. I, sec. 8, clauses 8 and 14 ("The Congress shall have Power . . . To define and punish . . . Offenses against the Law of Nations and to make Rules for the Government and Regulation of the land and naval Forces").

50. *Manual for Courts-Martial, United States* (1998 ed.), Rules 921(c) (2) and (3).

51. In re G. [Goran Grabez], Military Tribunal, Division 1, Lausanne, Switzerland, April 18, 1977; see Andreas R. Ziegler, "International Decision," *American Journal of International Law* 92 (1998): 78.

52. See Associated Press, "Rwanda: Ex-Mayor Gets Life," *New York Times*, May 1, 1999, A6 (Rwandan Mayor Fulgence Niyonteze convicted by Swiss military court for murder, attempted murder, incitement to murder, and war crimes in the 1994 Rwanda genocide, after seeking asylum in Switzerland).

53. Ex parte *Quirin*, 317 U.S. 1 (1942).

54. Ex parte *Milligan*, 71 U.S. (4 Wall.) 2 (1866). See also *Johnson v. Eisentrager*, 339 U.S. 763, 779–80 (1950) (*Quirin* defendants were "tried by a Military Commission sitting in the District of Columbia at a time when civil courts were open and functioning normally" for "acts committed in the United States").

55. See *United States v. Tiede*, 86 F.R.D. 227, 254 (U.S. Court for Berlin 1979) (*Quirin* "held that petitioners were not entitled to a jury trial because they were charged with violations of the law of war").

56. See *Berlin Democratic Club v. Rumsfeld*, 410 F. Supp. 144 (DDC 1976).

57. See *Reid v. Covert*, 354 U.S. 1 (1957) (requiring trial by jury in a capital murder case for U.S. dependents not enlisted in the armed forces). Justice Hugo Black famously observed that "No agreement with a foreign nation can confer power on the Congress, or on any other branch of Government, which is free from the restraints of the Constitution" (354 U.S. 16).

58. See *United States v. Tiede*, 86 F.R.D. 227, 254 (U.S. Court for Berlin 1979) (*Quirin* "held that petitioners were not entitled to a jury trial because they were charged with violations of the law of war").

59. See *Hawaii v. Mankichi*, 190 U.S. 197 (1903); *Dorr v. United States*, 195 U.S. 138 (1904).

60. *United States v. Verdugo-Urquidez*, 494 U.S. 259 (1990).

61. *United States v. Alvarez-Machain*, 504 U.S. 655 (1992).

62. See American Bar Association Task Force on an International Criminal Court and New York State Bar Association, "Establishment of an International Criminal Court," 269 ("In the situation where the U.S. national had committed the crime abroad and the United States agreed to his prosecution before an international criminal court sitting outside the United States and imposing punishment outside of the United States instead of prosecution before the courts of the country where he committed the crime, arguably there would be no grounds for constitutional objection merely because the United States might cooperate in the prosecutorial effort—such cooperation also might occur if he were tried before the courts of the [foreign] territorial state").

63. See Note on Assignment of Defence Counsel, ICTR/INFO, February 22, 1999, http://www.ictr.org/english/pressrel/defence.htm ("Based on a decision from the ICTR bench . . . the ICTR recently implemented a *temporary* moratorium on the appointment of defence counsel from Canada and France"—emphasis in original); "Rwanda Tribunal Lifts Ban on French and Canadian Lawyers," *Africa News*, October 27, 1999 ("The decision to rescind the ban came almost two months after judges . . . overruled the ban and granted convicted Rwandan genocide participant, Jean Paul Akayesu, a Canadian defence counsel on appeal").

64. Decision of the Appeals Chamber, Jean-Bosco Barayagwiza, ICTR-97-19, November 3, 1999; *modified upon rehearing*, March 31, 2000. The Appeals Chamber found ultimately that much of the delay was due to the actions of Cameroon, where the defendant had fled, and to the decision of Barayagwiza's defense counsel to postpone arraignment. The appeals judges also noted that the prosecutor of the International Tribunal had failed to muster these facts in the initial appeal, a neglect that ordinarily would bar their presen-

tation in a second hearing. Only the "wholly exceptional circumstances of this case" permitted the review, to prevent a "possible miscarriage of justice."

65. Statute, art. 72, art. 87(7), and art. 93(4).

66. Statute, art. 72(7) (a) (ii) and art. 72(7) (b) (ii).

67. The ICC enjoys international personality (Statute, art. 4[1]) and can enter into cooperation agreements with member states.

68. European Treaty partners have asked for assurances that the death penalty will not be imposed in extradition cases, even where there was no provision for the demand under the bilateral treaty. See *Soering v. United Kingdom*, 161 Eur. Ct. H.R. (ser. A) (1989), reprinted in *European Human Rights Report* 11 (1989): 439, and in *International Legal Materials* 28 (1989): 1063; discussed in Richard B. Lillich, "The Soering Case," *American Journal of International Law* 85 (1991): 128; and see *Short v. Kingdom of Netherlands, International Legal Materials* 29 (1990): 1388 (jurisdiction over spousal murder ceded by Dutch authorities only after charge reduced to noncapital offense); discussed in Major John E. Parkerson Jr. and Major Steven J. Lepper, *Short v. Kingdom of Netherlands, American Journal of International Law* 85 (1991): 698. Assurances have been obtained by the United States in bilateral extradition that a defendant convicted *in absentia* would enjoy the right to a new trial; see Marjorie M. Whiteman, *Digest of International Law* 6, ch. 16, § 39, 1051–52, and *Gallina v. Fraser*, 278 F.2d 77, 78 (2d Cir.), cert. denied, 364 U.S. 851 (1960) (American courts will not "inquire into the procedures which await the [defendant] upon extradition").

69. Statute, art. 33.

70. Statute, art. 103(3) (b).

71. Statute, art. 106(3), stating that "in no case shall such conditions [for ICC defendants] be more or less favorable than those available to prisoners convicted of similar offences in the State of enforcement."

72. Statute, art. 104(2).

73. Compare Judgement on Appeal, *Prosecutor v. Tadic*, IT-94-1, July 15, 1999.

74. *War Crimes Act of 1996*, 18 U.S.C. § 2441 (1998) (allowing prosecution in U.S. courts of any grave breaches of the Geneva Conventions, violations of Geneva common Article 3, or violations of the Fourth Hague Convention, where the victim or the offender was a U.S. national or was a member of the U.S. armed forces, whether the act was committed inside or outside the United States).

75. *Genocide Convention Implementation Act of 1997*, 18 U.S.C. § 1091(d) (1998) (allowing prosecution of genocide committed within the United States or by U.S. nationals).

76. See *Petite v. United States* 361 U.S. 529, 530–31 (19), and United States Attorney's Manual section 9–2.142 ("No federal case should be tried when there has been a state prosecution for substantially the same act or acts without a recommendation having been made to the Assistant Attorney General demonstrating compelling Federal interests for such prosecution"). Compare *Blockburger v. United States*, 284 U.S. 29 (1932) ("the test to be applied to determine whether there are two offenses or only one, is whether each provision requires proof of an additional fact which the other does not"), with *Ashe v. Swenson*, 397 U.S. 436, 453–54 (1970) (concurring opinion by Justice William Brennan) ("the Double Jeopardy Clause requires the prosecution, except in most limited circumstances, to join at one time all the charges against a defendant which grow out of a single criminal act, occurrence, episode, or transaction").

77. Most bilateral extradition treaties forbid the transfer of a defendant who has already been tried for the offense. Marjorie M. Whiteman, *Digest of International Law* 6, chap. 16, at § 40 at 1054; *Sindona v. Grant*, 619 F.2d at 177, citing *Galanis v. Pallanck*, 568 F.2d 234, 238–39 (2d Cir. 1977) ("'the position . . . adopted by the Secretary of State' in including double jeopardy clauses in extradition treaties 'accords with the policy adopted by the Department of Justice in response to concerns expressed by the Supreme Court in the federal-state context.'").

78. See "Decision on the Prosecutor's Motion Requesting Protective Measures for Victims and Witnesses," *Prosecutor v. Tadic*, IT-94-1-T; Monroe Leigh, "The Yugoslav Tribunal: Use of Unnamed Witnesses Against Accused," *American Journal of International Law* 90 (1996): 235; compare Christine Chinkin, "Due Process and Witness Anonymity," *American Journal of International Law* 91 (1997): 75.

79. Compare *Van Mechelen v. Netherlands, European Human Rights Report* 25 (1998) (Eur. Ct. Hum. Rts. 1997): 647 (conviction cannot be based solely or to decisive extent on anonymous statements); *Doorson v. Netherlands, European Human Rights Report* 22 (1996) (Eur. Ct. Hum. Rts. 1996) (anonymous witnesses permitted where fear of retaliation by drug dealers and defense counsel took part in interrogation); *Windisch v. Austria*, (1991), *European Human Rights Report* 13, 281 (Eur. Ct. Hum. Rts. 1990) (reliance on anonymous witnesses questioned only by police was impermissible); *Kostovski v. Netherlands*, (1990), *European Human Rights Report* 12, 434 (Eur. Ct. Hum. Rts. 1989) (disallowing reliance on anonymous witnesses at trial); *Holmes v. Laird* (servicemen transferred to German authorities on rape charge despite claim that "[t]hey were not permitted confrontation . . . because they were excluded while the prosecutrix testified").

80. 252 U.S. 416 (1920).

81. See *United States v. Hudson and Goodwin*, 11 U.S. (7 Cranch) 32 (1812). The Supreme Court, however, has found sufficient specificity in Congressional reliance on internationally defined crimes; see *United States v. Smith*, 18 U.S. 153, 157 (1820) (approving act of Congress punishing "the crime of piracy, as defined by the law of nations").

82. See *United States v. Melia*, 667 F.2d 300 (2d Cir. 1981) (extradition to Canada for conspiracy to commit murder in Connecticut, where phone calls were made from Connecticut to coconspirators in Canada); *Austin v. Healey*, 5 F.3d 598 (2d Cir. 1993) (extradition to United Kingdom for conspiracy and murder, for acts in United States procuring murder in United Kingdom); *Valencia v. Scott*, 1992 U.S. Dist. Lexis 3886 (E.D.N.Y. 1992) (extradition to France for acts in New York City furthering an international narcotics conspiracy); *Bozilov v. Seifert*, 983 F.2d 140 (9th Cir. 1993). Compare *Government of the United States v. McCaffery*, House of Lords, [1984] 2 All England Reports 570 (1984) (Lord Diplock) (approving extradition of McCaffery to the United States on charge of financial fraud where "all the physical acts that he did personally in furtherance of this international fraud were . . . done by him in England"). Extradition requires that both countries recognize the same form of extraterritorial jurisdiction. See, e.g., *United States v. Melia*, supra, 667 F.2d at 303 (extradition treaty with Canada allows surrender for acts "outside of the requesting country" if requested country could take jurisdiction "over such an offense committed in similar circumstances").

83. *Strassheim v. Daily*, 223 U.S. 280, 285 (1911) ("acts done outside a jurisdiction, but intended to produce and producing detrimental effects within it, justify a State in punishing the cause of the harm as if he had been present at the effect").

84. American Bar Association Task Force on an International Criminal Court and New York State Bar Association, "Establishment of an International Criminal Court," 269.

8

American Servicemembers and the ICC

Robinson O. Everett

When the Statute to establish the International Criminal Court (ICC) was being considered in Rome, the United States was concerned that American servicemembers deployed overseas might be tried by that Court. In that event, the servicemembers would not have the benefit of the jury trial and the other procedural safeguards available in a federal district court or in a state court. Nor would the servicemembers be tried in a tribunal that had the understanding of the unique requirements of the military society that the members of a U.S. court-martial would possess. Because the Statute as drafted did not guarantee that the United States would have exclusive—or at least primary—jurisdiction to try alleged war crimes committed by American servicemembers, the United States—under strong pressure from the Department of Defense—declined to sign the treaty. Moreover, unless some solution can be found for the concerns of the United States, it would be surprising if the Senate ratified the treaty, even if the Clinton administration changed its position.

STATUS OF FORCES AGREEMENT

The current effort to ensure that American servicemembers serving overseas would be tried by an American tribunal for any alleged war crimes is similar to the effort made by the United States after World War II to minimize the possibility that American servicemembers deployed in Europe and in Asia would be tried by foreign tribunals. At that time it was clear that hundreds of thousands of American servicemembers and quite a few of their dependents would be stationed overseas for long periods of time; and in many instances, their host countries would have systems of criminal justice quite different from the system familiar to Americans. Even though U.S. courts-martial do not provide the accused some of the procedural safeguards available in civil courts, they do offer protections that in some respects exceed those available in foreign courts. The fear at the time was that servicemembers might fare even worse if, instead of being tried by courts-martial, they were prosecuted in foreign courts. This fear was heightened regarding the possibility that the victim of a servicemember's alleged crime was a citizen of the host country. On the other hand, if Americans were the only victims of a servicemember's crime and if the only basis for jurisdiction of a foreign court were the crime's occurrence within that country's territory, a foreign prosecutor might have little interest in the case; and a serious crime might go unpunished.

To help allay such concerns, the United States negotiated with the other North Atlantic Treaty Organization (NATO) countries a Status of Forces Agreement (SOFA), which in Article 7 dealt with issues of jurisdiction over persons in the visiting forces. Under the provisions of that article, an American servicemember who engages in conduct that violates military law but that is not punishable under the law of the host country is subject to the exclusive jurisdiction of U.S. courts-martial. On the other hand, courts of the host country have exclusive jurisdiction to try American servicemembers for conduct prohibited by the law of that country but not prohibited by U.S. military law. Ironically, some of those involved in negotiating the SOFA treaty were apparently under the misconception that the host country would never have exclusive jurisdiction, and their premise was that any conduct that violated the law of the foreign country would automatically be a violation of the Uniform Code of Military Justice.[1]

Under Article 7, for conduct that violates both U.S. military law and the law of the host country, there is concurrent jurisdiction. In that event, U.S. courts-martial are granted the primary right to exercise jurisdiction to try crimes committed against the security or property of the United States or against U.S. personnel or their property, as well as crimes arising out of actions taken "in the performance of official duty." In all other instances of concurrent jurisdiction, the host country has the primary right to exercise that jurisdiction. However, in deference to U.S. concerns, the host country is obligated to give "sympathetic consideration" to any U.S. request for waiver of the primary right to exercise jurisdiction if the United States claims such waiver "to be of particular importance."[2] Apparently the Senate considered that in every case involving concurrent jurisdiction, a waiver would be "of particular importance," for, in ratifying the NATO SOFA, it attached a reservation contemplating that U.S. military authorities would request on a routine basis that a host country waive its primary right to exercise jurisdiction.

Under the SOFA, servicemembers are protected against double jeopardy; trial by a local court precludes trial by court-martial for the same conduct and vice versa. This preclusion of trial by two sovereigns for the same misconduct is an interesting contrast to U.S. law, which, absent a statutory prohibition, permits trial by both a federal court and a state court for the same criminal conduct.[3] Article 7 also requires that an accused be provided these important safeguards: (1) speedy trial; (2) notice before trial of the specific charge; (3) confrontation by witnesses; (4) the right to subpoena witnesses; (5) legal representation; (6) aid of an interpreter; and (7) opportunity to communicate with the servicemember's own government and the right to have a representative thereof present at trial when the rules of court permit.[4]

The NATO SOFA made provision for a "civilian component" of the visiting armed forces—civilian dependents and employees—and for purposes of criminal jurisdiction they were treated in the same manner as servicemembers. At the time of entry into the SOFA, the United States assumed that these members of the "civilian component" would be subject to trial by U.S. court-martial, as authorized by Article 2 of the Uniform Code of Military Justice.[5] Therefore, just as for servicemembers, the United States had a basis for insisting that such civilians be tried by U.S. courts-martial, rather than by courts of the host countries. However, in 1957, the Supreme Court ruled that Article 2 was unconstitutional insofar as it sought to extend court-martial jurisdiction to include persons who did not possess the status of being members of the armed forces.[6] Thereafter, civilians accompanying the armed forces overseas could be tried only in the courts of the host countries because the congressional grant of jurisdiction to courts-martial was unconstitutional and no jurisdiction had been granted to federal district courts to try crimes committed by civilian dependents and employees overseas.[7]

With the precedent of the NATO SOFA to rely on, the United States negotiated similar treaties with Japan and various other countries where U.S. troops were deployed. Some of these agreements went even further than the NATO SOFA in limiting the extent to which American servicemembers would be subject to the jurisdiction of the host country. In each instance, the United States, which has more of its servicemembers deployed overseas than any other country, was concerned to limit the risk that they might be subjected to trials lacking the procedural safeguards these servicemembers would enjoy in U.S. courts. However, if both the United States and the host country claimed primary jurisdiction to try a servicemember and the United States decided to waive its claim, that decision was not subject to judicial review.[8]

THE STATUTE OF THE ICC

Just as the United States was concerned half a century ago about the exposure of American servicemembers to trial in foreign courts, the forthcoming establishment of the ICC has led to concerns that American servicemembers may become subject to trial in that Court. The extent of that exposure depends in part on the scope of the ICC's jurisdiction, which, according to Article 5 of the Statute of the ICC, is limited "to the most serious crimes of concern to the international community as a whole." Subject to that limitation, Article 5 grants the Court "jurisdiction in accordance with this Statute with respect to the following crimes: (a) the crime of genocide; (b) crimes against humanity; (c) war crimes; (d) the crime of aggression." As detailed in Bartram Brown's chapter in this volume (chapter 4), the first three of these crimes are defined by the Statute. The *crime of aggression* is to be defined subsequently by the Assembly of the States Parties—those States that ratify the Statute—and the ICC shall exercise jurisdiction over this crime only after it has been defined.

Genocide encompasses killings and certain other acts "committed with intent to destroy, in whole or in part, a national, ethnical, racial, or religious group, as such."[9] *Crimes against humanity* refers to murder, "extermination," "enslavement," torture, rape, persecution, "apartheid," or various other acts "committed as part of a widespread or systematic attack directed against any civilian population, with knowledge of the attack."[10]

The Statute's Article 8, which concerns "war crimes," has special significance for those concerned about possible trial of American servicemembers by the ICC. This Article grants the Court jurisdiction "in respect of war crimes in particular when committed as part of a plan or policy or as part of a large scale commission of such crimes." The ensuing definition of *war crimes* is quite extensive. It includes "grave breaches of the Geneva Convention of 12 August 1949" and a number of "other serious violations of the laws and customs applicable in international armed conflict, within the established framework of international law." Various acts are encompassed within the definition of war crimes even though such acts take place in "an armed conflict not of an international character."[11] However, Article 8 makes clear that the term *war crime* does not apply to "situations of internal disturbances and tensions, such as riots, isolated and sporadic acts of violence or other acts of a similar nature."[12] The "elements" of the various crimes within the ICC's jurisdiction are to be adopted by the Assembly of the States that ratify the Statute.[13]

The ICC Statute creates the office of the Prosecutor,[14] who "may initiate investigations proprio motu on the basis of information on crimes within the jurisdiction of the Court" and who, in analyzing "the seriousness of the information received . . . may seek additional information from States, organs of the United Nations, intergovernmental or non-governmental organizations, or other reliable sources that he or she deems appropriate, and may receive written or oral testimony at the seat of the Court."[15] If the Prosecutor initiates charges that ultimately are tried by the ICC, many procedural safeguards will apply—some akin to those available in U.S. trials, whether civil or military.[16]

Nonetheless, trial of an American servicemember by the ICC would be quite different from trial by court-martial or by a federal district court. For example, the trial would be conducted entirely by Judges,[17] rather than by jurors or by members of a court-martial.[18] Obviously, viewpoints differ as to whether trial by experienced judges would be as likely as trial by jury or court-martial to produce an accurate and just result. It precludes the occasional "jury nullification" that prevents punishment of a guilty accused, and it ensures that there will be no favoritism for persons of the same nationality as the fact-finders. On the other hand, the Judges selected for the ICC will probably lack the understanding of the military society and its needs that would be possessed by people who were in the armed services or who had military experience. Moreover, some of the ICC Judges might even be hostile to American servicemembers.

In at least one situation, however, the establishment of the ICC might serve to benefit American servicemembers. If an American servicemember fell into the hands of a foreign government and was accused of a crime that was committed on the foreign government's territory or that involved its nationals, that government might wish to try the servicemember for the crime. In that event, the United States—because of its traditional concerns about assuring a fair trial for its servicemembers—could request extradition of the accused to the United States for trial in an American court, with the accompanying procedural safeguards.[19] The foreign government might then refuse the request for extradition to the United States for trial.[20] On the other hand, the foreign government might be willing to surrender the servicemember to the ICC for trial in order to eliminate a political confrontation with the United States and without appearing to surrender its own interests in having the alleged crime vigorously prosecuted. This scenario would be somewhat similar to that recently presented by the negotiations for the trial at The Hague of two Libyans accused of blowing up a Pan American airplane over Lockerbie, Scotland, in December 1988.

COMPLEMENTARITY AS A LIMITATION ON ICC JURISDICTION

Even though trial of an American servicemember by the ICC, with its procedural safeguards, may seem preferable to trial by some foreign courts, the obvious first choice of the United States is that the servicemember be tried by a U.S. tribunal.[21] Indeed, the willingness of American officials to deploy armed forces overseas, for peacekeeping purposes or otherwise, might be diminished if that deployment would subject American servicemembers to the jurisdiction of the ICC. Therefore, it is important to consider what means are available to reduce—or, if possible, to eliminate—the risk that American servicemembers will be tried by the ICC.

In this regard, great assistance is afforded by Article 1 of the ICC Statute, which states that the Court "shall be complementary to national criminal jurisdictions." The concept of *complementarity* is implemented by Article 17, which provides that the ICC "shall determine that a case is inadmissible where:

1. The case is being investigated or prosecuted by a State which has jurisdiction over it, unless the State is unwilling or unable genuinely to carry out the investigation or prosecution;

2. The case has been investigated by a State which has jurisdiction over it and that State has decided not to prosecute the person concerned, unless the decision resulted from the unwillingness or inability of the State genuinely to prosecute;

3. The person concerned has already been tried for conduct which is the subject of the complaint, and a trial by the Court is not permitted under article 20, paragraph 3;[22] or

4. The case is not of sufficient gravity to justify further action by the Court."

In light of Article 17, the ability of the United States to prevent the trial of American servicemembers by the ICC will be greatly enhanced if U.S. courts have jurisdiction to try servicemembers for any crime that falls within the ICC's jurisdiction. Moreover, since Article 17 by its terms applies to a "State," and not only to a "State Party," the United States—whether or not it becomes a party to the ICC—may block the exercise of jurisdiction by that Court (1) if the crime for which the servicemember might be tried by the ICC is within the jurisdiction of a U.S. court, civil or military, and (2) if U.S. authorities proceed in good faith to investigate the circumstances of the crime and, should they find it appropriate, try the crime in a U.S. court. Accordingly, it is important to ascertain when conduct by a servicemember that would constitute a crime under the ICC Statute would also be a crime in a U.S. court. This inquiry, in turn, may lead to a recommendation that the existing jurisdiction of U.S. courts be broadened in order to limit the potential exercise of ICC jurisdiction over American servicemembers.

With respect to American servicemembers still on active duty, the Uniform Code of Military Justice provides wide-ranging authority for courts-martial to punish almost any type of misconduct. For example, murder, rape, maiming, arson, and burglary are specifically dealt with by punitive articles of the Uniform Code.[23] Therefore, the conduct that constitutes a war crime may in many instances be charged as a collection of separate violations of the code's punitive articles, for example, a collection of murders and rapes.[24] In addition, Article 133 of the Code, 10 U.S.C. 933, prohibits "conduct unbecoming an officer and a gentleman," a prohibition that, regarding officers, would probably include some of the conduct prohibited by the Statute of the ICC.

Finally, Article 134 of the code, the "General Article," forbids "all disorders and neglects to the prejudice of good order and discipline in the armed forces, all conduct of a nature to bring discredit upon the armed forces, and crimes and offenses not capital." In many instances, conduct by an American servicemember that violates the ICC Statute would be prohibited by the second clause of Article 134, which concerns service-discrediting conduct. For example, a servicemember's participation in a "war crime" should be considered service-discrediting. Moreover, the third clause of Article 134 also creates a broad liability because it includes all "crimes and offenses not capital"—a phrase that refers to violations of federal criminal statutes.[25]

In light of Article 134's breadth of coverage with respect to the conduct of servicemembers, a firm basis exists for invoking the principle of complementarity to preclude the ICC from trying servicemembers who are still on active duty. Almost any conduct by a servicemember that could warrant trial in the ICC could also justify the preferring of charges for trial by court-martial. A good-faith investigation of those charges and a trial by court-martial—if warranted by the evidence discovered in the investigation—would then preclude trial in the ICC.[26]

Subject to the provisions of any applicable statute of limitations, Article 3(a) of the Uniform Code authorizes a general court-martial to try a former servicemember charged with an offense against the Uniform Code that is "punishable by confinement of five years or more and for which the person cannot be tried in the courts of the United States or any State or Territory thereof or of the District of Columbia." The statutory purpose was to eliminate an embarrassing jurisdictional gap revealed after World War II when occasionally no tribunal— military or civilian, American or foreign—had jurisdiction to try former servicemembers for offenses committed while they had been on active duty.[27] The Supreme Court, however, in 1956 ruled in *Toth v. Quarles* that retention of court-martial jurisdiction after military status ceased was not permitted by the Constitution.[28] Therefore, no tribunal was available that could consider the charges against Toth; and his participation in killing a North Korean became for him a crime without punishment.[29] This holding left U.S. courts-martial without jurisdiction to try discharged servicemembers for any alleged war crimes or misconduct in Korea or in Vietnam.[30] Expansion of federal district court jurisdiction to include crimes committed by servicemembers before their discharge would allow invoking complementarity to preclude their trial in the ICC.

Conducting military operations overseas often requires the presence of highly skilled technicians and experts who are not members of the armed forces. If such civilians are alleged to have committed war crimes, it also might be desirable to assure that these persons could be tried for those crimes in federal district courts— rather than by the ICC.

THE WAR CRIMES ACT

Some recent additions to the federal criminal code have provided more opportunities for invoking complementarity on behalf of servicemembers and have created an opportunity to utilize that principle to prevent the ICC from trying (1) former servicemembers for their conduct while on active duty or (2) civilians who might otherwise be subject to the Court's jurisdiction. In 1996, Congress enacted the War Crimes Act, which made punishable "a grave breach of the Geneva Conventions,"[31] whether committed within or outside the United States, if the victim or the perpetrator is a U.S. servicemember or "national."[32] A year later, Congress passed the Expanded War Crimes Act, which replaced the term *grave breach* with *war crime*, a term defined to include violations not only of the Geneva Conventions, but also of the Amended Protocol on Land Mines, at such time as the United States ratifies it; of certain articles of the Annex to Hague Convention IV; and of Common Article 3 of the Geneva Conventions.[33]

The legislative history of the War Crimes Act makes clear that its enactment resulted chiefly from a desire to establish U.S. criminal jurisdiction over people who perpetrated war crimes against Americans.[34] However, its language also applies to American servicemembers who commit war crimes. Probably the "crimes and offenses not capital" clause of Article 134 of the Uniform Code incorporates the War Crimes Act and thereby creates jurisdiction for courts-martial to try American servicemembers for violating the act. The chief issue would be whether the War Crimes Act's provision for a death penalty "if death results for the victim" would preclude its incorporation by the third clause of Article 134, which concerns only offenses "not capital." However, if a death penalty were not being sought, the argument is persuasive that the authorization of capital punishment in the War Crimes Act is severable and should be disregarded.[35]

THE LAW OF WAR

In defining the jurisdiction of general courts-martial, Article 18 of the Uniform Code of Military Justice states specifically:

> Subject to article 17 [Jurisdiction of courts-martial in general], general courts-martial shall have jurisdiction to try persons subject to this code for any offense made punishable by this code and may, under such limitations as the President may prescribe, adjudge any punishment not forbidden by this code, including the penalty of death when specifically authorized by this code. General courts-martial shall also have jurisdiction to try any person who by the law of war is subject to trial by a military tribunal and may adjudge any punishment permitted by the law of war.[36]

This language signifies that general courts-martial may exercise not only jurisdiction derived from Article I, Section 8, Clause 14 of the U.S. Constitution—which pertains to crimes committed by members of the "land and naval forces"—but also jurisdiction derived from Article I, Section 8, Clause 10—which empowers Congress to define and to punish "offences against the law of nations" and which is independent of the military status of the person who commits the "offence." Therefore, the jurisdictional limitation imposed by *Reid v. Covert* (1957) would not apply to a general court-martial exercising jurisdiction predicated on the "law of war."

The jurisdiction of courts-martial under the law of war is also recognized implicitly by Article 21 of the Uniform Code, which states:

The provisions of this code conferring jurisdiction upon courts-martial shall not be construed as depriving military commissions, provost courts, or other military tribunals of concurrent jurisdiction in respect of offenders or offenses that by statute or by the law of war may be tried by such military commissions, provost courts, or other military tribunals.[37]

Articles 104 and 106[38] are also intended to authorize courts-martial to exercise jurisdiction predicated on the law of war as a component of the "Law of Nations." The former article authorizes "death or such other punishment as a court-martial or military commission may direct" with respect to "any person" who "aids, or attempts to aid, the enemy" in several specified ways. The latter article, entitled "Spies," provides that a mandatory death penalty shall be imposed upon trial and conviction "by a general court-martial or by a military commission" of "[a]ny person who in time of war is found lurking as a spy or acting as a spy in or about" certain types of military installations. In light of these provisions of the Uniform Code, it seems clear that Congress has authorized a general court-martial or a military commission to try a servicemember for war crimes. Likewise, civilians who engage in conduct prohibited by the law of war—presumably including war crimes—may be tried by a general court-martial or by a military commission.[39]

During and after World War II, the Supreme Court had several occasions to consider whether certain conduct violated the law of war and was subject to trial by a military tribunal. The first occasion was in 1942 when the Court in ex parte *Quirin* upheld the jurisdiction of a military commission established by President Franklin Roosevelt to try some saboteurs who had been landed on the Atlantic coast from German submarines.[40] The trial was being conducted in Washington, and the defendants argued that trial by a military commission at a time and place when civilian courts were open violated the Constitution. In this connection, they relied especially on ex parte *Milligan* (1866),[41] which had ruled that a military commission convened in Indiana when civil authorities were in full control lacked jurisdiction to try a suspected Confederate sympathizer. However, as the Court pointed out, unlike *Milligan*, which involved martial law and emergency measures when civil authority could not function, the German saboteurs were being tried under the law of war, which was a branch of the "Law of Nations." Under Article I, Section 8, Clause 10 of the Constitution, Congress could "define and punish" violations of the law of war and could authorize their trial by court-martial or military commission. The trial of the German saboteurs was within the parameters set by Congress in the exercise of this power.[42]

A similar result was reached by the Supreme Court in re *Yamashita* (1946).[43] There it upheld the jurisdiction of a U.S. military commission to try a Japanese general accused of war crimes in the Philippines—crimes consisting chiefly of his failure to prevent his troops from committing many violent offenses against occupants of the territory they controlled.[44] According to the Court, the use of a military commission, rather than a general court-martial, to punish such misconduct was an option authorized by Congress.

In *Madsen v. Kinsella* (1952),[45] the Supreme Court considered whether the United States Court of the Allied High Commission for Germany, a tribunal created by the United States in connection with its postwar occupation of a part of Germany, had jurisdiction to try an American civilian dependent. She was charged with murdering her husband, who was an American army officer. Reasoning that under the law of war a victorious nation had the right to administer justice in occupied territory by such means as it saw fit, the Court held that the occupation court had jurisdiction even with respect to an American civilian present in the occupied territory. As a result, Mrs. Madsen received neither the procedural safeguards that would have been present in a U.S. civil court nor those she would have enjoyed in a trial by court-martial.

Analysis of these precedents leads to certain conclusions. In the first place, the Constitution gives Congress the power under both Article I, Section 8, Clause 14, and Article I, Section 8, Clause 10, to provide that American servicemembers may be tried by court-martial for war crimes. Any conduct by a servicemember that would be subject to trial by the ICC as a war crime probably could also be made subject to trial by a general court-martial. Indeed, to a considerable extent, the existing provisions of the Uniform Code of Military Justice and the War Crimes Act have already created jurisdiction over war crimes on the part of U.S. courts-martial—at least if the death penalty provisions of that Act do not preclude a "war crime" from being considered a "crime and offense not capital" within the meaning of Article 134 of the Code. Therefore, the principle of complementarity set out in the ICC Statute would provide the United States a basis for maintaining that American servicemembers accused of crimes prohibited by the Statute should be tried by a U.S. court-martial, rather than by the ICC. As a matter of caution, some additions to the Uniform Code and to the Manual for Courts-Martial might be desirable in order to make even firmer the conclusion that, as to American servicemembers, the jurisdiction of courts-martial would be coextensive with that of the ICC.[46]

The United States also may try in a federal district court a servicemember—or a civilian—who has been charged with a violation of the War Crimes Act.[47] Accordingly, if an American servicemember or civilian is charged with conduct that falls within the Act, the principle of complementarity would authorize the United States to demand that the accused be tried in a federal district court, rather than in the ICC. Currently, the War Crimes Act does not cover many of the crimes that are the subject of the Statute. Moreover, under the War Crimes Act, an issue may arise as to whether the alleged misconduct occurred during a conflict that constitutes a "war." Therefore, Congress might wish to consider whether this Act should be amended in a way that would ensure that the conduct it prohibits is coextensive with that as to which the ICC would have jurisdiction.[48] Admittedly, it may seem distasteful to modify U.S. criminal statutes to include crimes initially defined by others; but even so, this alternative should be considered in order to ensure the benefits of complementarity.

Quirin and *Yamashita* also established that the United States might use military commissions, rather than courts-martial, to try civilians for offenses against the law of war. Thus, even if American civilians were accused of conduct that violated the law of war as recognized in treaties, court decisions, and otherwise, but that was not specifically prohibited by the War Crimes Act, the United States could plausibly contend that, pursuant to the principle of complementarity, it is entitled to establish military commissions to try the accused, rather than leaving them subject to trial by the ICC.[49] Indeed, the possible advantage to be derived from having military commissions available as a means to try civilians accused of war crimes would provide an additional reason for the Supreme Court to reaffirm the existence of such jurisdiction on the part of military commissions in the event of a challenge thereto.[50]

CONCLUSION

Complementarity does not provide American servicemembers deployed overseas any absolute protection against being brought to trial before the ICC. However, this principle recognized in the ICC Statute does make available to the United States a means for insisting that U.S. authorities—not the ICC—have the opportunity to investigate and to prosecute alleged crimes by servicemembers against the "Law of Nations." Perhaps, therefore, the threat to American servicemembers posed by the Statute may be less ominous than many have supposed.

Whether the Statute of the ICC is ratified by the United States may well depend on Congress's evaluation of the extent of that threat and on a consideration of the means that may be available for reducing such threat. Thus, in preparation for deciding whether to join with other nations in ratifying the Statute, Congress should undertake a careful review of existing U.S. legislation concerning the jurisdiction of U.S. courts—civil or military—to deal with conduct that would come within the jurisdiction of the ICC. To the extent such conduct is not currently subject to punishment by any U.S. tribunal, Congress should then determine whether the Uniform Code of Military Justice and other federal penal statutes need to be amended to prohibit such conduct.

Complementarity will not invariably preclude the trial of American servicemembers by the ICC. Some cases involving claimed war crimes by American servicemembers may be politically infeasible even to investigate—much less to prosecute—because to do so might be construed as the acceptance by the United States of a false premise that the conduct involved was criminal. Nevertheless, providing the United States with the best possible basis for invoking complementarity to forestall trial by the ICC of American servicemembers or civilians appears to be a worthwhile endeavor.

NOTES

1. Thus, a Senate report commented, "It should be noted that, as a practical matter, no such case is likely to arise respecting United States troops, because the Uniform Code of Military Justice, which Congress enacted for United States Armed Forces, permits any offense against the law of the country where the troops are stationed to be treated as an offense against the Code." See U.S. Senate, Executive Report No. I, 83d Cong., 1st sess., p. 5. I am unaware of any provision of U.S. military law that automatically makes punishable by court-martial conduct that violates the law of a host country. Probably, the cited report was construing a reference to "crimes and offenses not capital" in Article 134 of the Code, 10 U.S.C. sec. 934, to include any "crime" or "offense" under the law of the State or foreign country where the servicemember's conduct occurred. However, the quoted language has consistently been construed to apply only to "crimes and offenses" under Federal statutes. Robinson Everett, *Military Justice in the Armed Forces of the United States* (Harrisburg, Pa.: Military Service Publishing, 1956), 41, 66.

2. Statute, art. 7, par. 3.

3. In U.S. constitutional law, self-incrimination is treated differently than double jeopardy; and a witness cannot be compelled by federal officials to give testimony that would be incriminating under state law, and vice versa. However, self-incrimination under the laws of a foreign sovereign may be disregarded. *United States v. Balsys*, 118 S.Ct. 2218 (1998).

4. Some have suggested that the provision for these protections in the NATO Status of Forces Agreement constituted the first international "Bill of Rights."

5. 10 U.S.C. sec. 802. By its terms, the Uniform Code applied to "all persons serving with, employed by, or accompanying the armed forces without the continental limits of the United States and without the following territories: That part of Alaska east of longitude one hundred and seventy-two degrees west, the Canal Zone, the main group of the Hawaiian Islands, Puerto Rico, and the Virgin Islands." Art. 2 (11), U.C.M.J., 10 U.S.C. sec. 2(11); Public Law 506, 81st Cong., c. 169, sec. 1, 64 Stat. 108.

6. *Reid v. Covert*, 354 U.S. 1 (1957); *Kinsella v. Singleton*, 361 U.S. 234 (1960); *McElroy v. Guagliardo*, 361 U.S. 281 (1960).

7. On various occasions, Senator Sam Ervin of North Carolina, who chaired the Subcommittee on Constitutional Rights of the Senate Committee on the Judiciary, proposed legislation to authorize federal district courts to try civilian dependents and employees for conduct that would constitute a violation of the punitive articles of the Uniform Code of Military Justice if it had been committed by a servicemember. His purpose was to eliminate the jurisdictional void created by *Reid v. Covert* (1957) and to provide a basis for the United States to request that American civilian dependents and employees overseas be tried in a federal district court, rather than by a foreign tribunal or else not tried at all. Senator Ervin also proposed legislation to fill the jurisdictional void created by *Toth v. Quarles* (350 U.S. 11 [1955]), which held that servicemembers who committed crimes during their

enlistment were no longer subject to court-martial after they had separated from the armed forces.

8. In *Wilson v. Girard* (354 U.S. 524 [1957]), the Supreme Court declined to review the decision by the United States to waive its claim of primary right to exercise jurisdiction over an American soldier who had killed a Japanese woman at a time when he was serving on duty as a guard.

9. Statute, art. 6.

10. Statute, art. 7.

11. Statute, art. 8, pars. 2(c), 2(e).

12. Statute, art. 8, pars. 2(d), 2(f).

13. Statute, art. 9, par. 1.

14. Statute, art. 42.

15. Statute art. 15.

16. Likewise, article 7 of the NATO SOFA requires that certain rights be granted to a servicemember tried by a host country.

17. Statute, art. 36, par. 4(b). The ICC will have eighteen full-time members elected for nine-year terms, and the candidates will be nominated by the States Parties. Each State Party may put forward one candidate for any election. If the United States does ratify the Statute, probably one Judge will be an American. However, if the United States does not ratify, no American will serve on the Court because any candidate put forward must be "a national of a State Party."

18. In a U.S. court-martial, an accused who so elects may be tried by a military judge alone if the judge approves. See U.C.M.J. art. 16, 10 U.S.C. sec. 816. Waiver of jury is also allowed in most U.S. civil courts.

19. Of course, this request can only be made if a U.S. court would have jurisdiction over the offense and if the offense is one specified in the extradition treaty.

20. Likewise, if the alleged misconduct occurs in a country that has a SOFA with the United States, the foreign government might claim that it has either exclusive jurisdiction or the primary right to exercise concurrent jurisdiction over the servicemember and might refuse to surrender him or her to U.S. military authorities for trial by court-martial. This would present a situation similar to the one that existed in *Wilson v. Girard*, supra.

21. Sometimes a servicemember might prefer to be tried for a war crime by the ICC, where a death penalty is not authorized, rather than be tried in a U.S. court under the War Crimes Act, 18 U.S.C. sec. 2441, which permits a federal district court to impose the death penalty for a war crime involving willful killing.

22. Statute, article 20, paragraph 3, forbids trial by the ICC for "the same conduct unless the proceedings in the other court" were to shield the accused from responsibility for crimes within the ICC's jurisdiction or "were not conducted independently or impartially in accordance with the norms of due process recognized by international law."

23. Statute, arts. 118, 120, 124, 126, 129, 10 U.S.C. secs. 918, 920, 924, 926, 929.

24. The murders and assaults at My Lai, Vietnam, of which Lieutenant William Calley was convicted were probably war crimes; *United States v. Calley*, 48 C.M.R. 19, 22 U.S.C.M.A. 534 (1973). See Gary D. Solis, *Son Thang: An American War Crime* (Annapolis, Md.: Naval Institute Press, 1997).

25. As has already been noted, this language does not include violations of foreign law.

26. Statute, art. 20, par. 3.

27. Under the Articles of War as they existed during World War II, no provision was made for retention of court-martial jurisdiction to try ex-servicemembers; and extradition to a foreign country might not be authorized by any treaty with the country where the crime took place. Cf. *United States v. Icardi*, 140 F.Supp. 383 (D.D.C. 1956).

28. *Toth v. Quarles* (1956).

29. Robinson Everett and Laurent Hourcle, "Crime without Punishment," *Air Force JAG Law Review* 13 (1971): 184. However, Article 3(a) has been invoked to authorize trial of servicemembers who committed a crime while on active duty, were discharged, and thereafter reenlisted.

30. As will be discussed later, it is arguable that under the law of war, a military commission or general court-martial might have had jurisdiction over any war crimes committed in Vietnam by a former servicemember.

31. 18 U.S.C. Sec. 2441—"Conduct defined as a grave breach in any of the international conventions relating to the laws of warfare signed at Geneva 12 August 1949 or any protocol to any such convention to which the United States is a party."

32. The Act uses *national* as defined in Section 101 of the Immigration and Nationality Act, 8 U.S.C. 1101.

33. This contains rules governing internal conflict as well as conflict between separate countries.

34. The War Crimes Act of 1996 was introduced by a freshman North Carolina congressman, Walter Jones Jr., as the result of a conversation with a former prisoner of war who believed that he had been the victim of war crimes by his North Vietnamese captors and who was concerned about the apparent lack of jurisdiction for U.S. courts to try such persons.

35. When testifying as a witness in favor of the War Crimes Act of 1996, I suggested that the death penalty provision be removed. Although I have no conscientious objection to capital punishment, my concern was that the death penalty provision would probably be seldom applied but that its presence in the act might create problems of various types—such as in seeking extradition, in incorporating the War Crimes Act under the third clause of Article 134, and in countering claims that human rights are violated if an accused is sentenced to death. Possibly, Congress should now enact some specific provision to authorize severance of the death penalty provision from the act in situations where its presence creates a problem.

36. 10 U.S.C. 818.

37. 10 U.S.C. 821.

38. 10 U.S.C. secs. 904 and 906.

39. When the War Crimes Act of 1996 was being considered, I suggested that it should contain an express provision that it did not repeal by implication the jurisdiction of general courts-martial and military commissions with respect to violations of the law of war. Article 21 would provide the precedent for such a provision. Legislative counsel informed me that this was unnecessary because under such circumstances implied repeal does not take place. However, the legislative history does include a statement that the Act was not intended to repeal any existing jurisdiction of military tribunals.

40. 317 U.S. 1 (1942).

41. 71 U.S. 2 (1866).

42. One of the defendants claimed to be an American citizen; but even if this claim were true, the Court concluded that it had no effect on the jurisdiction of the military commission.

43. 327 U.S. 1 (1946).

44. *Yamashita* is an important precedent because the defendant was convicted and executed because of his failure to maintain control of his troops, rather than because of active misconduct on his part. Article 28 of the ICC Statute provides specifically for command responsibility.

45. 343 U.S. 341 (1952).

46. Although the Manual for Courts-Martial is promulgated by executive order of the president—who has no authority to legislate—the manual's interpretation of the punitive articles of the Uniform Code of Military Justice is often given considerable weight in construing those articles. The manual has traditionally contained extensive discussions of the elements of offenses prohibited by the code.

47. 18 U.S.C. Sec. 2441.

48. When I testified concerning the House bill that became the War Crimes Act of 1996, I expressed the view that the act should be extended to invoke the principle of universality and to grant jurisdiction to a U.S. district court to try any of the prohibited war crimes, whether or not the perpetrator or victim was an American servicemember or national. I still believe this broadening of jurisdiction would be desirable, subject perhaps to some requirement of special approval by the U.S. attorney general if Americans were not directly involved in the war crime. However, creation of the ICC might reduce the occasions for invoking universal jurisdiction.

49. The same argument invoking complementarity could be made with respect to war crimes allegedly committed by servicemembers. However, trial by military commission, rather than by general court-martial, would deprive the servicemember of many safeguards available in a court-martial. Among those safeguards would be the appellate review that Congress has prescribed for trials by court-martial. Thus, trial by court-martial is preferable, even if a military commission would be constitutionally permissible.

50. As with servicemembers, it would be preferable to try alleged war crimes of civilians by court-martial—for which trial procedure and appellate review are familiar and well defined by the code and the Manual for Courts-Martial—rather than by ad hoc military commissions.

9

The ICC and the Deployment of U.S. Armed Forces

William L. Nash

In all likelihood, President Bill Clinton's goal of creating an International Criminal Court (ICC)[1] will be achieved, but without the participation of the United States—or China, Iraq, Israel, Libya, Qatar, and Yemen. Over active U.S. opposition, a large majority of nations—including close U.S. allies—voted in July 1998 to support the establishment of an ICC. Since that vote, governments have set in motion the political and legal processes that seem likely to lead to the Court's establishment.

This chapter begins by reviewing some key characteristics of current U.S. uses of force that help explain the U.S. position toward the Court. It then considers the underlying Pentagon concerns about the ICC, exploring its potential impact on the use of military force by the United States—both during the decision-making process and in the execution of a military operation. The chapter concludes that the impact is likely to be less than Court opponents predict. U.S. military concerns must be placed in perspective, realistically evaluated both in terms of their likelihood and in the context of today's requirements for effective U.S. leadership. From that perspective, American servicemembers and national interests are better served by joining the Court and helping it fulfill its stated purpose—prosecuting individuals who commit the most egregious international crimes.

U.S. LEADERSHIP AND THE USE OF FORCE

To begin this examination, it is important to understand the current environment in which the United States deploys force. The United States is the predominant military force in the world today. It enjoys a position of dominance that is perhaps unequaled in world history, and it is the only nation with the capability to project power throughout the world and, with few exceptions, to achieve regional

153

dominance at any place of its choosing. In addition to physical dominance, the United States has unmatched superiority in its doctrine, leadership, intelligence, logistics, and communications that, when combined with its ability to strike opponents from long, over-the-horizon distances, would leave a potential enemy with little military recourse in a direct confrontation.

The United States has demonstrated a willingness to use its military power—lethal and nonlethal—to an unprecedented degree in the past decade. The U.S. Army estimates that its operational tempo has increased by three hundred percent as it has responded to over twenty real-world contingencies (compared to seven during the entire Cold War). All services have reported recruiting and retention problems partially attributed to the increased pace of training and to operational deployments. This has occurred in the absence of a peer competitor to the United States.

U.S. deployments in the post–Cold War era have been in the national interest, but not a narrowly defined interest. From Saudi Arabia to Somalia, from Haiti to Iraq to Bosnia, the United States has acted on behalf of both vital national interests and values that traditionally fell outside that definition. Moral imperatives, largely humanitarian in nature, often lay behind U.S. decisions to act militarily since the fall of the Berlin Wall. Some have gone so far as to argue for a new understanding of "national" interest. Vaclav Havel, president of the Czech Republic, said of the intervention of the North Atlantic Treaty Organization (NATO) in Kosovo, "It is fighting in the name of human interest for the fate of other human beings. . . . This war gives human rights precedence over the rights of states."[2] Although it is not my purpose to argue for such a policy, it is clear that the use of American military power has not declined with the dissolution of the Soviet Union, nor is it likely to decrease in the years ahead.

Judging from recent experiences, the contemporary use of force by the United States is likely to have several characteristics. The first is that the United States will seek to shape the political and legal context within which force is used. U.S. leadership is stronger, and its military actions more effective, if the international community provides an endorsement of U.S. actions. One of the reasons behind the success of Desert Shield/Desert Storm was the unequivocal support from the international community through a U.N. Security Council resolution (and ultimately the U.S. Congress and public). Wherever possible, the United States has sought international sanction for its military actions. Failure to achieve such support has not precluded military action—the air campaign in Kosovo lacked formal international approval (although this action created a precedent that the United States may regret when applied by other nations). The ability of the United States to win international endorsement of its use of force is affected by many factors, which will be discussed later in this chapter. Political and legal support from the international community is useful for a variety of reasons, not the least of which is that it enhances the prospect of assembling a strong coalition effort.

In fact, most recent U.S. interventions have been undertaken with other nations. Whether it is a "coalition of the willing" as in Desert Storm or a formal alliance operation as in Kosovo, the United States has chosen to build and to lead a coalition. This approach reflects the desire to enhance the legitimacy of force and to share the costs and the risks of intervention. Coalition operations are normally difficult, and often contentious. The United States will be faulted if it fails to take the lead, but it will be equally faulted if its leadership is perceived as arrogant and insensitive to other nations' prerogatives.

The second characteristic of interventions today is that they fail to achieve success if addressed solely by military means. Political, economic, and social challenges dominate the ultimate, and often the short-term, success of larger interventions. In fact, with the exception of Somalia, military successes have come quickly of late. In Bosnia, NATO forces completed the military tasks prescribed in the Dayton Accord within 120 days. Civilian implementation addressing the political, economic, and social woes of the country continues to this day. The prospects in Kosovo look no better. As of this writing, no significant recent interventions have been concluded successfully.[3] The ultimate success of such efforts hinges on actors and institutions other than the U.S. military. In most instances, success will not be the sole responsibility of the United States; it will be the result of combined efforts of international and regional institutions ranging from the World Bank to the U.N. High Commissioner for Refugees, as well as regional organizations, nongovernmental organizations (NGOs), private businesses, indigenous political institutions, and local and national leadership. Catalyzing, promoting, and helping to coordinate the nonmilitary elements of an intervention are much easier and more likely to succeed if the initial military intervention has been regarded as legitimate.

Thus U.S. military power is more effectively employed when its actions are endorsed as consistent with international norms and broadly shared objectives and when U.S. forces act in coalition and in conjunction with nations and institutions that undertake political, social, and economic efforts. Securing international support, while not determining, has become increasingly important for advancing U.S. security interests.

How the United States exercises leadership in its current position of military, political, and economic strength will affect more than military successes; it will significantly determine the future role of the United States in the world. It is in this broader context that this chapter considers the U.S. position toward the ICC.

It is true—perhaps we can say it only to other Americans—that the United States has accepted unparalleled responsibilities around the globe. And while there may be elements of U.S. "indispensability" that ring true, it is simply not useful to say it publicly and haughtily. In the eyes of many, that is what the United States did in Rome. Foreign governments believed that as its price for serving as the world's police force, the United States was demanding an exemption from accountability.

The overwhelming vote against the U.S. proposal to allow states to shelter their nationals from the ICC shows that most nations, including some of the strongest allies of the United States, recoil at what they perceive as an open display of U.S. exceptionalism. This perception is dangerous. Over the long term, it undermines the capacity of the United States to lead. The ICC unfortunately is not the only issue fueling this perception. But because it goes to the heart of accountability to international norms and because it is the first new international security institution in decades, it is a particularly resonant issue by which to measure U.S. attitude toward global leadership. This places a heavy burden on opponents of the ICC to demonstrate why it is not in U.S. interests to join the Court.

MILITARY CONCERNS

The U.S. military has reason to be wary of an ICC. The concept of allowing a civilian court to evaluate what essentially may be professional military judgments runs contrary to the core of the U.S. military system. The idea that the laws of war, so clearly and diligently ingrained in U.S. military doctrine and training, might be reinterpreted by an outsider is worrisome. As Robinson Everett explains in chapter 8, even the shared jurisdiction embodied in Status of Forces Agreements (SOFAs), which are now considered the key prerequisite for ensuring protection of American servicemembers deployed abroad, once was viewed with suspicion. At a more fundamental level, the military rightly expects that its civilian leaders will be sufficiently clear and committed in their direction of military force that the execution of policy will not be a contentious issue subjected to second-guessing.

Americans should expect these concerns to surface in the context of the ICC. They are all the more legitimate in the context of America's leading military role. Active international engagement means that American citizens are exposed on many fronts. Our forward-deployed soldiers (and diplomats) may be engaged by enemy fire, taken hostage, or attacked by terrorists in the course of their duties. U.S. leaders and citizens understand this to be an integral part of the burden of responsibility; and while they take the associated risks every day, they also strive to minimize those risks.

Moreover, the United States will be the target of international criticism for unilateral actions, such as U.S. attacks on Libya in reprisal for the Berlin disco bombing or the bombing of the Al Shiffa pharmaceutical plant in Sudan. Even when endorsed by the United Nations or supported by a large majority of nation-states, U.S. actions can engender enemies and criticism. One need only consider the charges levied against the United States for causing civilian casualties in operations against Iraq. The nature of the attacks in Kosovo also highlighted questions about the humanity of a strategy that appeared to minimize military casualties at the cost of risking greater civilian loss of life.

In the end, the mandate and the structure of the Court, particularly its requisite deference to national judicial capabilities, coupled with the training and the conduct of the U.S. armed forces adequately address many of these legitimate concerns.

The U.S. military, as much as, if not more than, any other military establishment, trains its servicemembers in the law of war and has integrated a serious program on international and human rights law in all of its training and education programs. Concerns about the Court should be mitigated by confidence in this commitment to the training and the caliber of American soldiers, sailors, airmen, and marines.

U.S. commanders are professionals who know how to do their jobs. Commanding a modern military operation requires great and sustained attention to legal issues. This is not just because it behooves members of the military to understand their rights under the Geneva Conventions and other applicable norms—which are critically important. It is also because the reciprocal nature of the laws of war requires that the U.S. military internalize the rules and constraints when conducting its own operations. One need only recall the legal basis the U.S. claims for the humane treatment and return of captured American servicemembers, whether in Iraq or Kosovo, to understand why the military cares deeply about international law.

In preparing American forces for the Bosnia operation in 1995, a great deal of effort was devoted to avoiding inappropriate or inhumane action, including potential violations of the laws of war. Many hours were spent identifying "protected sites" so that the United States would not destroy them. Lawyers were included in all relevant planning and decision making. During the initial Bosnia intervention, day-to-day decisions often required moving the artillerymen to the back benches and moving the lawyers up front. This is the way of modern military operations. The United States places a high priority on following the laws of war because it is important, right, and prudent. And the United States will continue to do so regardless of whether an ICC with related jurisdiction comes into being.

The U.S. government will never commit genocide. Furthermore, it will never purposefully or systematically commit war crimes or crimes against humanity. This doesn't mean that others will always concur that U.S. use of force does not raise potential violations of international law, including those that fall under ICC jurisdiction. For example, a serious issue revolves around Geneva Convention provisions regarding disproportionate force and the war crime of "[i]ntentionally launching an attack in the knowledge that such attack will cause incidental loss of life or injury to civilians."[4] The ICC's Statute specifies that the Court will have jurisdiction "in particular" when such an attack is committed "as part of a plan or policy or as part of a large-scale commission of such crimes."[5] But the Statute does not say that the Court will have jurisdiction "only" in such cases. Given the difference of perspectives between the United States and many other nations, there can be serious international debate about whether a specific bombing campaign would constitute a "large-scale commission" of a crime and whether it would be reasonable to believe that such bombing would cause incidental civilian casualties.

Kosovo demonstrated that in the present urbanized world, the total avoidance of collateral damage is impossible, even with the precision weapons used today. So there may be ongoing questions about whether bombing, even when undertaken with great effort to minimize harm to civilians, would be a legitimate concern of an ICC. In addition, any military campaign will be flawed. The United States and its allies will make mistakes, such as bombing the Chinese Embassy in Belgrade. These are reasons why U.S. efforts to require that the detailed elements of crimes be applied by judges at the outset—before consideration of general international law—are so important.

Nonetheless, the U.S. military justice system is best positioned to evaluate criminality and negligence regarding the use of force. If it is appropriate to investigate mistakes to determine who was responsible or if particular actions merit investigation of criminal charges, the U.S. military will do so. The United States was correct to insist on strong provisions to ensure that ICC jurisdiction would be complementary to that of national justice systems.

As Judge Robinson Everett argues, the ICC's complementarity provisions provide a means for demanding that U.S. authorities—not the ICC—have the opportunity to investigate and to prosecute alleged crimes by American servicemembers against the "Law of Nations." Everett notes that there is no absolute protection against Americans ever being brought to trial before the ICC. With regard to the American who might participate as a mercenary in a foreign genocidal campaign, his fate might be best served by an ICC. Americans abroad currently fall under the jurisdiction of foreign courts, unless they are servicemembers deployed under a SOFA. And even in the case of a SOFA, complications may arise regarding jurisdiction that is shared between the United States and the host nation. So absolute protection from prosecution overseas is, in reality, an unreasonable expectation, particularly in the context of what already have been defined as international crimes that any nation may prosecute.

Moreover, in order to actually investigate a case, the ICC would have to demonstrate that the United States was unwilling to genuinely investigate or prosecute. A matter of legitimate concern regarding violations of international law will be investigated and prosecuted vigorously by U.S. military authorities. The criminal embarrassments of Vietnam, and possibly of Korea, are of another age. It is very difficult to imagine any reasonable institution or people who would not conclude that the U.S. military is committed to upholding international law.

Thus, the prospect of an American soldier actually being prosecuted and sentenced by the ICC is reasonably remote. The more realistic apprehension about the Court is that it will be used as a political forum for raising questions about U.S. foreign policy. Concern about the ICC is at the strategic level, and it is fundamentally political. The legal vulnerability of an American soldier is not the chief threat.

The political concern has merit. One consequence of the disproportionate might of the United States is that it is rarely subject to direct military challenge by its enemies. Foes will search out asymmetrical responses to U.S. strength. Care should be taken then regarding the creation of alternate means (in this context, the ICC) that can be used by opponents to disrupt operations of the United States, to imperil its ability to act, and to undermine its accomplishments.

Certainly enemies of the United States, or an ICC Prosecutor, could raise questions about U.S. military actions by threatening to hold military or political leaders accountable for violations of international law. It is not unreasonable to fear that U.S. actions, or even threats of actions (such as hints of a U.S. attack to prevent terrorist action), could prompt a complaint to the Court or result in the ICC announcing its intention to investigate. This issue has arisen in the context of requests that the International Criminal Tribunal for the Former Yugoslavia (ICTY) investigate the NATO bombing of Kosovo. But as Bartram Brown's chapter (chapter 4) explains, many procedural safeguards to prevent frivolous prosecution have been built into the Court's jurisdiction and operation. Moreover, there are other forums and means to challenge U.S. policy; the ICC will not be the only vehicle for so doing, and it may well prove to be a less effective venue than a press conference. Treating the ICC as though it will become the prime mechanism to challenge American global leadership is to vest more power in the Court than it could ever have.

IMPACT ON DECISION MAKING

In terms of policy decisions, Clinton administration officials already have warned that because an ICC could be used to challenge U.S. policy, it could inhibit U.S. activism overseas. They argue that the ICC's existence could make the United States reluctant to conduct military operations that are not vital for American security. By this argument, the operations most at risk would be those at the humanitarian or peacekeeping end of the spectrum of military engagement (particularly given the current attitudes of many in Congress who both oppose such operations and oppose the ICC). The initial American intervention in Somalia bore no relationship to traditional security interests; it aimed to save human lives. U.S. relief efforts in Rwanda after the genocide were conducted for humanitarian reasons. These types of deployments and even disaster assistance to non-Americans would be most easily sacrificed for fear of the ICC.

But Kosovo demonstrates that such predictions of military recalcitrance are likely overblown. The ICTY had jurisdiction over Kosovo, and NATO intervened on a large scale. It is true that the ICTY is a creature of the U.N. Security Council and that the United States was familiar with its personnel and rulings. Nonetheless, no commentator appears willing to contend that if an ICC had existed, the United States would have refrained from acting against Slobodan Milosevic. The campaign was roundly criticized for many reasons. North American academics submitted a complaint to the ICTY charging NATO with inappropriately targeting civilian infrastructure, using inhumane weaponry, and causing unnecessary civilian casualties. But the main source of international governmental concern appeared to be the fact that NATO acted without U.N. Security Council authorization. Ironically, perhaps, the ICTY's indictment of Milosevic may have done more to legitimize the bombing of Serb targets than any other event surrounding NATO engagement.

The Court's overall impact on the United States in deciding whether to deploy forces will be marginal. It is doubtful that an ICC would ever constitute the sole reason not to undertake a military mission. It will be disregarded when circumstances require and used as a rationale for inaction when other interests dominate. If there were a strong consensus about the importance of U.S. military action among American policymakers, the impact of the ICC would not be significant.

OPERATIONAL IMPACT

The ICC could have impact at the operational level, ranging from the virtually imperceptible to the extremely negative, depending on the Court's actions. For example, the United States certainly will revise (or finish revising) all of its SOFAs to ensure that they include protections from ICC jurisdiction, providing greater assurance for servicemembers and reinforcing the principle of complementarity. In the future, before conducting a training exercise, overflying territory, or mounting a territorial defense, the military will routinely determine whether the host nation, its neighbors, or an anticipated adversary is a "State Party" to the ICC. Thus, the ICC will become another routine piece of the complex mosaic of standing legal protections and associated deployment prerequisites.

The ICC could have more potentially significant effects if it were to routinely pursue allegations against U.S. policies. Such a posture is unlikely, given the degree to which a new ICC likely will be guided by U.S. allies and will be eager to establish its credibility. Moreover, ICC actions would not proceed as long as the

United States were undertaking its own investigation. But the very act of launching an investigation, however short-lived, could give credence to allegations of wrongful acts by the United States. Such actions could have two effects on U.S. military operations.

First, U.S. concern about avoiding such charges could lead to unwise operational constraints. For example, if the military were directed to adopt as operational policy stricter interpretations of "proportionality," this could reduce the speed, mass, and dominance that have characterized U.S. military operations in the past decade (and lower casualties). Concerns about incidental loss of life could result in even more conservative targeting. Some would call this a positive development, but repeated piecemeal efforts increase the risks to both parties and are usually more harmful in the long run. Returning to the recent Kosovo experience, the slow and limited buildup of NATO's air campaign can explain, in part, the length of the war and the resulting "incidental loss of life"—an unintended consequence of "proportionality." In fact, the United States already subjects its military operations to a high degree of sensitivity to target selection and other related legal concerns.

Second, a more likely effect of ICC interference in U.S. policy would be to increase the frequency and visibility of internal U.S. military investigations. The Clinton administration has implied that it would not investigate the legality of military operations that it regards as valid official actions to enforce international law.[6] If the United States ultimately felt compelled to better insulate itself from ICC jurisdiction by investigating ICC concerns, the Department of Defense (DOD) could find itself launching investigations on the flimsiest of charges. Investigations might be considered a relatively inexpensive insurance policy, but they would absorb time and money. If taken to extremes, internal investigations would undermine morale and appear to constitute second-guessing of military decision making. They could ruin individual careers and ultimately decrease public confidence in the military.

Of course, these potential negative effects hinge on an assumption that the ICC will overreach and pursue matters that are not within its intended purpose of holding the worst international criminals to account.

LEADERSHIP IN PARTNERSHIP

The United States does not conduct coalition operations because it could not achieve its military objectives without the assistance of other nations. Put bluntly, the United States can accomplish virtually any strictly military task it is ordered to carry out. Rather, the United States works in partnership with others to accomplish a variety of objectives—and political objectives are at the forefront. Leading coalitions can be trying, time-consuming, and resource intensive. The associated costs and uncertainties cannot be predicted. But leadership of the United States, and its ability to sustain its credibility and effectiveness as a leader in the twenty-first century, hinges in no small part on its willingness to lead with and through other nations.

A footnote from my own experience: In Bosnia the U.S. division comprised forces from twelve nations. Leading this coalition force required an enormous amount of time on a helicopter to meet with national commanders to consult, listen, propose, discuss, redraft, persuade, and compromise. It was a lot of work, and the end result wasn't always the initial plan. But the strength born of unity almost always allowed the U.S. division to accomplish objectives that otherwise would not have been possible. Turkish and Russian troops side by side searching a Bosnian village made it impossible for either Muslims or Serbs to cry foul. Translating a political consensus into military cohesion at the point of an operation allows one to accomplish a great deal.

This is not the essay in which to fully explore the advantages of collective action, but suffice it to say here that U.S. national security does not consist only of winning specific military campaigns. This is why the United States has worked for decades to expand political and economic freedoms and to strengthen laws and institutions that promote national security through nonmilitary means. This effort has involved compromises and uncertainties, but it serves larger security objectives.

There is no doubt that genocide, crimes against humanity, and violations of the laws of war deserve punishment. The International Criminal Court, as a vehicle for holding accountable the perpetrators of the most horrific internationally recognized crimes, offers another way to strengthen the international rules that the United States has worked to uphold. By allowing the international community to guarantee individual responsibility, the Court may help avert wider conflicts. By promoting justice, it may help end a cycle of violence in a particular historical conflict. To the extent that the Court helps accomplish any of these objectives, it may reduce demands for U.S. military action.[7] Many proponents overstate the ICC's potential positive effects, much as many opponents inflate the risks. But the Court certainly has the potential to contribute to the kind of international environment the United States has long sought.

In addition, the ICC is the first security-related international institution since the United Nations. U.S. absence from the Court would be a significant and supremely isolating act. It will underscore U.S. ambivalence about joining in collective efforts and institutions to enhance security, an attitude that, however reasonably presented, weakens the claim of the United States to international leadership. Other nations increasingly question the intentions of a leading power that appears willing to lead exclusively on its own terms. The United States loses leverage and credibility by fueling impressions that its cooperation in international politics requires an exemption from the rules.

Finally, the Rome Statute will, in the eyes of the international community, apply to Americans—including U.S. military personnel—regardless of whether the United States signs or ratifies the Treaty. U.S. assertions of exemption from the Court's reach are, as Michael Scharf writes in chapter 13 of this volume, unlikely to convince most other nations. Thus, the potential that the Court will be a forum to which politically motivated charges are brought remains alive regardless of the U.S. view on the Court's jurisdiction. This means that, for all practical purposes, the Court's possible negative impact will be just as great if the United States refuses to join.

CONCLUSION

From a purely pragmatic standpoint, the United States can do more to advance national interests (and the interests of U.S. servicemembers) by signing the Treaty than it could by continuing to oppose the ICC. To no small degree, the Court's efficacy and impact will hinge on the appointment of capable, fair, and apolitical officials. The United States has everything to gain from helping to choose those individuals. The United States will be in a better position to ensure an appropriate U.N. Security Council role regarding the definition of *aggression* if ever the Assembly of States Parties were to entertain discussions on that contentious issue. Ignoring the Court accomplishes little. It seems, on balance, prudent to sign the Treaty.

The United States has lost much of the moral high ground in the effort to shape the ICC. While much time can be spent lamenting U.S. actions and rhetoric before, during, and after the Rome Conference, the future offers the only possibility for change. The sources of military concern are understandable, but they hinge on a need to believe the absolute worst of an institution and a process instead of on a commitment to ensure that it works as intended. Moreover, by trumpeting its uniqueness and appearing to demand special treatment, the United States corrodes its own power and authority.

NOTES

1. Remarks by the president to the fifty-second session of the United Nations General Assembly, September 22, 1997.

2. Address to both houses of Parliament, Ottawa, Canada, April 29, 1999.

3. Desert Storm was certainly a military success, but the ongoing confrontation with Saddam Hussein's regime shows no likelihood of near-term resolution. The United States left Somalia without achieving even its revised goals, and the country remains in chaos. U.S. intervention forces have left Haiti, but the intervention's ultimate success remains debatable.

4. Statute, art. 8, 2 (b) (iv).

5. Statute, art. 8, 1.

6. See Ambassador David Scheffer's chapter (chap. 6) in this volume.

7. It is also true that the ICC may create pressure *for* U.S. engagement by handing down international indictments. The United States will have to evaluate carefully the feasibility or the wisdom of seeking to apprehend alleged criminals (as has been the case in Bosnia).

10

The United States and Genocide Law: A History of Ambivalence

Samantha Power

The U.S. position toward the International Criminal Court (ICC) reveals a stark contrast between the long-standing rhetorical commitment of the United States to preventing genocide and its willingness to join in international efforts to transform this promise into a reality. This ambivalence about binding the United States to international law that might deter mass atrocity or might enable punishment of its perpetrators is also manifest in its historical relationship with the Genocide Convention. It might have been possible to cast congressional hostility toward the Genocide Convention as a historical anomaly.[1] However, the parallels between arguments against the Genocide Convention and those lodged in opposition to the ICC reveal that the United States has not changed its calculus of interests in the face of genocide. Despite U.S. public and political opposition to genocide, this country is reluctant to endure risk on behalf of this cause.

ABOUT COURSE ON THE GENOCIDE CONVENTION

In 1946, in the aftermath of the Holocaust, several State Department lawyers teamed up to draft the first version of the international genocide ban that they hoped would banish from the earth the crime that had so "shocked the conscience" of mankind that a new word had been invented in 1944 to describe it. The U.S. representative at the United Nations spoke strongly on behalf of the Convention in the General Assembly and joined in voting for its approval in 1948. Few doubted that the United States would be one of the first countries to ratify it. Indeed, in the General Assembly, the United States was the first country to sign the document. In June 1949, President Harry Truman heartily endorsed the Convention. He called on U.S. senators to supply the two-thirds vote required for ratification on the grounds that the United States had "long been a symbol of freedom and democratic progress to peoples less favored" and because it was time to outlaw the "world-shocking crime of genocide."[2] Dean Rusk, then deputy undersecretary of state, stressed that ratification was needed to "demonstrate to the rest of the world that the United States is determined to maintain its moral leadership in international affairs."[3] Ratification seemed a mere formality.

Although the Genocide Convention appeared destined for quick Senate approval, it would in fact yield only controversy, skepticism, and defeat. When it made its way to the U.S. Senate, American leadership evaporated. It took forty years for the U.S. Congress to ratify the Convention, and that ratification included five understandings, a declaration, and two reservations, which combined to reduce the U.S. signature to a hortatory expression of disapproval of the crime.

The reservations most significantly weakened the Convention. The first reservation held that, before being a party to any case before the International Court of Justice (ICJ) the president would have to provide his or her specific consent to the court's jurisdiction. This directly undermined the act of ratifying the Convention, which is intended to supply *advance* consent and to empower the ICJ to interpret and apply the Genocide Convention without requesting a state's permission. The second reservation held that the Genocide Convention could not authorize any legislation or action by the United States if that legislation or action were prohibited by the U.S. Constitution. This provision has become a standard accompaniment to U.S. ratifications of international human rights treaties. It is problematic because it leaves the executive again free to decide, if a case of genocide arises, whether compliance with the treaty in the case at hand violates some provision of the Constitution. This paves the way for the reopening of some of the very debates that stalled ratification in the first place. With this pair of reservations, the U.S. Senate made it clear that it did not see the law as meaningfully "binding."[4]

As Senator Jesse Helms of North Carolina, now chairman of the Senate Foreign Relations Committee and then an outspoken critic of the law, remarked during the ratification process in 1986: "[T]he treaty has been defanged in terms of the dangerous defects in its original version. . . . [T]his Genocide Convention upon which we are about to vote is purely symbolic. We might as well be voting on a simple resolution to condemn genocide—which every civilized person does."[5]

The Senate's failure to swiftly ratify the Convention deprived U.S. leaders of a useful tool of diplomacy. For forty years, American diplomats had weaker moral and political standing to speak out against genocide. Failure to ratify also made it impossible for the United States to bring genocide charges to the ICJ. And even after ratification, the Senate's reservations to the Convention continued to deprive the United States of legal standing to bring another state before the ICJ on genocide charges. In at least two cases (the Khmer Rouge's Cambodia and Saddam Hussein's Iraq), American presidents have urged legal proceedings against genocidal regimes. And in both cases, the United States was relegated to hoping that some other nation would file a case at the ICJ. The failure of the United States to heartily endorse the Treaty weakened the Convention's potential effect on individual and state behavior.

PARALLEL ARGUMENTS

An unwieldy but highly effective alliance of lawyers and southerners succeeded in convincing key senators to block the Genocide Convention's passage. Opponents of the ban focused on two interrelated aspects of the Convention's so-called "dangerous defects." One issue involved the definition of the term *genocide* and fears that it would be erroneously ascribed to Americans for actions at home or during military operations abroad. Another set of concerns focused on the threats to U.S. sovereignty posed by international law and institutions.

Definitional Defects

Genocide Convention opponents feared that enemies would use the new legal instrument to target U.S. citizens. The enemy most feared during the 1950s and 1960s was not an external foe but a domestic one: civil rights activists. Opponents of the Convention encouraged southern Senators to believe that activist lawyers might use the Convention to target the architects and implementers of southern segregation.[6] The Genocide Convention did list the infliction of mental harm as one of the acts that would signal genocide, but the law required that this act and others (killing, physical destruction, etc.) be accompanied by an intent to destroy all or part of the group in question. Nonetheless, senators were afraid that they, their law enforcement officials, or the United States as a whole would be vulnerable to condemnation at the ICJ and even to prosecution in some future criminal court.[7] Because the Genocide Convention would only make parties accountable for crimes committed prospectively, Senate critics did not raise the possibility that genocide charges might be filed against the U.S. government for actions against the Native American population.[8]

By the 1970s, the southerners' specific fear of being charged with "genocide" had been supplanted by broader concerns. The shadow once cast over the Convention by the civil rights movement darkened as domestic and foreign advocates increasingly mischaracterized U.S. foreign policy as "genocide." In 1967 Bertrand Russell and Jean-Paul Sartre convened their own makeshift "International War Crimes Tribunal" and "in the interest of humanity and for the protection of civilization" staged a "prosecution" of the U.S. government for committing genocide in Vietnam.[9] In 1969 North Vietnam threatened to charge American prisoners of war (POWs) with genocide, which the *New York Times* covered prominently.[10]

This politicized use of the term *genocide* made it possible to stoke fears of show trials in which Americans ended up unjustly pinned into the defendant's box. Senator Sam Ervin Jr., the leader of the Convention opposition, testified in 1970 before the Senate Foreign Relations Committee that ratification "would make American soldiers fighting under the flag of their country in foreign lands triable and punishable in foreign courts—even in courts in our warring enemy—for killing and seriously wounding members of the military forces of our warring enemy."[11] In some senses this was a moot claim because the Vietnamese could charge prisoners in their custody regardless of whether the U.S. Senate ratified the treaty or not. But Ervin and others were determined to prevent the introduction of any measure that might give Vietnamese charges an air of legality or international legitimacy.

Today, the concern that international law could be used to target U.S. foreign policy dominates discussion about the ICC. Some ICC opponents even resurrect the race issue. In a long polemic in the *New American*, William Jasper asked, "Could not American officials, mayors, governors, police chiefs, sheriffs, police officers, National Guardsmen, or private American citizens be charged with genocide for actions taken to protect lives and property during a race riot?"[12] But the central fear of most Court opponents does not revolve around domestic injustices as spotlighted by the U.N. High Commissioner for Human Rights (on the death penalty) or Human Rights Watch (on police brutality). Rather it is the fear that an independent ICC Prosecutor will indict—for the express purpose of challenging the United States—American soldiers who operate abroad.

The Pentagon, which did not significantly engage the issue of the Genocide Convention, has been a major player in the ICC debate. In the spring of 1998, it summoned more than one hundred foreign military attaches to the Department of Defense in order to warn them of the threat that the ICC posed to their soldiers. A Pentagon memo informed diplomatic officials that the United States backed the formation of a Court but was "intent on avoiding the creation of the wrong kind of court."[13]

Pentagon concerns prominently shaped the U.S. position at ICC negotiations in Rome. In the interest of sheltering U.S. soldiers from ICC prosecution, the United States demanded that the Prosecutor's autonomy be limited and that cases proceed only after a referral from the Security Council or from a State Party to the Treaty. Washington wanted nonsignatories to the Treaty to be immune from prosecution except in cases of genocide.

It is notable that the United States is not objecting to ICC jurisdiction for genocide, the crime that once daunted and deterred U.S. legislators. Clinton administration officials seem confident that Americans would not be wrongly charged with committing genocide. If Americans were unjustly charged, U.S. officials appear to have concluded that the Court would be unable to meet the extreme standards of intent and action required for a genocide conviction. Still, if the administration's fears about being held accountable for war crimes or crimes against humanity are examined, they evoke those that were once prompted by the Genocide Convention. Specifically, U.S. government leaders are concerned that crimes could be redefined and misapplied by enemies with a political agenda. "America does not shrink from accountability," Ambassador David Scheffer said, "but we will resist politically motivated or frivolous complaints against our armed forces."[14] U.S. leaders fear that U.S. forces operating overseas would be under the constant threat of erroneous prosecution. They therefore sought to craft an ICC from which Americans could be immunized.

The United States has sought to clarify definitions of the crimes in question. But the most refined language cannot provide absolute guarantees. Judicial interpretation is critical. Although it is known that the decisions that emerge from international or national courts will not forestall definitional disputes, they will create a body of legal precedent. At a minimum, these decisions will help judges navigate the definitional terrain in future judgments, and they may reduce blatant misuses of a term of law, thereby over time mitigating the danger of politicized, unfounded prosecution. Already, the ICC can draw on the body of precedent generated by the ad hoc tribunals and national courts, and it will slowly produce its own jurisprudential terms of reference. But the administration's concern about the ICC's politicization transcends the issue of definitions of crimes; it includes concern about vesting power in an independent, non-American institution.

Intrusions on U.S. Sovereignty

This concern echoes the second main line of argument that was made against the Genocide Convention—the need to preserve U.S. sovereignty. The concept of sovereignty remained a key political issue, even as the government dismissed its relevance as a constitutional issue.

In the early decades of the ratification debate, the American Bar Association (ABA) constituted a relentless source of opposition. Before finally shifting its position and endorsing the treaty in 1976, the ABA dispatched one constitutional lawyer after another to Washington to convince the Senate Foreign Relations Committee members that the Genocide Convention would trump the U.S. Constitution and therefore imperil the independence of the American republic. Successive teams of State and Justice Department lawyers dismissed this argument, but they never succeeded in overriding the fears of those alienated by incursions on U.S. sovereignty and petrified of creeping notions of world government.

As the debate continued, concerns about the politicization of international bodies figured prominently. In 1985, the ICJ ruled that it had jurisdiction in *Nicaragua v. United States*. Senator Richard Lugar, a member of the last generation of Convention critics, claimed the decision showed that the ICJ could "be used for blatant political attacks."[15] When the Senate Republican opposition succeeded in attaching reservations to the law in the form of a "Sovereignty Package," Senator Helms declared that this "defanging" of the law meant that "the sovereignty of our Nation and the freedom of our people have been protected against assault by the World Court."[16]

Much has changed in the context of the ICC debate. Today, the ABA is a strong proponent of the Court. International law has evolved considerably, addressing many of the definitional and procedural questions that were more pertinent in the early life of the Genocide Convention. Other powerful international institutions, including the World Trade Organization, have emerged to play significant roles in adjudicating international disputes without arousing hostility to the concept that they are so empowered. Yet many observers and senators echo the same constitutional and sovereignty fears regarding the ICC. In chapter 7 Ruth Wedgwood explores some of the issues related to fears that the United States will sacrifice its constitutional integrity on the altar of a new international Court. Many senators continue to believe that sovereignty remains a central issue. The context may have changed, but the concerns are constant.

BEHIND THE ARGUMENTS

It has been fifty-five years since General Dwight Eisenhower and American troops liberated the Buchenwald concentration camp. Eisenhower's memorable cable to Army Chief of Staff George Marshall said: "We are told that the American soldier does not know what he is fighting for. Now, at least, he will know what he is fighting against."[17] But to the extent that Americans ever were willing to make sacrifices to suppress genocide, the willingness appears to have vanished—trumped, as evidenced by the "trials" of the Genocide Convention and the ICC Statute, by the perceived need to protect Americans and to preserve American sovereignty. Underlying elements of this dynamic must be addressed if the outcome is to be changed.

Foolproof and Effective Institutions

Opponents of the ICC enter the debate with the same presumptions held by opponents of the Genocide Convention—first, that fellow states and Court officials will prove ill-intentioned or incapable, and, second, that it is feasible to construct a functional, durable, and just institution from which the United States can be shielded.

The first presumption is problematic because assuming the worst of the individuals who comprise an institution makes it virtually impossible to contemplate vesting power in it. The former head prosecutor for the U.N. International Criminal Tribunal for the Former Yugoslavia, Louise Arbour, was right to remind critics that "an institution should not be constructed on the assumption that it will be run by incompetent people, acting in bad faith from improper purposes."[18]

The fears of the United States about the ICC must be placed in context. Every institution rises and falls on the quality of the individuals comprising it. Concerns about the competence of many Americans generated fierce debate about establishing a representative democracy in the United States. No matter how efficient a system of checks and balances, John Stuart Mill wrote long ago, "The goodness of the administration of justice is in the compound ratio of the worth of the men composing the tribunals, and the worth of the public opinion which influences or controls them."[19] Americans should be reminded of the inherent and worthwhile risks of creating common institutions.

Of course, the United States also cannot afford to assume the best of individuals who comprise national or international bodies. Particularly given the status of the United States as a political target in the world, U.S. officials are justified in insisting on checks and balances for international institutions—just as the Framers of the Constitution did when creating the constitutional structure of the United States two centuries ago. They received many checks and balances in Rome. Ambassador David Scheffer has lamented the "casualness" of the claims of nongovernmental organizations and member states that the safeguards already built in to the Rome Treaty will protect U.S. troops. Yet all the other major democracies have concluded that the ICC's rules and procedures provide reasonable assurance that the Court will behave responsibly. The United States remains unconvinced. "We can't work off of mere assumptions that things won't happen," said Scheffer. "We have to see a document that provides us with the assurance that this court will not be a politically motivated court."[20]

In saying that it wants to protect itself from a political ICC, the United States is seeking more than reasonable assurances about the Court's responsible execution of its mandate. The United States is reserving the right to define the term *political* in the context of the Court's actions. Of the 180 U.N. members who do not hold a veto on the Security Council, only some will share America's definition. Many deem the Security Council as the epitome of a politically motivated institution and want an independent ICC precisely because they believe it will not be driven strictly by great power politics.

Because the United States wants to decide what would constitute political action, it has sought to guarantee its exemption from the ICC's reach, even at great cost to the Court's effectiveness. The very presumption that the ICC could provide complete assurances to the United States is problematic for a Court that aims to be universal.

U.S. officials initially sought to obtain an exception to ICC jurisdiction by centralizing power—proposing that all ICC action be approved by the Security

Council, where the United States holds a veto. This approach would have compromised the Court's ability to act—a criminal need have only one Permanent Member as a patron to block prosecution. When this approach failed, leaving the Court free to act independently of the Security Council, the United States proposed that a state be able to exempt its nationals from the Court's jurisdiction as long as the state assumed responsibility for the alleged crimes. This solution would render the Court helpless whenever a mass murderer retained the reins of state.

Institutional independence can mean different things. Court advocates hear "independent" and think, "depoliticized, egalitarian, and neutral with checks and balances built in." Court critics hear "independent" and think, "politicized, unaccountable, and unreliable." Though the United States has been at the forefront of the charge for international justice, it has never been willing to place itself at the mercy of a system it did not trust. And it has never been willing to trust a system it did not control.

The drafters of the Rome Treaty did a great deal to respond to U.S. fears, as explained by many of the authors in this volume. The Treaty enshrines the principle of complementarity, builds delays and checks into the judicial process, and significantly limits its jurisdiction to the most heinous international crimes. But infinite checks cannot be built into an institution without shortchanging other principles. No charter can offer perfect assurances and no institution can be made foolproof without imperiling the very principles for which it is created.

Calculations of Interest

Some Court supporters act as if opponents are taking issue with the ICC's purpose. But as Senator Helms pointed out during consideration of the Genocide Convention, every civilized person condemns genocide. Even opponents of the ICC abstractly oppose impunity for the worst international crimes. The reality is that they accord greater weight to the costs and risks of joining the Court than they do to the value of international justice.

Just before the Rome Conference began, Ambassador Scheffer described his approach: "The U.S. delegation has been and will continue to be guided by our paramount duty: to protect and advance U.S. interests."[21] Prosecuting those responsible for mass atrocities does not outweigh concerns about other U.S. interests.

The United States does not see the Court as supplying any direct benefit to Americans. Administration officials do not entertain the possibility that an American soldier or citizen could commit an atrocity and escape adequate punishment in the U.S. court system. They see no need for the Court to concern itself with reining in American perpetrators.

But they also have no fear that Americans will become victims. The United

States does not fear that the types of mass violence that the ICC is designed to counter will occur in the United States or against Americans. Early proponents of the Genocide Convention—Brian McMahon and Raphael Lemkin, a Polish Jew who immigrated to the United States and coined the word *genocide*—recognized the slim likelihood that Americans would ever need the Convention's protection. As McMahon, chairman of the first hearings on the Convention, put it: "In the history of our country, we have never had an act of genocide in the United States, and as far as I can see we will never have one."[22] Lemkin wrote that "[f]or America, Genocide is an outside crime. It is like African leprosy."[23] Americans are confident that if outside powers were to commit mass atrocity against them, the United States would punish the responsible state or perpetrators.

It therefore is fair to say that while the likelihood of the ICC being used against U.S. citizens is small, the Court is even less likely to directly, tangibly improve an individual American's security. The benefits of international justice are real, but they are abstract, distant, and indirect. However remote the risk of Americans being unjustly targeted for prosecution, the harm—if it were to occur—would be concrete, immediate, and direct.

CONCLUSION

Court supporters believe that the Court's safeguards render the risk to Americans negligible. But, more fundamentally, they believe that the risk is worth taking in the interest of creating an institution empowered to lock up a Saddam Hussein or a Ratko Mladic. American policymakers, while backing the creation of a Court to prosecute international criminals, focus on avoiding the associated risks to the United States and its citizens. They seem to have concluded that the gains secured when another state's genocidaires are prosecuted do not outweigh the risks of enduring—or responding to—frivolous or politically motivated charges against Americans.

The ICC debate revolves around different and competing priorities within the national interest: fully protecting American troops and citizens from unjust prosecution and creating a universal, apolitical, legal body that will help deter and prosecute the commission of crimes against humanity. Even one of the twentieth century's most eloquent moral voices, Albert Camus, could conclude, "I believe in justice, but I will defend my mother before justice."[24] Court opponents, with their focus on risks to Americans, have dominated the domestic ICC debate. But it is questionable whether the majority of Americans would share that narrow interpretation of interests. The task is to convince Americans that their mothers and compatriots—because they have been protected from unfair prosecution to the greatest extent that is reasonably possible—would accept that risk to achieve the Court's purpose.

NOTES

1. For a detailed examination of the battle in the Senate over the Genocide Convention, see Lawrence J. LeBlanc, *The United States and the Genocide Convention* (Durham, N.C.: Duke University Press, 1991).

2. "Special Message to the Senate Transmitting Convention on the Prevention of the Crime of Genocide," June 16, 1949, *Public Papers of the Presidents of the United States,* January 1 to December 31, 1949 (Washington, D.C.: U.S. Government Printing Office, 1964).

3. See William Korey, *NGOs and the Universal Declaration of Human Rights* (New York: St. Martin's, 1998), pp. 203–28.

4. The Senate understandings, while limiting, largely accorded with the intentions of the original drafters of the Genocide Convention. The Senate understood the words "intent to destroy, in whole or in part" (Article II) as the intent to destroy "in whole or in *substantial part*" the group concerned. The Senate understood the words "mental harm" (Article II[b]) as the "permanent impairment of mental facilities through drugs, torture, or similar techniques." In its third understanding, the Senate resolution stated that extradition laws would take effect only between states that deemed the act in question criminal. It also stated that the Convention should not interfere with the state's right to try its own nationals for acts committed outside the state. The fourth Senate understanding provided that, in order to constitute genocide, acts in armed conflict had to be committed with a *specific intent* to destroy. And finally, the Senate understood that the United States would not participate in any future international criminal tribunal without ratifying a separate treaty to that effect. The "declaration" simply held that the U.S. government would not deposit its instrument of ratification for the Genocide Convention until it had passed implementing legislation, which it did not do until 1998. In this legislation the Senate would define "substantial part" as "a part of a group of such numerical significance that the destruction or loss of that part would cause the destruction of the group as a viable entity within the nation of which such a group is a part."

5. *Congressional Record,* 132 Cong. Rec. S1369 (daily ed., February 19, 1986), 99th Cong. 2d sess.

6. In 1970, for instance, Eberhard Deutsch of the American Bar Association (ABA) alarmed senators by testifying that the Supreme Court's language in *Brown v. Board of Education* (347 U.S. 483, 1954), which found that racial separation "generates a feeling of inferiority as to their status in the community that may affect their hearts and minds in a way unlikely ever to be undone . . . and has a tendency to retard their education and mental development," left the senators exposed to charges of genocide by mental harm.

7. In 1951 and again in 1970, the Civil Rights Congress, a black activist organization, published a book called *We Charge Genocide,* which alleged that "the oppressed Negro citizens of the United States" were the victims of genocide. It claimed that the living conditions of the black race proved the existence of a plan to deliberately inflict "on the group conditions of life calculated to bring about its destruction in whole or in part." Civil Rights Congress, *We Charge Genocide* (New York: n.p., 1951), xi, 5, 19. Deutsch of the ABA made one hundred copies of the book available to the Senate.

8. In his book *A Little Matter of Genocide* (San Francisco: City Light Books, 1997), Ward Churchill takes issue with the Senate silence on this score. He argues that in the

1950s and 1960s, one might have lodged a current (and not a retrospective) case against the United States on the basis of forced sterilization of Native American women or the establishment of compulsory boarding schools for Native American children. While this case is not less plausible than that raised by maltreatment of African Americans, it bears little resemblance to the scope of the crime and the intent demanded by the law itself.

9. The first session was held May 2–10, 1967, in Stockholm; the second November 20–December 1 in Roskilde, Denmark. See Jean-Paul Sartre, *On Genocide* (Boston: Beacon, 1968).

10. Charles Mohr, "Hanoi Charges Genocide by the U.S." *New York Times*, November 26, 1969, p. 10.

11. Senate Committee on Foreign Relations, *Hearings on the Genocide Convention before a Subcommittee of the Senate Commission on Foreign Relations,* 91st Cong., 2d sess., 1970, 204.

12. William F. Jasper, "A UN Criminal Court Is a Dangerous Idea in the Making," *New American*, April 13, 1998, p. 21.

13. Eric Schmitt, "Pentagon Battles Plans for International War Crimes Tribunal," *New York Times*, April 14, 1998, p. A11.

14. Transcript of Scheffer speech, "Seeking Accountability for War Crimes: Past, Present, and Future," at the Commonwealth Club, San Francisco, California, May 13, 1998. Available: <http://www.state.gov/www/policy_remarks/1998/980513_scheffer_war_crimes.html>, (January 11, 2000).

15. Opening statement, *Hearings on the Genocide Convention before the Senate Committee on Foreign Relations,* 99th Cong., 1st sess. 1985, 1.

16. *Congressional Record*, 132 Cong. Rec. S1369 (daily ed., February 19, 1986), 99th Cong., 2d sess.

17. Gerald Parshall, "Freeing the Survivors," *U.S. News & World Report*, April 3, 1995, p. 50.

18. Remarks at Harvard University, October 6, 1998.

19. John Stuart Mill, *Considerations on Representative Government* (New York: Prometheus Books, 1991), 40.

20. Transcript of Scheffer speech, "U.S. Position on the International Criminal Court," Foreign Press Center Briefing; Washington, D.C., July 31, 1998. Available: <http://www.useu.be/archive/scheffer731.html> (January 11, 2000).

21. Scheffer, "Seeking Accountability."

22. "Approval of Pact on Genocide Urged," *New York Times*, April 13, 1950, p. 15. McMahon urged ratification with four understandings that he hoped would take care of the objections of the opposition.

23. Letter from Raphael Lemkin to Gertrude Samuels, June 6, 1950. Microfilm Reel 1, The Papers of Raphael Lemkin, New York Public Library Collections.

24. Albert Camus, remarks at the acceptance of the 1957 Nobel Prize for Literature, discussed in *Resistance, Rebellion, and Death* (New York: Vintage International, 1995), 113.

Part III

The ICC and National Approaches to Justice

11

Justice versus Peace

Michael P. Scharf

This chapter examines the question of whether the International Criminal Court (ICC) has the potential of requiring too much justice. Notwithstanding the popular catch phrase of the 1990s, "no peace without justice," achieving peace and obtaining justice are sometimes incompatible goals. In order to end an international or internal conflict, negotiations often must be held with the very leaders who are responsible for war crimes and crimes against humanity. When this is the case, insisting on criminal prosecutions[1] can prolong the conflict, resulting in more deaths, destruction, and human suffering.

Reflecting this reality, during the past several years, Argentina, Cambodia, Chile, El Salvador, Guatemala, Haiti, Sierra Leone, South Africa, and Uruguay, as part of a peace arrangement,[2] have each granted amnesty to members of the former regime that committed international crimes within their respective borders. With respect to four of these countries—Cambodia, El Salvador, Haiti, and South Africa—the United Nations pushed for, helped negotiate, and/or endorsed the granting of amnesty as a means of restoring peace and democratic government. The term *amnesty* is derived from the Greek word *amnestia*, meaning "forgetfulness or oblivion."[3] In the present context, amnesty is an act of sovereign power immunizing persons from criminal prosecution for past offenses.[4]

At the negotiations of the Rome Statute, the United States and a few other delegations expressed concern that the ICC could hamper efforts to halt human rights violations and to restore peace and democracy in places like Haiti and South Africa. At the ICC preparatory conference in August 1997, the U.S. delegation circulated a "nonpaper" regarding amnesties. It suggested that the proposed Court, in the interest of international peace and national reconciliation, should take amnesties into account when deciding whether to exercise jurisdiction over a situation or to prosecute a particular offender.[5] According to the U.S. text, the policies favoring prosecution of international offenders must be balanced against the

179

need to close "a door on the conflict of a past era" and "to encourage the surrender or reincorporation of armed dissident groups," thereby facilitating the transition to democracy.[6]

While the U.S. proposal was met with criticism from many quarters, the final text of the Rome Statute potentially could be interpreted as codifying the U.S. proposal. This chapter examines the policy and the legal issues related to an "amnesty exception" to the ICC's jurisdiction and evaluates whether the text of the Rome Statute should be read as embodying such an exception. It concludes that the existence of the ICC should not be viewed as completely removing the possibility of amnesty as a bargaining chip of last resort available to mediators attempting to end an international or internal conflict.

PRACTICAL CONSIDERATIONS

Interests Favoring Amnesty

As Payam Akhavan of the office of the prosecutor of the International Criminal Tribunal for the Former Yugoslavia (ICTY) has observed, "It is not unusual in the political stage to see the metamorphosis of yesterday's war monger into today's peace broker."[7] This is because cooperation of the leaders of the various parties to a conflict is needed to put an end to the fighting and the violations of international humanitarian law. Yet, it is not realistic to expect them to agree to a peace settlement if, directly following the agreement, they would find themselves or their close associates facing potential life imprisonment. As evidenced in the recent cases of Haiti and South Africa, the offer of amnesty may be a necessary and, I will argue, justified bargaining chip to induce human rights violators to agree to peace and to relinquish power.

From 1990 to 1994, Haiti was ruled by a military regime headed by General Raoul Cedras and Brigadier General Philippe Biamby, which executed over three thousand civilian political opponents and tortured scores of others.[8] The United Nations (U.N.) mediated negotiations that in July 1993 resulted in the "Governors Island Agreement." Haiti's military leaders agreed to relinquish power and to permit the return of the democratically elected president in return for a full amnesty for the regime and a lifting of the economic sanctions imposed by the U.N. Security Council.[9] Under pressure from the U.N. mediators, President Jean-Bertrand Aristide agreed to the amnesty clause.[10] The U.N. Security Council immediately "declared [its] readiness to give the fullest possible support to the Agreement,"[11] which it later said "constitutes the only valid framework for resolving the crisis in Haiti."[12]

Because Haitian military leaders failed to comply with the Governors Island Agreement, the Security Council on July 31, 1994, took the extreme step of authorizing an invasion of Haiti by a multinational force.[13] On the eve of the invasion on September 18, 1994, a deal was struck whereby General Cedras agreed to retire his command "when a general amnesty will be voted into law by the Haitian parliament."[14] The amnesty deal had its desired effect: Aristide was permitted to return to Haiti and to reinstate a civilian government, the military leaders left the country, much of the military surrendered their arms, and most of the human rights abuses promptly ended—all with practically no bloodshed or resistance.[15]

Africa's experience with amnesty was fundamentally different, but it illustrates a similar point: amnesty may be critical to peace. From 1960 to 1994, thousands of black South Africans were persecuted and mistreated under that country's apartheid system. With the prospect of a bloody civil war looming over political negotiations about the nation's future, "The outgoing leaders made some form of amnesty for those responsible for the regime a condition for the peaceful transfer to a fully democratic society."[16] The leaders of the majority black population decided that the commitment to afford amnesty was a fair price for a relatively peaceful transition to full democracy.[17] In accordance with the negotiated settlement, the South African Parliament on July 19, 1995, created a Truth and Reconciliation Commission, which included a Committee on Amnesty.[18] Amnesty would be available only to individuals who personally applied for it and fully disclosed the facts of their apartheid crimes. After conducting 140 public hearings and considering 20,000 written and oral submissions, the South African Truth and Reconciliation Commission published a 2,739-page report of its findings on October 29, 1998.[19] Most observers believe the amnesty in South Africa headed off increasing tensions and a potential civil war.

The granting of amnesty from prosecution is commonly misconstrued as the absence of accountability and redress. But in the cases of Haiti and South Africa, amnesties were tied to accountability mechanisms. These mechanisms were less invasive than domestic or international prosecution, but they accomplished important goals. Both Haiti and South Africa included, in connection with amnesty arrangements, monetary reparations to victims and their families, truth commissions to document abuses (and sometimes identify perpetrators by name), and employment bans and purges (referred to as "lustration") to keep perpetrators from positions of public trust.[20] Of the two cases, South Africa's Truth and Reconciliation Commission was more powerful, with the ability to subpoena witnesses and to grant immunity. Haiti went further in lustration: all members of the military with the rank of colonel and above were expelled from the armed forces. While not the same as criminal prosecution, these mechanisms do encompass much of what justice is intended to accomplish: prevention, deterrence, punishment, and rehabilitation. Indeed, some experts believe that these mechanisms do not constitute just "a second-best approach" when prosecution is impractical, but that in many situations they may be better suited to achieving the aims of justice.[21] It would have been appropriate for the ICC to defer to amnesty granted in the cases of Haiti and South Africa. Nonetheless, deference to amnesties should not be granted lightly. The related issues and suggested guidelines for ICC decision making are discussed later.

The Benefits of Prosecution

While providing amnesty to perpetrators sometimes may be necessary to achieve peace, there are several important countervailing considerations favoring prosecution that suggest that amnesty should be a last resort reserved for the most compelling situations. In particular, prosecuting persons responsible for violations of international humanitarian law can serve to discourage future human rights abuses, to deter vigilante justice, and to reinforce respect for law and a new government.

While prosecutions might initially provoke resistance, many analysts believe that national reconciliation cannot take place as long as justice is foreclosed. As Professor Cherif Bassiouni, chairman of the U.N. investigative commission for Yugoslavia, has stated, "If peace is not intended to be a brief interlude between conflicts," then it must be accompanied by justice.[22]

Failure to prosecute leaders responsible for human rights abuses breeds contempt for the law and encourages future violations. The U.N. Commission on Human Rights and its Subcommission on minorities have concluded that impunity is one of the main reasons for continuing grave violations of human rights throughout the world.[23] Reports indicate that the granting of amnesty or de facto impunity has led to increased abuses in Chile and El Salvador.[24]

What a new or reinstated democracy needs most is legitimacy, which requires a fair, credible, and transparent account of what took place and who was responsible. Criminal trials (especially those involving proof of widespread and systematic abuses) can generate a comprehensive record of the nature and the extent of violations, how they were planned and executed, the fate of individual victims, who gave the orders, and who carried them out. The most authoritative rendering of the truth is the crucible of a trial that accords full due process. Justice Robert Jackson, the chief prosecutor at Nuremberg, underscored the logic of this proposition in concluding that the Nuremberg Trial's most important legacy was the documentation of Nazi atrocities "with such authenticity and in such detail that there can be no responsible denial of these crimes in the future."[25]

In addition to truth, there is a responsibility to provide justice. While a state may appropriately forgive crimes against itself, such as treason or sedition, serious crimes against persons, such as rape and murder, are an altogether different matter. Holding the violators accountable for their acts is a duty owed to the victims of these atrocities. Prosecuting and punishing the violators would give significance to the victims' suffering and would serve as partial remedy for their injuries. Moreover, prosecutions help restore victims' dignity and prevent private acts of revenge by those who, in the absence of justice, would take it into their own hands.

While prosecution and punishment can reinforce the value of law by displacing personal revenge, failure to punish former leaders responsible for widespread human rights abuses encourages cynicism about the rule of law and distrust of the political system. To the victims of human rights crimes, amnesty represents the ultimate in hypocrisy: while they struggle to put their suffering behind them, those responsible are allowed to enjoy a comfortable retirement. When those with power are seen to be above the law, the ordinary citizen will never come to believe that the rule of law is a fundamental necessity in a democratic country.

Finally, where the United Nations gives its imprimatur to an amnesty, there is a risk that rogue regimes in other parts of the world will be encouraged to engage in gross abuses. For example, the international amnesty given to the Turkish officials responsible for the massacre of over one million Armenians during World War I may have encouraged Adolf Hitler to conclude that Germany could pursue genocidal policies with impunity. In 1939, in relation to the acts of genocide and aggression committed by German forces, Hitler remarked, "Who after all is today speaking about the destruction of the Armenians?"[26] Richard Goldstone has stated that the failure of the international community to prosecute Pol Pot, Idi Amin, Saddam Hussein, and Mohammed Aidid, among others, encouraged the Serbs to launch their policy of ethnic cleansing in the former Yugoslavia with the expectation that they would not be held accountable.[27] When the international community encourages or endorses an amnesty for human rights abuses, it sends a signal that others have nothing to lose by instituting repressive measures; if things start going badly, they can always bargain away their crimes by agreeing to peace.

THE LIMITED INTERNATIONAL LEGAL OBLIGATION TO PROSECUTE

Of the crimes covered by the ICC (genocide, grave breaches of the Geneva Conventions, violations of the laws and customs of war, and crimes against humanity), there exists an international obligation to prosecute only two: genocide and grave breaches of the Geneva Conventions. A state's failure to prosecute these crimes can amount to a breach of international law. Amnesty for such crimes committed by members of the former regime could be invalidated before domestic courts[28] or an international forum.[29] It would be inappropriate for the ICC to defer to a national amnesty in such a situation. The ICC should not violate obligations contained in the very international conventions that make up its subject matter jurisdiction.

In contrast, while international law may permit all states to exercise universal jurisdiction to prosecute perpetrators of violations of the laws and customs of war and of crimes against humanity, states are not required to prosecute under international law. Thus, in these cases the ICC would have more flexibility in deciding whether to defer to an amnesty for peace arrangement.

The Genocide Convention

Most of the countries of the world are Party to the Genocide Convention (whose substantive provisions also have been deemed customary international law binding on all states).[30] The Genocide Convention provides an absolute obligation to prosecute persons responsible for genocide as defined in the Convention.[31] It also requires Parties "to provide effective penalties for persons guilty of genocide."[32]

Both the Convention and the Rome Statute define genocide as one of a list of enumerated acts when committed "with intent to destroy, in whole or in part, a national, ethnical, racial, or religious group, as such." There are several important limitations inherent in this definition. It is not enough that abuses were intended to repress opposition or to target individuals. The goal must be literally to partly or completely destroy the target group. Even more important, the victims must constitute one of the four types of groups enumerated in the Convention. The drafters of the Genocide Convention deliberately excluded from the definition of genocide acts directed against "political groups."[33] This significantly limits the types of situations that qualify as genocide and carry with them the attendant duty to prosecute.

The 1949 Geneva Conventions and Violations of the Laws of War

The four Geneva Conventions were negotiated in 1949 to codify international rules relating to the treatment of prisoners of war and civilians in occupied territory. Almost every country of the world is party to these Conventions. The Conventions distinguish between "grave breaches" and "other" war crimes. Although states may prosecute offenders of both categories of war crimes, the Geneva Conventions require prosecution (or extradition) only with respect to "grave breaches." They also require parties "to provide effective penal sanctions for persons committing, or ordering to be committed, any of the grave breaches of the Convention." Grave breaches include willful killing, torture, or inhuman treatment; willfully causing great suffering or serious injury to body or health; extensive destruction of property not justified by military necessity; willfully depriving a civilian of the rights of fair and regular trial; and unlawful confinement of a civilian. The Rome Statute reproduces this list in Article 8(a).[34] The official history of the Geneva Conventions negotiations confirms that the obligation to prosecute grave breaches is "absolute," meaning, inter alia, that States Parties can under no circumstances grant perpetrators immunity or amnesty from prosecution for these crimes.[35]

For this discussion of amnesties granted in the context of internal conflict, it is important to note the limitations of the definition of *grave breaches* and the attendant obligation to prosecute. They apply only in the context of international armed conflict involving two or more states or of a partial or total occupation of the territory of one state by another. Furthermore, the Geneva Conventions do not create a corresponding obligation to prosecute "other violations of the laws and customs of war" applicable in international armed conflicts, which are listed as part of the ICC's jurisdiction in Article 8(b). Thus, there is no requirement to prosecute either war crimes that are committed in a civil war or war crimes that do not amount to "grave breaches" in an international conflict.

Customary International Law: Crimes against Humanity

The Rome Statute in Article 7 defines *crimes against humanity* as a specific list of "inhuman acts" when committed as part of a widespread or systematic attack against any civilian population, with knowledge of the attack.

Unlike grave breaches of the Geneva Conventions and the crime of genocide, there exists no treaty requiring states to prosecute crimes against humanity. Traditionally, those who committed crimes against humanity were treated like pirates, as hostis humani generis (an enemy of all humankind), and any state could punish them through its domestic courts.[36] In the absence of a treaty containing the aut dedere aut judicare (extradite or prosecute) principle, this so-called "universal jurisdiction" is generally thought to be permissive, not mandatory. Yet several commentators and human rights groups recently have taken the position that customary international law not only establishes permissive jurisdiction over perpetrators of crimes against humanity, but also requires their prosecution and conversely prohibits the granting of amnesty to such persons.[37]

Customary international law, which is just as binding on states as treaty law is, arises from "a general and consistent practice of states followed by them from a sense of legal obligation" referred to as opinio juris.[38] Under traditional notions of customary international law, "deeds were what counted, not just words."[39] Yet those who argue that customary international law precludes amnesty for crimes against humanity base their position on nonbinding General Assembly Resolutions,[40] hortative declarations of international conferences,[41] and international conventions that are not widely ratified,[42] rather than on any extensive state practice consistent with such a rule. The trouble with such an approach is "that it is grown like a flower in a hot-house and that it is anything but sure that such creatures will survive in the much rougher climate of actual state practice."[43] Indeed, to the extent that any state practice in this area can be said to be widespread, it is the practice of granting amnesties or de facto impunity to those who commit crimes against humanity.[44] That the United Nations itself has felt free of legal constraints in endorsing recent amnesty for peace deals in situations involving crimes against humanity confirms that customary international law has not yet crystallized in this area.

AMNESTY AND THE ROME STATUTE

The preceding discussion indicates that in some circumstances there are no international legal constraints to the negotiation of an amnesty-for-peace deal. In the cases of genocide and grave breaches, there appears to be an overriding duty to prosecute crimes under ICC jurisdiction. Yet it is worth noting that the ICC Statute does not specify whether it codifies the procedural aspects as well as the substantive provisions of the Genocide and Geneva conventions. In other words, it would be possible to argue that even in the case of incorporating into its jurisdiction a treaty-based crime, the ICC Statute did not incorporate the treaty's absolute obligation to prosecute for that crime. The ICC Statute therefore does not definitively resolve the question of whether or when the Court should defer to an amnesty. According to the chairman of the Rome Diplomatic Conference, Philippe Kirsch, the adopted provisions reflect "creative ambiguity" that potentially could allow the ICC Prosecutor and Judges to interpret the Rome Statute as permitting recognition of an amnesty exception to the jurisdiction of the Court.[45] These provisions are discussed later.

The Preamble

On the one hand, the Preamble of the Rome Statute suggests that deferring a prosecution because of a national amnesty would be incompatible with the purpose of the Court, namely to ensure criminal prosecution of persons who commit serious international crimes. In particular, the Preamble:

> Affirm[s] that the most serious crimes of concern to the international community as a whole must not go unpunished and that their effective prosecution must be ensured. . . .
>   Recall[s] that it is the duty of every State to exercise its criminal jurisdiction over those responsible for international crimes.
>   [And] emphasiz[es] that the International Criminal Court established under this Statute shall be complementary to national criminal jurisdictions.[46]

Preambular language is important because international law provides that "a treaty shall be interpreted in good faith in accordance with the ordinary meaning to be given to the terms of the treaty in their context and in the light of its object and purpose."[47] The object and purpose of the Rome Treaty is clearly set forth in its Preamble, which should be given great weight in an international court.

Yet notwithstanding this preambular language, other articles of the Rome Statute might be read as permitting the Court under certain circumstances to recognize an amnesty exception to its jurisdiction. The apparent conflict between these articles and the Preamble reflect the schizophrenic nature of the negotiations at Rome: entirely different drafting groups negotiated the preambular language and the procedural provisions.

Article 16: Action by the Security Council

With respect to a potential amnesty exception, the most important provision of the Rome Statute is Article 16. Under that article, the ICC would be required to defer to a national amnesty if the Security Council adopted a resolution under Chapter VII of the U.N. Charter requesting the Court not to begin any proceedings or to defer those already commenced.[48]

The Security Council has the legal authority to require the Court to respect an amnesty if two requirements are met, namely: (1) the Security Council has determined the existence of a threat to the peace, a breach of the peace, or an act of aggression under Article 39 of the U.N. Charter; and (2) the resolution requesting the Court's deferral is consistent with U.N. purposes and principles with respect to all of the following (sometimes competing) goals: maintaining international peace and security, resolving threatening situations in conformity with principles of justice and international law, and promoting respect for human rights and fundamental freedoms under Article 24 of the U.N. Charter.

In the Tadic case, the ICTY Appeals Chamber held that the Tribunal was empowered to review the legitimacy of the Security Council's Resolution establishing the ICTY. This suggests that the ICC could claim independent authority to assess Security Council decision making regarding amnesty as part of the Court's incidental power to determine the propriety of its own jurisdiction (competence de la competence).[49] This aspect of the ICTY Appeals Chamber decision has been characterized by one commentator as "strongly supporting those who see the U.N. Charter not as unfettered license for police action but as an emerging constitution of enumerated, limited powers subject to the rule of law."[50] It is possible, then, that the ICC would not be compelled by the existence of a Security Council resolution to terminate an investigation or prosecution were it to find that an amnesty contravenes international law in the cases of genocide or grave breaches.

Article 53: Prosecutorial Discretion

The Court's Prosecutor may choose to respect an amnesty-for-peace deal by declining to initiate an investigation (even when a State Party has filed a complaint) where the Prosecutor concludes there are "substantial reasons to believe that an investigation would not serve the interests of justice."[51] However, the Prosecutor's decision is subject to review by the Court's Pre-Trial Chamber. In reviewing whether respecting an amnesty would better serve "the interests of justice," the Pre-Trial Chamber would have to evaluate the amnesty's context and provisions and consider whether there is an international legal obligation to prosecute the offense. It presumably could not be concerned entirely with peace.

Article 17: Complementarity

The concerned state also could argue that the amnesty precludes ICC action. The Court must dismiss a case where "the case is being investigated or prosecuted by a State which has jurisdiction over it, unless the State is unwilling or unable genuinely to carry out the investigation or prosecution."[52] It is significant that Article 17 requires an investigation but does not specify that it be a criminal investigation. The concerned State could argue that a truth commission (especially one modeled on that of South Africa) constitutes a genuine investigation. On the other hand, subsection 2 of the article provides that the standard for determining that an investigation is not genuine is whether the proceedings are "inconsistent with an intent to bring the person concerned to justice"[53]—a phrase that might be interpreted as requiring criminal proceedings.

Article 20: *Ne Bis in Idem*

Finally, the accused can attempt to raise the issue under Article 20, which codifies the *ne bis in idem* principle (the international law version of the prohibition against double jeopardy). Relying on this provision, the accused could argue that his or her confession before a truth commission, and any attendant penalties, are the functional equivalent of having been tried and convicted for the same offense with which he or she is charged by the ICC.

There are two problems with this argument, however. First, the provision speaks of trial by "another court," and a truth commission is not a court; and second, Article 20 is not applicable to proceedings "inconsistent with an intent to bring the person concerned to justice," which again implies that criminal proceedings are required.

CONCLUSION

David J. Scheffer, the U.S. ambassador-at-large for war crimes issues, has remarked that "one must understand that amnesty is always on the table in [peace] negotiations."[54] The preceding discussion indicates that Ambassador Scheffer largely is correct in that there frequently are no international legal constraints to the negotiation of an amnesty-for-peace deal. This is because the procedural law imposing a duty to prosecute is far more limited than the substantive law establishing international offenses. While there was a requirement to prosecute grave breaches of the Geneva Conventions in Bosnia and the crime of genocide in Rwanda, there was no obligation to prosecute crimes against humanity and war crimes in internal armed conflict in Chile, El Salvador, Guatemala, Haiti, Sierra Leone, South Africa, or Uruguay.

The Rome Statute is purposely ambiguous on the question of whether the ICC should defer to an amnesty-for-peace arrangement where there is no international duty to prosecute. While amnesties often are a necessary bargaining chip in negotiations for the peaceful transfer of political power, amnesties vary greatly. Some, as in Haiti and South Africa, are linked closely to mechanisms for providing accountability and redress; others, as in Sierra Leone, Chile, and Argentina, are simply a mindful forgetting. The ICC should take only the former types of amnesties into account under Articles 16, 17, 20, and 53 of its Statute.

Thus, in determining whether to defer to an amnesty arrangement, the ICC should consider the following questions: (1) Do the alleged offenses constitute violations of the Genocide Convention or grave breaches of the Geneva Conventions, which carry with them an international duty to prosecute? (2) Would an end to the fighting or transition from repressive rule have occurred without some form of amnesty agreement? (3) Has the state instituted a mechanism designed to discover the truth about victims and to attribute individual responsibility to the perpetrators? (4) Has the state provided victims with adequate reparation and/or compensation? (5) Has the state implemented meaningful steps to ensure that violations of international humanitarian law and serious human rights abuses do not recur? (6) Has the state taken steps to punish those guilty of committing violations of international humanitarian law through noncriminal sanctions, such as imposition of fines, removal from office, reduction of rank, and forfeiture of government or military pensions and/or other assets?[55] Even when the answers to these six questions suggest that the particular amnesty arrangement serves the interests of both peace and justice, the ICC should defer prosecution only in the most compelling of cases in light of its core purpose as reflected in the Preamble to the Rome Statute.

NOTES

1. As an anonymous government official stated: "The quest for yesterday's victims of atrocities should not be pursued in such a manner that it makes today's living the dead of tomorrow." Anonymous, "Human Rights in Peace Negotiations," *Human Rights Quarterly* 18 (1996): 258.

2. See Michael P. Scharf, "The Letter of the Law: The Scope of the International Legal Obligation to Prosecute Human Rights Crimes," *Law and Contemporary Problems* 59 (1996): 41; Naomi Roht-Arriaza, "State Responsibility to Investigate and Prosecute Grave Human Rights Violations in International Law," *California Law Review* 78 (1990): 451, 458–61, 484 n.187.

3. See Norman Weisman, "A History and Discussion of Amnesty," *Columbia Human Rights Law Review* 4 (1972): 520.

4. See Commission on Human Rights, *Progress Report on the Question of the Impunity of Perpetrators of Human Rights Violations*, July 19, 1993, U.N. Doc. E/CN.4/Sub.2/1993/6:12.

5. See ICC PrepCom—August 1997, U.S. Delegation Draft (Rev.), on file with the author.

6. See ICC PrepCom—August 1997, U.S. Delegation Draft (Rev.), on file with the author.

7. Payam Akhavan, "The Yugoslav Tribunal at a Crossroads: The Dayton Peace Agreement and Beyond," *Human Rights Quarterly* 18 (1996): 259, 271.

8. See Michael P. Scharf, "Swapping Amnesty for Peace: Was There a Duty to Prosecute International Crimes in Haiti," *Texas International Law Journal* 31 (1996): 1, 4–5.

9. See "The Situation of Democracy and Human Rights in Haiti, Report of the Secretary-General," July 12, 1993, U.N. Doc. A/47/975, S/26063 (reproducing the text of the Governors Island Agreement) and the supplementary New York Pact, signed on July 16, 1993, "The Situation of Democracy and Human Rights in Haiti, Report of the Secretary-General," August 13, 1993, U.N. Doc. A/47/1000, S/26297.

10. See Irwin P. Stotzky, "Haiti: Searching for Alternatives," in *Impunity and Human Rights in International Law and Practice*, ed. Naomi Roht-Arriaza (New York: Oxford University Press, 1995), 188.

11. See "Statement of the President of the Security Council," July 15, 1993, reprinted in *Resolutions and Decisions of the Security Council 1993*, 48 SCOR at 120, U.N. Doc. S/26065 (1993).

12. See "Statement of the President of the Security Council," October 25, 1993, reprinted in *Resolutions and Decisions of the Security Council 1993*, 48 SCOR at 126, U.N. Doc. S/26633 (1993).

13. U.N. Security Council Resolution 940 (July 31, 1994), par. 4.

14. "Haitian Lawmakers Pass Partial Amnesty to Pressure Cedras," *Commercial Appeal* (Memphis), October 8, 1994, 1A (LEXIS, News Library, Curnws File).

15. Maggie O'Kane, "After the Yanks Have Gone," *Guardian*, February 18, 1995, 24 (LEXIS, News Library, Curnws File).

16. Martha Minow, *Between Vengeance and Forgiveness* (Boston: Beacon, 1998), 52.

17. Minow, *Between Vengeance*, 52.

18. The National Unity and Reconciliation Act, Act No. 34, 1995, Republic of South Africa, *Government Gazette*, vol. 361, no. 16579 (Cape Town, July 26, 1995).

19. The text of the South African Truth Commission's Report is available at: <http://www.truth.org.za> (November 10, 1999).

20. Naomi Roht-Arriaza, *Impunity and Human Rights in International Law and Practice* (New York: Oxford University Press, 1995), 281–304.

21. Minow, *Between Vengeance*, 9 (contending that prosecutions "are slow, partial, and narrow").

22. M. Cherif Bassiouni, "Searching for Peace and Achieving Justice: The Need for Accountability," *Law and Contemporary Problems* 59 (1996): 9, 13.

23. U.N. Commission on Human Rights, "Report on the Consequences of Impunity," U.N. Doc. E/CN.4/1990/13, reproduced in *Transitional Justice: How Emerging Democracies Reckon with Former Regimes* 3, ed. Neil Kritz (Washington, D.C.: U.S. Institute of Peace, 1995), 18, 19.

24. See, e.g., Report Prepared by the Special Rapporteur on the Situation of Human Rights in Chile in Accordance with Paragraph 11 of the Commission on Human Rights Resolution 1983/38 of March 1983, U.N. Doc. A/38/385, par. 341 (1983).

25. Report to the President from Justice Robert H. Jackson, Chief of Counsel for the United States in the Prosecution of Axis War Criminals, October 7, 1946, reprinted in *American Journal of International Law* 39 (supp. 1945): 178, 184.

26. Adolf Hitler, "Speech to Chief Commanders and Commanding Generals," August 22, 1939, quoted in M. Cherif Bassiouni, *Crimes against Humanity in International Criminal Law* (Irvington-on-Hudson, N.Y.: Transnational, 1992), 176 n. 96.

27. Michael Scharf, "The Case for a Permanent International Truth Commission," *Duke Journal of Comparative & International Law* 7 (1997): 398 n.128.

28. "The newly created Constitutional Court rejected challenges to the South African amnesty on the grounds that it violated the rights of families to seek judicial redress for murders. The Court held that neither the Constitution nor any applicable treaty prevented granting amnesty in exchange for truth." See *Azanian Peoples Organization v. President of the Republic of South Africa*, Case CCt 17.96, Constitutional Court of South Africa, July 25, 1996.

29. Challenges to amnesty laws enacted in Argentina, Chile, El Salvador, Suriname, and Uruguay have been lodged with the Inter-American Commission on Human Rights of the Organization of American States. See Dianne Orentlicher, "Settling Accounts: The Duty to Prosecute Human Rights Violations of a Prior Regime," *Yale Law Journal* 100 (1991): 2540 n. 5.

30. Reservations to the Convention on the Prevention and Punishment of the Crime of Genocide, 1951 I.C.J. 15, 23 (May 28) ("The principles are recognized by civilized nations as binding on States, even without any conventional obligation"); Case Concerning Barcelona Traction, Light and Power Co. (*Belgium v. Spain*), 1970 I.C.J. 3, 32 (February 5) (noting that the prohibition of genocide is jus cogens); Application of the Convention on the Prevention and Punishment of the Crime of Genocide (*Bosnia v. Yugoslavia*) 1993 I.C.J. 325, 440 (September 13) (separate opinion of J. ad hoc Lauterpacht) ("the prohibition of genocide has long been regarded as one of the few undoubted examples of jus cogens").

31. Article 4 of the Genocide Convention states: "Persons committing genocide or any of the acts enumerated in article 3 shall be punished, whether they are constitutionally responsible rulers, public officials, or private individuals." Convention on the Crime of Genocide, December 9, 1948, 78 U.N.T.S.

32. Genocide Convention, art. V.

33. The exclusion of "political groups" was due in large part to the fact that the Convention was negotiated during the Cold War, during which the Soviet Union and other totalitarian governments feared interference in their internal affairs. Leo Kuper, *Genocide* (New Haven, Conn.: Yale University Press, 1981), 30.

34. Geneva Convention for the Amelioration of the Condition of the Wounded and Sick

in Armed Forces in the Field, August 12, 1949, art. 49, 75 U.N.T.S. 31. Rome Statute for the International Criminal Court, art. 8(a), A/Conf. 183/9, July 17, 1998.

35. See Virginia Morris and Michael P. Scharf, *An Insider's Guide to the International Criminal Court for the Former Yugoslavia* (Irvington-on-Hudson, N.Y.: Transnational, 1995), 114 n. 356 and accompanying text, and 341; see also Theodore Meron, *Human Rights and Humanitarian Norms as Customary Law* (New York: Oxford University Press, 1989), 215.

36. Naomi Roht-Arriaza, "Sources in International Treaties of an Obligation to Investigate, Prosecute, and Provide Redress," in *Impunity and Human Rights in International Law and Practice*, ed. Naomi Roht-Arriaza (New York: Oxford University Press, 1995), 25. See Carla Edelenbos, "Human Rights Violations: A Duty to Prosecute?" *Leiden Journal of International Law* 7 (1994): 5, 15; Orentlicher, "Settling Accounts," 2585; M. Cherif Bassiouni, *Crimes against Humanity in International Criminal Law* (Boston: Martinus Nijhoff, 1992): 492, 500–501; America's Watch, *Special Issue: Accountability for Past Human Rights Abuses* (December 1989), 2.

37. See Edelenbos, "Human Rights Violations: A Duty to Prosecute?," 5, 15; Orentlicher, "Settling Accounts," 2585; Bassiouni, *Crimes against Humanity*, 492, 500–501; America's Watch, *Special Issue*, 2.

38. Restatement (Third) of the Foreign Relations Law of the United States, sect. 102(2) (1987); Statute of the International Court of Justice, art. 38(1)(b), 59 Stat. 1055, 1060 (1945) (sources of international law applied by the Court include "international custom, as evidence of a general practice accepted as law").

39. Bruno Simma, "International Human Rights and General International Law: A Comparative Analysis," in *Collected Courses of the Academy of European Law*, no. 4, bk. 2 (The Hague: Martinus Nijhoff, 1995), 223.

40. See, e.g., Declaration on Territorial Asylum, G.A. Res. 2312, 22 U.N. GAOR Supp. (No. 16) at 81, U.N. Doc. A/6716 (1967) ("states shall not grant asylum to any person with respect to whom there are serious reasons for considering that he has committed a . . . crime against humanity"); U.N. Resolution on War Criminals, G.A. Res. 2712, 25 U.N. GAOR Supp. (No. 28) at 78–79, U.N. Doc. A/8028 (1970) (adopted by a vote of 55 in favor to 4 against with 33 abstentions) (condemns crimes against humanity and "calls upon the States concerned to bring to trial persons guilty of such crimes"), reprinted in Bassiouni, *Crimes against Humanity*, 698; G.A. Res. 2840, 26 U.N. GAOR Supp. (No. 29), at 88, U.N. Doc. A/8429 (1971) (adopted by a vote of 71 in favor to none against with 42 abstentions) (affirming that a State's refusal "to cooperate in the arrest, extradition, trial, and punishment" of persons accused or convicted of crimes against humanity is "contrary to the United Nations Charter and to generally recognized norms of international law"); Principles of International Cooperation in the Detection, Arrest, Extradition, and Punishment of Persons Guilty of War Crimes and Crimes against Humanity, G.A. Res. 3074, GAOR Supp. (No. 30) at 79, U.N. Doc. A/9030 (1973) (adopted by a vote of 94 in favor to none against with 29 abstentions) (crimes against humanity "shall be subject to investigation and the persons against whom there is evidence that they have committed such crimes shall be subject to tracing, arrest, trials, and, if found guilty, to punishment"), reprinted in *International Legal Materials* 13 (1974): 230; Principles on the Effective Prevention and Investigation of Extra-Legal, Arbitrary, and Summary Executions, G.A. Res. 1989/65 (1989) (states shall bring to justice those accused of having participated in extra-legal, arbitrary, or summary executions); Declaration on the Protection of All Persons from Enforced Dis-

appearances, G.A. Res. 47/133 (1992) (equating disappearances to a crime against humanity and requiring states to try any person suspected of having perpetrated an act of enforced disappearance). It is noteworthy that large numbers of countries abstained during voting on the above listed resolutions and thereby did not manifest their acceptance of the principles enumerated therein.

41. The final Declaration and Programme of Action of the 1993 World Conference on Human Rights affirms that "[s]tates should abrogate legislation leading to impunity for those responsible for grave violations of human rights such as torture and prosecute such violations, thereby providing a firm basis for the rule of law." World Conference on Human Rights, Declaration and Programme of Action, Vienna, June 1993, U.N. Doc. A/Conf./57/23, second part.

42. Convention on the Non-Applicability of Statutory Limitations to War Crimes and Crimes against Humanity, New York, done in November 26, 1968, 754 U.N.T.S. 73 (entered into force November 11, 1970) (no statutory limitation shall apply to crimes against humanity, irrespective of the date of their commission), reprinted in *International Legal Materials* 8 (1969): 68 (ratified by just 39 states).

43. Simma, "International Human Rights," 223.

44. Scharf, "The Letter of the Law," 41, 57–58.

45. The author discussed this issue with Philippe Kirsch over dinner during an international conference in Strasbourg, France, on November 19, 1998.

46. Rome Statute, Preamble (emphasis added).

47. Vienna Convention on the Law of Treaties, opened for signature May 23, 1969, art. 31(1), 1155 U.N.T.S. 331, 8 I.L.M. 679, 691–92.

48. Rome Statute, art. 16.

49. *Prosecutor v. Tadic*, Case No. IT-94-1-AR72 (Appeals Chamber, Decision on the Defence Motion for Interlocutory Appeal on Jurisdiction, October 2, 1995), 6.

50. Jose E. Alvarez, "Nuremberg Revisited: The Tadic Case," *European Journal of International Law* 7 (1996): 245, 249.

51. Rome Statute, art. 53.

52. Rome Statute, art. 17(a).

53. Rome Statute, art. 17(2).

54. Remarks by David Scheffer at International Law Weekend (November 2, 1996), quoted in Scharf, "The Letter of the Law," 60.

55. See Norman Dorsen and Paul van Zyl, *Justice without Punishment: Guaranteeing Human Rights in Transitional Societies* (unpublished manuscript on file with the author).

12

Complementarity and Conflict: States, Victims, and the ICC

Madeline Morris

The Rome Treaty for an International Criminal Court (ICC)[1] promises a Court that will be complementary to national jurisdictions. But the Treaty does not adequately define what purposes the ICC is to be complementary in achieving. The Treaty reflects an intention that the Court shall serve the justice interests of the victims of genocide, war crimes, and crimes against humanity[2] and the interests of the states principally affected by those crimes, as well as the interests of the broader community of states in relation to those crimes. But the Treaty fails to anticipate how the interests of these three different groups predictably may diverge.

Decision making on fundamental issues requiring prioritization of the interests of the three categories of intended beneficiaries therefore will fall by default largely to the ICC Prosecutor. That Prosecutor will operate within a structure, framed by the Treaty, that encourages him or her to be attentive to the interests of the majority of States Parties to the ICC Treaty and to certain elements of the Court's broader international audience but much less so to the interests of principally affected states or victim populations. The interests of victim populations and principally affected states therefore may tend to be overlooked. To avoid this outcome, clear and carefully developed policies need to be articulated at the "legislative" level.

INTERESTS AND INFLUENCE

The reason for the creation of the ICC, as stated in the Treaty's Preamble, is that "the most serious crimes of concern to the international community as a whole must not go unpunished and . . . their effective prosecution must be ensured by taking measures at the national level and by enhancing international cooperation."[3] The Treaty emphasizes that, in pursuing those purposes, the Court "shall be complementary to national criminal jurisdictions."[4]

The intended meaning of ICC complementarity with national jurisdictions, however, is not adequately elaborated in the Treaty. A fundamental question underlying an inquiry into the meaning of ICC complementarity is: Whose interests is the Court intended to serve? It may be useful to conceptualize courts and prosecutors as analogous to fiduciaries entrusted with faithfully serving the interests of specified others.[5] In national jurisdictions, courts and prosecutors are bound to serve the interests of society in general and, to some ambiguous and debated degree, the interests of victims. In that debate, it is recognized that victims have interests that are in part distinct from the broader societal interests in criminal justice. The balancing of those two sometimes-divergent sets of interests is a chronic source of complexity in the administration of criminal law at the municipal level. The balancing of interests in the operations of an *international* criminal court is even more complex and problematic because there is an additional layer of interests at stake: not only the principally affected state and the victims but also the broader community of States that are Parties to the ICC Treaty will have potentially divergent interests in the handling of crimes within ICC jurisdiction. Because of the array of overlapping but also divergent interests at stake, the meaning of the ICC's complementarity with national courts is neither obvious nor inconsequential.

The potential divergence of interests between the different categories of ICC beneficiaries has very significant implications for ICC prosecutorial policy and practice. The purposes of penal sanctions are commonly identified as deterrence, retribution, incapacitation, and rehabilitation.[6] The interests of victim populations may feature retribution—a just punishment for a wrong committed—more prominently than would the interests of the majority of States Parties to the Rome Treaty ("majority states"), which may tend more to focus on deterrence.[7] In addition, the interests of majority states may focus heavily on prosecution of political leaders, while the interests of victims may emphatically include prosecution not only of leaders but also of those lower in the hierarchy who personally committed the atrocities. Consistent with those differences in emphasis, the interests of victim populations may require a larger number of prosecutions and, possibly, a broader cross section of defendants than would those of the majority states. The interests of the state most affected by a particular context of mass crimes ("principally affected state") and those of the victim population and the majority states also may diverge. For example, principally affected states may wish to confer amnesties to which victim populations may object. Or principally affected states may wish to utilize plea-bargaining arrangements whose functioning may be impeded by the operation of the ICC, as I shall demonstrate. Because the interests of majority states, principally affected states, and victim populations may diverge in these and other ways, clear policy must be articulated as to the combination and the priority of interests that the ICC is intended to serve.

States that are signatories to the Rome Treaty appear to intend that the ICC serve the interests of victims and principally affected states as well as majority states. Reflecting an intention that the Court should serve the interests of victims, Article 75 of the Treaty provides that the Court shall establish and implement principles for victim reparations. Article 79 provides that the States Parties shall establish a trust fund for the benefit of victims and their families. Article 53 provides that the interests of victims should be taken into account in evaluating whether prosecution is in the interests of justice. Article 68 provides that, in the course of a trial, "[w]here the personal interests of the victims are affected, the Court shall permit their views and concerns to be presented. . . ."

Reflecting deference to the interests of principally affected states, the Treaty provides that the ICC will operate only where national justice systems are "unable" or "unwilling" genuinely to prosecute the cases in question.[8] This positions the ICC essentially as a substitute for national courts, to fulfill their functions when they are unavailable, and would seem to imply that, at least in some respects, priority of place is given to national-level justice interests.

Although, in the provisions just surveyed, the ICC Treaty does reflect an intention that the ICC should serve victims' and principally affected states' interests as well as those of majority states, the Treaty's overall structure does not ensure either that the Court will be responsive to victims' interests or that the Court will serve the interests of the states for whose national courts it substitutes. Quite the reverse, the Treaty creates a structure in which the interests of victims and principally affected states are likely to be largely overlooked.

Because the Treaty is silent on the overall priority of interests to be served by the Court and on major policy issues such as the number and array of defendants to be prosecuted, appropriate relations with active national courts, and the like, decisions on these fundamental issues will fall by default largely to the ICC Prosecutor. The Treaty creates an incentive structure in which that Prosecutor will be attentive, to some extent, to the interests of the majority states, but much less so to those of principally affected states or victims. The Treaty's provisions on election, removal, and discipline of the Prosecutor and Judges make the Court loosely accountable to the States Parties.[9] On these matters, the will of the majority (or supermajority) of States Parties will govern.[10] The Prosecutor is likely also to be somewhat attentive to the views of the Court's broader international audience. That broader audience would include media that cover the Court's work and thereby shape international public opinion about the Court (and about the Prosecutor). It would include also the international legal and diplomatic communities, of which the Prosecutor will be a member. Nongovernmental organizations (NGOs) also will watch the Court and attempt to influence its policies. The broader audience to which the Prosecutor will be attentive may also even include states (especially powerful states) that are not parties to the Rome Treaty, particularly when their cooperation with the Court may be important. None of those influences on the Prosecutor, with the possible exception of some NGO lobbying, is likely to represent the interests of victims or principally affected states. The tendencies set in place by the Treaty's accountability structure and the Prosecutor's likely attentiveness to the Court's broader international audience thus are unlikely to favor the interests of principally affected states or victim populations. The net result is that the ICC may largely fail to serve the interests of two of its three intended categories of beneficiaries—victims and principally affected states—and, as shall be demonstrated, may even impede efforts by states to serve those interests.

COMPLEMENTARITY AND ITS DISCONTENTS

The complementarity provisions of the ICC Treaty will result in the Court's potentially operating in two distinct postures: (1) sole active jurisdiction, where international prosecutions before the ICC are carried out in the absence of national prosecutions, and (2) active concurrent jurisdiction, where international prosecutions before the ICC are carried out concurrently with national prosecution of other cases arising from the same context of mass crimes.

Sole Active Jurisdiction

When the ICC acts as the sole active forum for the prosecution of crimes committed in a particular context of mass crimes, the cases that it handles will be, by definition, the only ones prosecuted. Where the ICC bears exclusive responsibility for prosecutions, the danger arises that the ICC will tend to bring too few cases to serve adequately the interests of victims and, perhaps, principally affected states. This tendency would spring from the fact that the Prosecutor, attentive to the majority states and also to the Court's broader international audience, is likely to aim for a few high-profile trials, even though this may not fulfill the interests of the states most affected and, particularly, the victim populations. The Prosecutor is likely to be satisfied by a rather small number of trials for two reasons. First, the majority states and the Court's broader international audience may be focused only passingly on the crimes in question and, where that is true, will likely have the impression that those responsible have been punished if a few prominent trials occur. Second, the majority states' interest in prosecuting genocide, war crimes, and crimes against humanity is likely to be heavily focused on deterrence. With the crimes already having been committed, the majority states are likely to focus on the use of punishment to help ensure that such mass crimes do not occur again. Deterrence is exemplary, and a relatively few examples may be thought to suffice.[11]

By contrast, the victim population's interests are unlikely to be satisfied by a small number of trials. Retribution, meaning a just punishment for a wrong committed,[12] is a fundamental function of criminal justice that is likely to be of particular importance to victim populations.[13] Indeed, the "sense of justice" would seem to have a great deal to do with retribution—the condemnation and punishment of the perpetrator—and much less to do with a forward-looking concern with using the present instance of the crime as an opportunity to deter future occurrences. The justice interests of victim populations are likely to include a substantial retributive element precisely because of the immediate and personal relationship of victims to the crimes committed.[14] This does not make victims "vengeful," as has occasionally been implied. Rather, it means that those who have suffered enormously as the victims of genocide, war crimes, and crimes against humanity have legitimate interests that may be different in emphasis from those of the broader international community that, while not oblivious to the crimes, has not experienced them personally. Where crimes have been committed on a mass scale, by numerous perpetrators against many victims, the interests of victims—including not only deterrence but also retribution—will not be met by a few trials.[15]

Provisions exist within the ICC Treaty that could be interpreted as providing a statutory basis for the ICC taking a very low-volume prosecutorial approach. Article 1 of the Treaty states that the ICC is intended to "exercise its jurisdiction over persons for the most serious crimes of international concern. . . ."[16] Consistent with Article 1, Article 5 delineates the Court's subject-matter jurisdiction as encompassing genocide, crimes against humanity, particularly serious war crimes (as defined by the Treaty), and aggression.[17] Article 17 lists as a basis for inadmissibility of a case before the ICC that the case, even while coming within the Court's subject jurisdiction, is "not of sufficient gravity to warrant further action by the Court."[18] The listing of "insufficient gravity" as a basis for inadmissibility of cases otherwise within the Court's jurisdiction necessarily implies that some instances of genocide, crimes against humanity, serious war crimes, and aggression are not sufficiently grave to warrant the Court's action. Reading Articles 1, 5, and 17 together suggests that the ICC is intended to exercise its jurisdiction only over grave *instances* of the (delineated) most-serious crimes. One not-implausible interpretation of this gravity requirement would be that the ICC should try a very small number of the most culpable perpetrators.

For reasons I have already mentioned, such an interpretation of the Treaty would be a damaging one. And, while it sounds plausible, the minimalist approach is by no means mandated by the Treaty. While the trial of a handful of notorious perpetrators would be consistent with the language of the Treaty, so equally would be the trial of a larger, quite substantial number of perpetrators who were responsible for grave cases of the crimes covered. If some forms of collaboration or even some crimes of violence would be considered less than grave, multiple murders and tortures undoubtedly constitute grave cases of the crimes within the Court's jurisdiction.

Addressing the interests of victim populations and principally affected states may often require a greater number of prosecutions than would be required to satisfy the interests of majority states. Ultimately, in the ICC as in national courts, resource limitations will constrain the number of prosecutions that can be brought. The argument made here is not that resource constraints can or should be overlooked but rather that ICC budget projections and resource allocations should be made in a manner reflecting the full range of interests intended to be served.

A problem closely related to the prosecution of too few cases is the possibility of the ICC's failing to prosecute an appropriate array of cases. The provisions of the ICC Treaty previously discussed,[19] specifying in effect that the ICC should handle only grave instances of the most serious crimes, could easily be interpreted—misinterpreted, in my view—to mean that the ICC should prosecute only leadership-level defendants.

If majority states and the broader international audience would likely be satisfied by a few prominent prosecutions, the likely presumption would be that those few prosecutions should be of top-level leaders. They generally are the most notorious, widely known wrongdoers. In political terms, they bear the broadest responsibility in the sense that, while they may not be the individuals most responsible for specific atrocities (specific rapes, tortures, and murders may have been the creations of followers), the leaders are most responsible for creating the political context in which the crimes were fostered. These factors would likely make the leaders appear to the international community like the appropriate group to prosecute.

This is not necessarily so, however, in the perception of the victim population. In addition to being concerned with leaders, victims pervasively express a deep and heartfelt desire that their particular perpetrators be brought to justice.[20] It is familiar to hear of a holocaust survivor, for instance, who has spent a lifetime longing for (and perhaps working for) the discovery and punishment of a particular camp guard—the punishment not only of a Hitler or an Eichmann but also of the person who tortured him or killed his loved ones, the one whose face he cannot forget. Addressing the justice interests of victims, Judge Gabrielle McDonald, then president of the International Criminal Tribunal for the Former Yugoslavia (ICTY), recently said, "I've never heard a witness say, 'That person is not important enough.' I've never heard a victim say, 'I want someone with a higher rank.' Every individual wants justice in their own case."[21]

Obviously, not all leaders and not all followers can be prosecuted in most contexts of crimes of mass violence. But a prosecutorial design that includes followers as well as leaders would serve victim interests better than would a leaders-only design. Even for victims whose own individual perpetrators are not prosecuted, there may be some symbolic retribution value in the prosecution, condemnation, and punishment of a full cross section of perpetrators, including followers as well as leaders.

It has been suggested that it is not worthwhile to prosecute followers because they have merely been led astray by leaders, through propaganda and other forms of manipulation. But, while large numbers of actors in mass violence may be caught up in the current and commit heinous crimes, there are also always large numbers of individuals who refrain, and even a few heroes who save others. It is demeaning to common people—to *people*—to suggest that, while leaders are worth prosecuting, followers are not responsible moral agents.

I am not arguing against the availability of a duress defense. Where the elements of the defense are met (essentially, that the crime was committed to avoid the imminent threat of grave physical injury or death),[22] duress is an appropriate defense. What I am arguing against is the suggestion that, even in the absence of duress, followers should be presumed not to be responsible actors.

Prosecuting a cross-section of perpetrators may be desirable in terms not only of retribution but also of deterrence. In support of the strategy of prosecuting only the top leaders, the argument is often made that it is most important to prosecute the leaders because "without the leaders, these crimes would not occur." But that point is no more true than its converse, that without the followers, these crimes would not occur. Indeed, there are probably more than a handful of would-be leaders of crimes of mass violence whose dangerous aspirations are never realized for lack of followers. Applying deterrents at top, middle, and lower levels of criminal hierarchies ultimately may be a more effective deterrence strategy than exclusive prosecution of those in leadership positions. This is not to say that the leaders should not be prosecuted. Indeed, their prosecution is essential. Rather, the point is that applying deterrents only to the leaders may be a poor approach. Prosecuting a cross section of defendants may in many contexts be a preferable policy both for deterrence and for providing to the victim population a sense that justice has been done.

When the ICC operates as the sole active forum, it will bear sole responsibility for achieving justice in the context in question. If the ICC is to serve the interests of all of its intended beneficiaries when operating in this posture, the ICC's prosecutorial strategy must entail an adequate number and array of prosecutions reflecting the goals both of deterrence and of retribution and the responsibilities both of leadership and of followership.

Active Concurrent Jurisdiction

Variations in States' Motives

The second posture in which divergences of interest may arise among majority states, principally affected states, and victim populations will be where the ICC exercises jurisdiction concurrently with active national courts. There are a number of reasons for which a state might pursue cases arising from the same situation with which the ICC is occupied, as I will show. The appropriate response of the ICC to divergences of interest arising in the application of active concurrent jurisdiction will depend, in part, on the reasons for which state courts are operating concurrently with the ICC in a given instance. In serving the interests of victims and principally affected states as well as majority states, the ICC will have to be mindful of the interaction of its jurisdiction with that of active national courts. If a state is making bona fide efforts to achieve justice at the national level, then the ICC should take care to operate in a manner that is indeed complementary to those national efforts. If, on the other hand, the state's exercise of jurisdiction is not bona fide, then complementarity may require noncooperation with the national jurisdiction.

The Vestiges of Primacy

The International Criminal Tribunals (ICTs) for the former Yugoslavia and Rwanda (ICTY and ICTR, respectively), in their renditions of concurrent jurisdiction, have previewed some of the conflicts to be confronted when an international court tries some cases while national courts concurrently try others arising from the same context of mass crimes.[23] The complementarity framework laid out in the Rome Treaty is intended to avoid problems that were associated with the jurisdictional "primacy" governing the concurrent jurisdiction of the ICTs. But ICC complementarity, while a definite improvement, retains certain sore points of the old primacy regime.

The ICTs, by the terms of their Statutes, enjoy jurisdictional primacy, meaning that the ICTs may require national courts to relinquish jurisdiction over cases that the ICTs wish to prosecute.[24] In some instances, this arrangement has engendered acrimony between the ICTs and states wishing to prosecute defendants over whom the ICTs have taken jurisdiction.

ICC complementarity incorporates a vestigial form of the primacy of jurisdiction exercised by the ICTs. Under the ICC Treaty, the Court is to determine whether a case otherwise within its jurisdiction[25] is "admissible." A case is *in*admissible before the ICC if it has been or will be appropriately handled by a national jurisdiction.[26] If admissibility is challenged,[27] the ICC will make the final determination of admissibility.[28] ICC jurisdiction over an admissible case will be exclusive, precluding national prosecution of the case, under the Treaty's *ne bis in idem* provisions.[29] ICC complementarity thus incorporates a revised form of primacy in the sense that the ICC can assert exclusive jurisdiction even over the objection of a state. ICC primacy differs significantly from the ICTs primacy in that the ICC Treaty articulates narrow criteria to be employed in exercising that primacy. ICC primacy is to be exercised only in the absence of adequate handling of the case by a state. By contrast, the ICTs exercise their power to prosecute and preclude national prosecution without statutory guidance as to when that power should be applied.[30] Nevertheless, in the ICC as in the ICTs, it is the international tribunal that ultimately determines whether it will exercise jurisdiction over a particular case to the exclusion of national courts.

The ICC's taking jurisdiction over one prosecution, however, would not preclude a state's prosecuting other cases arising from the same context of mass crimes. Even if the ICC concludes that a state's justice system has collapsed or that the government is unwilling genuinely to prosecute—thus concluding, in effect, that the state is unable or unwilling to handle *any* cases arising from that context of mass crimes—the state may disagree and proceed with its own cases concurrently with those of the ICC. Where a state decides to do so, that state and the ICC will exercise concurrent jurisdiction over the crimes committed within the overall context of mass crimes in question.

Where, as in the case of the ICC, the international tribunal has primacy (that is, can insist on taking a particular case), that international tribunal will largely control the distribution of defendants between national and international fora. The ICC will therefore have major responsibility for the resolution of certain predictable conflicts involving the distribution of defendants that will tend to arise in the application of active concurrent jurisdiction.

While the ICC's admissibility rules (that national courts have priority of jurisdiction unless they are unwilling or unable to handle the cases appropriately) will limit the ICC's choice of defendants in some instances, in situations in which the ICC has determined that a national justice system has collapsed or that a government is unwilling genuinely to prosecute, all potential cases would be admissible before the ICC.[31] This is the posture in which the ICC would operate most often because, if the national justice system were neither defunct nor unwilling, then, in most situations, no cases would be admissible before the ICC.[32] In this posture, the ICC's choice of defendants will be constrained only by its own prosecutorial policies.

The prosecutorial policy that is embraced by the ICTs and that appears likely also to be adopted by the ICC is a stratified concurrent-jurisdiction approach to the distribution of defendants. Under this policy, the international forum seeks to prosecute the leadership stratum and leaves the lower strata defendants to be tried in national courts. This approach to the distribution of defendants predictably produces anomalous outcomes in the handling of leaders and followers, creates impediments to national plea-bargaining arrangements, and may tend to undermine national judicial authority.

Stratified concurrent jurisdiction systematically produces anomalous outcomes in the handling of leaders and followers because the leaders, who are tried in the international forum, generally receive more favorable treatment than the followers, who are tried in national courts. The advantages for defendants of international prosecution include absence of the death penalty (applicable in many national courts but inapplicable under the ICC Treaty), greater due process protections (including appointed defense counsel) than many national fora offer, better conditions of incarceration than those in some countries, and, not infrequently in postconflict contexts, greater assurance of impartiality than national courts can provide. A policy of stratified concurrent jurisdiction thus leads to anomalies of inversion in which these crucial advantages flow to the leaders who are, by hypothesis, most responsible for the mass crimes, while the followers are subject to harsher treatment.[33] Such anomalies of inversion were pronounced and problematic as the ICTR pursued its policy of stratified concurrent jurisdiction relative to Rwandan national courts.[34] In Rwanda, many defendants who were not high-level leaders in the Rwandan genocide have been sentenced to death in national courts[35] after summary trials, sometimes without defense counsel, while leaders of the genocide have received lighter sentences after trials with full due process at the ICTR.[36] Anomalous outcomes of this type will predictably occur where an international forum with primacy pursues a policy of stratified concurrent jurisdiction.

Stratified concurrent jurisdiction also tends to impede national plea-bargaining arrangements. National justice systems may see fit to grant defendants benefits (for instance, charge or sentence reductions) in return for guilty pleas or other cooperation. This may be done to facilitate investigations or to expedite prosecution of a large volume of cases. While plea bargaining may be an advantageous strategy, the leniency in sentencing that goes with plea agreements can easily create a perception that impunity has prevailed unless at least the leaders are fully prosecuted and punished. Herein lies the second problem with stratified concurrent jurisdiction. If the international forum takes jurisdiction over the leaders, then the national forum will lack leaders to prosecute. Indeed, the national government seeking to institute a plea-bargaining arrangement will have to acknowledge that, far from being "prosecuted to the full extent of the law," the leaders are away receiving substantial advantages in the international forum. With the leaders away receiving advantageous treatment and the followers getting "bargains" at home, a perception may be created, especially among the victim population, that the plea agreement program is really a program of impunity. National justice systems, consequently, may be impeded in their plea-bargaining arrangements.

This problem is exemplified, once again, by the Rwandan experience. The Rwandan government implemented a specialized plea-bargaining system to deal with the enormous volume of cases related to the Rwandan genocide of 1994.[37] The ICTR's repeatedly taking jurisdiction over the leadership-level suspects posed an obstacle to the political acceptability within Rwanda of the plea-bargaining system[38] and led to conflict between the government of Rwanda and the ICTR.[39]

Stratified concurrent jurisdiction may also tend to undermine the authority of the national justice system in a principally affected state by depriving it of the opportunity to try those who were the leaders of the mass crimes that affected the country. This problem may be particularly significant in postconflict situations in which a new democratic regime is attempting to establish a strong and authoritative judiciary.

Principles for the Application of Complementarity in Contexts of Active Concurrent Jurisdiction

Consistent with the principle of complementarity, the appropriate response of the ICC to divergences of interest arising in contexts of active concurrent jurisdiction will depend largely on the motives for the state's justice efforts. One motive for a state's exercising jurisdiction concurrently with the ICC would be that, while the state has a functioning judiciary, the state is unable to handle the particular cases being brought before the ICC because the state cannot obtain extradition of those defendants or cannot obtain the necessary evidence abroad for those cases. When this is the operative motive, avoiding anomalies of inversion, impediments to plea bargaining, or the undermining of national judicial authority should present little problem. The ICC, consistent with its role as a complement to national jurisdictions and thus acting only where states are unwilling or unable to act, would pursue only those cases that the state cannot because of lack of intergovernmental cooperation. In practice, this may result in the ICC disproportionately prosecuting leaders (because those are the individuals likely to have had the resources to flee the country and the political connections to block intergovernmental cooperation); but the leader-drain effect is likely to be far less pronounced than it would be under a deliberate policy of stratified concurrent jurisdiction. Therefore, the problems of anomalies of inversion, impediments to plea bargaining, and the undermining of judicial authority will be reduced, if not eliminated.

A different analysis is warranted where the second state motive for active concurrent jurisdiction applies. Here, a state actively exercises jurisdiction concurrently with the ICC because, while the ICC considers the state unable to prosecute because of a collapsed justice system, the government's constituencies, including victim populations, view the number or the character of the prosecutions brought by the ICC as inadequate, and the state therefore views it as worthwhile to proceed with prosecutions notwithstanding the impaired condition of its justice system. In this context, it may be wise for the ICC Prosecutor to negotiate with the national government to agree on an ICC prosecutorial strategy, regarding the number and the character of ICC cases, that would both satisfy the ICC's other goals *and* adequately fulfill the interests of that government and its constituencies, including victims, thus obviating the need for national trials. Such negotiations would not constitute improper influence on the Prosecutor or the Court. While there would be agreement on the overall approach as to the volume and the character of cases, the agreement need not involve commitments to prosecute particular defendants and, obviously, would not influence the outcome of the cases brought. Where such negotiations are successful and the state forgoes national prosecutions, not only will anomalies of inversion and plea-bargaining problems be averted, but the potential injustices inherent in prosecutions by an impaired national justice system also will be avoided.

Where negotiations are not successful in forestalling national prosecutions (and, given the political realities of such situations, this may frequently be the case), the ICC will have to shape its subsequent relations with the national jurisdiction according to the actual quality of the national justice efforts as they are carried out. If national prosecutions are conducted with impartiality and something approaching adequate due process, then the ICC should attempt to foster those national justice proceedings. Such measures to foster national justice efforts should include the ICC Prosecutor's taking into account potential anomalies of inversion, impediments to plea-bargaining, and the undermining of national judicial authority when designing criteria governing the defendants over whom the ICC will exercise jurisdiction. This will often require the ICC Prosecutor to pursue a prosecutorial policy other than stratified concurrent jurisdiction. If, on the other hand, national justice processes seriously lack impartiality or adequate due process, then the ICC may have to refuse to foster or to cooperate with those national proceedings. In such cases, it may be appropriate for the ICC to proceed pursuant to the same or virtually the same principles and policies, discussed earlier,[40] as would apply if the ICC were the sole active forum.

The situation is more complex where the third state motive for active concurrent jurisdiction applies. Here, a state actively exercises jurisdiction concurrently with the ICC because, while the ICC considers the state unable to prosecute because of a collapsed justice system, the government desires to consolidate the rule of law or to reinforce national judicial authority and therefore, on balance, views it as worthwhile to proceed, notwithstanding the impaired condition of its justice system. In this situation, the state is interested not only in assuring a certain range of prosecutions, but also, specifically, in conducting some or all of those prosecutions in its national courts in order to reap national benefits. Here, the available range of ICC prosecutorial approaches is wide, and the attendant political implications are widely divergent.

Where there is clearly no hope of any national prosecutions of acceptable quality occurring within an acceptable period, the ICC Prosecutor would do well to attempt to convince the state to forgo national trials. If such attempts at persuasion are unsuccessful, then, as in other cases where negotiations fail to forestall national prosecutions, the nature of the ICC's subsequent interactions with the national justice processes should depend on the quality of those processes as they are implemented.[41]

The completely collapsed justice system just discussed, however, represents the most extreme case. Not all countries with substantially collapsed justice systems will be completely incapable of conducting absolutely any satisfactory trials. Where a largely disabled justice system is capable of conducting one or two or a handful of adequate prosecutions (perhaps with substantial international assistance) and that state desires to pursue justice at the national level for rule of law-strengthening purposes, it may be possible to accommodate both national and international interests. Here, a useful strategy may be to reverse the traditionally envisioned order of things and to have the *national* courts conduct a very small number of high-profile prosecutions of prominent defendants while the ICC conducts a somewhat larger number of other prosecutions.

A different strategy may be necessary where the fourth reason for active concurrent jurisdiction applies. Where a state exercises jurisdiction concurrently with the ICC because state actors seek through national prosecutions to suppress, discredit, or wreak vengeance on political adversaries, the ICC Prosecutor may wish to negotiate with the national government regarding an ICC prosecutorial strategy that would fulfill legitimate state and victim interests sufficiently to obviate any real need for national trials. Obviously, however, where political suppression is the state's motive, it is less than likely (though not impossible, given the needs of states to maintain acceptable international appearances) that such an agreement could be reached.

ICC complementarity poses particularly complex issues when the ICC operates concurrently with active national fora. This concurrent operation may arise for reasons that are good, bad, or ambiguous. The ICC will have to employ a carefully constructed range of policy responses, some of which have been considered in the preceding pages, if it is to foster the interests of victims, principally affected states, and majority states both directly within the ICC and within the national fora with which it interacts.

CONCLUSION

The ICC Treaty's complementarity provisions are the product of political conflict and compromise. Like many such products, the provisions leave unaddressed issues that will be critical to their effective implementation.

In the absence of delineation of the necessary policies to govern the application of complementarity, fundamental decisions on the balancing and the prioritization of the interests of victims, principally affected states, and majority states will fall by default to the ICC Prosecutor. While an ICC Prosecutor may appropriately be vested with some latitude in the exercise of prosecutorial discretion, the delineation of major policy principles that go to the fundamental purposes of the Court requires prior articulation by a deliberative and representative body. Particularly because some approaches that best serve the full range of majority state, principally affected state, and victim interests may be untraditional and perhaps counterintuitive, one cannot be sanguine that an ICC Prosecutor, acting in the press of events, will pursue the most desirable prosecutorial approach. Even more fundamentally, the requirements of legitimate international lawmaking demand that the principal purposes and functions of a treaty-based body be decided by the parties themselves and not by an individual employed to execute one aspect of the Treaty.

There is currently no procedure foreseen for the elaboration of the kind of ICC policy that I have argued is required. These policy issues are matters that could in theory be taken up by the Assembly of States Parties, which is intended to provide oversight and guidance to the ICC.[42] However, given the politically sensitive nature of the issues and the absence, to date, of any indication of an intention to focus on these matters, it seems unlikely that the Assembly of States Parties will address these questions.

Failure to develop the needed policies to guide the work of the ICC could substantially undermine its likely value and effectiveness. In the absence of carefully developed and articulated policies to guide ICC practice on complementarity, there exists the very real risk that the ICC will create injustice rather than justice as it fails to serve the interests of states and victims and perhaps even impedes the fulfillment of those interests in state proceedings.

NOTES

This chapter is a condensed version of an article by this author that will appear in its full form as: "Complementarity and Its Discontents: States, Victims, and the International Criminal Court," in *Peace and Human Rights: Reflections on the Contributions of an International Criminal Court,* ed. Dinah Shelton, (Ardsley, N.Y.: Transnational, 2000).

The author is grateful for comments on earlier drafts of this work by Michael Byers, Robinson Everett, Jack Goldsmith, Donald Horowitz, Carl Kaysen, Dino Lorenzini, Gladys Rothbell, Sheldon Rothbell, Michael Scharf, Minna Schrag, Sarah Sewall, Scott Silliman, and Cory Skolnick and the participants in the Workshop on ICC and U.S. National Security, convened by the American Academy of Arts and Sciences, January 28–29, 1999.

1. On July 17, 1998, 120 countries meeting at a United Nations Diplomatic Conference in Rome adopted a treaty for the establishment of an International Criminal Court. Rome Statute of the International Criminal Court, *adopted* July 17, 1998, at the United Nations Diplomatic Conference of Plenipotentiaries on the Establishment of an International Criminal Court; available: <http://www.un.org/icc>. The treaty was adopted by a vote of 120 in favor and 7 against, with 21 abstaining. See "U.N. Diplomatic Conference Concludes in Rome with Decision to Establish Permanent International Criminal Court," U.N. Press Release L/ROM/22 (July 17, 1998); available: <http://www.un.org/icc>; accessed February 10, 2000. In the present chapter, I use the term "Rome Treaty" rather than "Rome Statute" to reflect that the document produced at Rome is an agreement among the parties, rather than a legislative act.

2. The Treaty provides for the Court eventually to have jurisdiction over the crime of aggression as well, but it precludes the Court's exercising jurisdiction over that crime until the Treaty is amended to include a definition of *aggression* and provisions specifying the conditions under which the Court shall exercise jurisdiction over that crime. ICC Treaty, supra note 1, art. 5.

3. See ICC Treaty, supra n. 1, preamble.

4. See ICC Treaty, supra n. 1, preamble, art. 1.

5. Cf. Kathleen Clark, "Do We Have Enough Ethics in Government Yet?: An Answer from Fiduciary Theory," *University of Illinois Law Review* (1996): 57.

6. Aryeh Neier, *War Crimes* (New York: Times Books, 1998), 81–84 (proposing de-

terrence, retribution, and incapacitation as purposes of criminal punishment); Richard G. Singer and Martin R. Gardner, *Crimes and Punishment: Cases, Materials, and Readings in Criminal Law* (New York: M. Bender, 1989), §2.03 (discussing deterrence, retribution, incapacitation, and rehabilitation as justifications for penal sanctions).

7. Incapacitation also would likely be a concern of victims, principally affected states, and majority states in situations where individual defendants pose a continuing threat. Rehabilitation may in some instances be of importance to majority states and perhaps to principally affected states but probably less so to victims.

8. ICC Treaty, supra n. 1, art. 17.

9. See ICC Treaty, supra n. 1, arts. 34–52.

10. See ICC Treaty, supra n. 1, arts. 34–52.

11. Of course, too few examples will not suffice, since every perpetrator who goes unpunished provides an example that it is possible to commit crimes with impunity. For a discussion of the optimal number of prosecutions to achieve an acceptable degree of deterrence given a particular severity of punishment, see Richard Posner, *Economic Analysis of Law*, 2d ed. (Boston : Little, Brown, 1977), 163–78.

12. See Immanuel Kant, *The Metaphysical Elements of Justice*, trans. J. Ladd (Indianapolis, Ind.: Bobbs-Merrill, 1965), 99–102; Paul Robinson, *Criminal Law* (New York: Aspen Law and Business, 1997), 15.

13. This is not to say that deterrence is unimportant to victims. Indeed, deterrence likely is a concern of victims, particularly if there is an imminent threat of the reemergence of violent persecution of their group. My point is not that victims have no interest in deterrence or that majority states have no interest in retribution but, rather, that there likely is a difference of emphasis by different groups in this regard.

14. Remarkably, there has been virtually no systematic study of the justice interests of victims of crimes of mass violence. An empirical study of that subject is currently under preparation by the present author.

15. Article 53 of the Treaty, discussed earlier, which provides for judicial review of a Prosecutor's decision not to prosecute after an investigation into a particular case has been initiated, does not solve this problem. In contexts of mass crimes, most victims' cases will never become the subject of ICC Prosecutors' investigations, much less of Article 53 reviews. Decisions regarding the number of cases to be brought will occur in policy making well prior to the point at which Article 53 would apply.

16. ICC Treaty, supra n. 1, art. 1.

17. See ICC Treaty, supra n. 1, art. 5.

18. ICC Treaty, supra n. 1, art. 17(1)(d).

19. See supra n. 16–18 and accompanying text.

20. See, e.g., Conversation of author with Alex Boraine and Paul VanZyl, vice chair and executive secretary, respectively, South African Truth and Reconciliation Commission (TRC), in New York City (November 8, 1998) (regarding the interests of victims who testified before the TRC) (notes on file with author).

21. Marlise Simons, "Then It Was the Klan, Now It's the Balkan Agony," *New York Times*, January 13, 1999, A4 (quoting Judge McDonald).

22. See Wayne LaFave and Austin Scott, *Criminal Law*, 2d ed. (St. Paul, Minn.: West Publishing, 1986), 432–41.

23. For an examination of the problems involving the concurrent jurisdiction of the ICTR, see Madeline Morris, "The Trials of Concurrent Jurisdiction: The Case of Rwanda,"

Duke Journal of Comparative and International Law 7 (1997): 349, 362–72. The problems of active concurrent jurisdiction confronted by the ICTs have arisen primarily in the Rwandan rather than the former-Yugoslav context. This is not surprising since the Rwandan government has attempted more actively to conduct extensive national prosecutions than have the former Yugoslav countries. See Fionnuala Ni Alain, "The Fractured Soul of the Dayton Peace Agreement: A Legal Analysis," *Michigan Journal of International Law* 19 (1998): 957, 996.

24. See "Statute of the International Criminal Tribunal for the Prosecution of Persons Responsible for Serious Violations of International Humanitarian Law Committed in the Territory of the Former Yugoslavia Since 1991," in *Report of the Secretary-General Pursuant to Paragraph 2 of Security Council Resolution 808*, Annex, Art. 9(2), at 39, U.N. Doc. S/25704 (1993); Statute of the International Criminal Tribunal for Rwanda, U.N. Security Council Res. 955, U.N. SCOR 49th Sess., 3453rd mtg., Annex, Art. 8(2), U.N. Doc. S/RES/955 (1994), reprinted in *International Legal Materials* 33 (1994):1598, 1605.

25. See ICC Treaty, supra n. 1, arts. 5–12.

26. See ICC Treaty, supra n. 1, art. 17.

27. Challenges to admissibility may be brought by a state or other party. See ICC Treaty, supra n. 1, art. 19.

28. See ICC Treaty, supra n. 1, art. 19.

29. The *ne bis in idem* provisions state, "No person shall be tried before another court for a crime . . . for which that person has already been convicted or acquitted by the Court." ICC Treaty, supra n. 1, art. 20 (2).

30. See Morris, "The Trials," supra n. 23, at 365.

31. See ICC Treaty, supra n. 1, art. 17.

32. See ICC Treaty, supra n. 1, art. 17.

33. For a discussion of the advantages flowing to leaders because of "anomalies of inversion," see Morris, "The Trials," supra n. 23, at 363–64, 371.

34. See Morris, "The Trials," supra n. 23, at 363–64, 371.

35. For example, on April 24, 1998, twenty-two individuals were executed pursuant to death penalties issued by Rwandan courts for genocide-related crimes. Among those executed were low-level government functionaries and peasants without significant political involvements. Interview with Faustin Ntezilyayo, Rwandan Minister of Justice, November 1996–January 1999, in Durham, N.C. (January 12, 1999).

36. See, e.g., *The Prosecutor v. Jean-Paul Akayesu*, Case No. ICTR-96-4-T (Trial Chamber, Sentence) 1998 (sentence of imprisonment for life); *The Prosecutor v. Jean Kambanda*, Case No. ICTR-97-23-S (Trial Chamber, Judgment and Sentence) 1998 (sentence of imprisonment for life).

37. See Organic Law No. 08/96 of August 30, 1996 on the "Organization of Prosecutions for Offences Constituting the Crime of Genocide or Crimes against Humanity Committed Since October 1, 1990," in *Official Gazette of Rwanda* 1 (September 1996), arts. 4–18.

38. See Morris, "The Trials," supra n. 23, at 363–64.

39. See Morris, "The Trials," supra n. 23, at 363–64.

40. See supra, 198–201.

41. See supra, 201–202.

42. See ICC Treaty, supra n. 1, art. 112.

Part IV

The ICC's Implications for International Law

13

The ICC's Jurisdiction over the Nationals of Non–Party States

Michael P. Scharf

On August 20, 1998, the United States launched an airstrike against the Al Shiffa pharmaceutical plant in Sudan, which U.S. officials claimed was a chemical weapons facility operated by Osama bin Laden, the terrorist behind the bombings of the U.S. embassies in Tanzania and Kenya a month earlier.[1] It subsequently was disclosed that the Al Shiffa plant produced legitimate pharmaceutical products, including antimalaria drugs under a U.N. contract specifically approved by the United States, and that Osama bin Laden had no financial or other connection to the plant.[2] Arguing that the bombing of a civilian pharmaceutical plant constituted a war crime, the president of Sudan called for international prosecution of the U.S. officials behind the airstrike.[3]

Anticipation of just such a scenario is what prompted the United States to join China, Libya, Iraq, Israel, Qatar, and Yemen as the only seven countries in the world voting in opposition to the Rome Treaty for an International Criminal Court (ICC).[4] As a Congressional Research Services Report for Congress concluded, "[A]t the core of the U.S. objection to the ICC Treaty is the fear that other nations would use the ICC as a political forum to challenge actions deemed legitimate by responsible governments."[5] Had the ICC been in existence in August 1998, Sudan could have initiated proceedings potentially leading to an international indictment and arrest warrant for the U.S. personnel responsible for the airstrike on the Al Shiffa plant (possibly including the president, the secretary of defense, and military commanders involved). As a nonparty to the Treaty of Rome, the United States would not be obligated to provide evidence or to surrender accused persons within its territory to the ICC in such a proceeding. However, under Article 12 of the Rome Treaty, U.S. refusal to become a party would not bar the ICC from issuing an indictment charging American citizens with war crimes or crimes against humanity committed in the territory of Sudan. Such an indictment obviously could do serious damage to U.S. foreign policy, even if there were little likelihood that the accused would ever face trial.[6]

The Clinton administration has argued that international law prohibits the ICC from exercising jurisdiction over the nationals of nonparties. Thus, U.S. ambassador-at-large for war crimes issues David Scheffer testified before the Senate Foreign Relations Committee that "the treaty purports to establish an arrangement whereby U.S. armed forces operating overseas could be conceivably prosecuted by the international court even if the United States has not agreed to be bound by the treaty. This is contrary to the most fundamental principles of treaty law."[7] Subsequently, Scheffer stated that this jurisdiction overreach constituted the "single most fundamental flaw in the Rome Treaty that makes it impossible for the United States to sign the present text."[8]

A few months later, in a speech before the annual meeting of the American Society of International Law,[9] Scheffer laid out several legal arguments in support of his contention. He argued that the ICC cannot exercise jurisdiction over U.S. nationals on the basis of the universality principle for three reasons: first, because the Rome Statute rejects that basis of jurisdiction by specifying that the consent of the state of the perpetrator's nationality or the state in whose territory the offense took place is required; second, because some of the crimes within the subject-matter jurisdiction of the Court are not recognized as crimes of universal jurisdiction under customary international law; and third, because universal jurisdiction cannot be delegated to a treaty-based collective international court. Ambassador Scheffer also stated that the ICC cannot exercise jurisdiction on the basis of the territoriality principle because a state cannot delegate its territorial jurisdiction to try an offender to an international court without the consent of the state of nationality.[10] On this basis Scheffer expressed the "hope that on reflection governments that have signed, or are planning to sign, the Rome Treaty will begin to recognize the proper limits to Article 12 and how its misuse would do great damage to international law and be very disruptive to the international political system."[11]

Echoes of this legal argument immediately appeared on Capitol Hill. On June 29, 1999, Representative Bob Ney (R-Ohio) introduced a bill (H.R. 2381) entitled "Protection of United States Troops from Foreign Prosecution Act of 1999," which inter alia would prohibit economic assistance for countries that ratify the ICC Statute. The preamble of the bill declares: "the treaty known as the Rome Statute of the International Criminal Court . . . by claiming the unprecedented power over . . . citizens of nations that are not party to the treaty—based upon events taking place in the territory of a nation party to the treaty, is entirely unsupported in international law."[12]

This chapter analyzes the validity of the American government's arguments in the context of historic precedent and of the principles underlying international criminal jurisdiction. The chapter concludes that it is not the jurisdiction of the

ICC over the nationals of non–party states but the U.S. administration's legal argument that rests on shaky foundations. This analysis demonstrates that the United States actually preserves very little by remaining outside the ICC Treaty regime, while the legal argument opposing ICC jurisdiction over the nationals of non–party states has the potential of undermining important U.S. law enforcement interests. Consequently, the best way to protect the United States from the specter of indictment of U.S. personnel by a potentially politicized tribunal is to ratify the Rome Treaty, to play an influential role in the selection of the Court's Judges and Prosecutor, and to provide U.S. personnel to work in the Office of the Prosecutor, as the United States has so successfully done with respect to the International Criminal Tribunal for the Former Yugoslavia (ICTY).

THE UNIVERSALITY PRINCIPLE OF JURISDICTION

Most commentators focus on the delegated territorial basis of the ICC as legitimizing its exercise of jurisdiction over the nationals of non–party states under Article 12 of the Rome Statute. But the universal basis of jurisdiction is also relevant, given the unique nature of the core crimes within the Court's subject-matter jurisdiction.

Universal jurisdiction provides every state with jurisdiction over a limited category of offenses generally recognized as of universal concern, regardless of where the offense occurred, the nationality of the perpetrator, or the nationality of the victim.[13] While other bases of jurisdiction require connections between the prosecuting state and the offense, the perpetrator, or the victim, the universality principle assumes that every state has a sufficient interest in exercising jurisdiction over those offenses that states universally have condemned.[14] The United States calls "paper thin"[15] the foundations for the argument that the universality principle permits the ICC lawfully to exercise jurisdiction over the nationals of non–party states. This section first examines the universal basis of jurisdiction incorporated into the Rome Treaty and then explores the precedent for the conferral of universal jurisdiction on an international tribunal.

The Universal Jurisdictional Basis of the Rome Treaty

Ambassador Scheffer maintains that the drafters of the Rome Statute rejected universal jurisdiction.[16] In his words, "The requirement of the consent of the state on whose territory the crime was committed would be unnecessary if the Court's basis for jurisdiction were universality."[17] This contention, however, is belied by a close examination of the negotiating record of the Rome Treaty.

No one at the Rome Diplomatic Conference disputed that the core crimes within the ICC's jurisdiction—genocide, crimes against humanity, and war crimes—were crimes of universal jurisdiction under customary international law (although there were debates about the scope and the definitions of those crimes).[18] Thus, the drafters did not view the consent of the state of territoriality or nationality as necessary as a matter of international law to confer jurisdiction on the Court. Rather, they adopted the consent regime as a limit to the exercise of the Court's competence over crimes of universal jurisdiction as a politically expedient concession to the sovereignty of states in order to garner broad support for the Statute.[19] As Leila Sadat has observed, when the Prosecutor or a state refers the case, "although the universality principle does not disappear, layered upon it is a State consent regime" requiring that either the territorial state or the state of the accused's nationality be party to the Rome Treaty or accept the jurisdiction of the Court on an ad hoc basis.[20]

According to Philippe Kirsch, the chairman of the Rome Diplomatic Conference, three options were considered with respect to the exercise of the ICC's jurisdiction.[21] The first option was a German proposal providing automatic jurisdiction over the core crimes in the Court's Statute, which enjoyed strong support.[22] The second option, which also garnered wide support, was a Korean proposal that provided jurisdiction if any of four states were party to the Court's Statute: the territorial state, the state of nationality of the accused, the state of nationality of the victim, or the state with custody of the accused.[23] The third option, proposed by the United States, would require the consent of the state of nationality of the offender as a precondition for the exercise of jurisdiction over war crimes and crimes against humanity, but not for genocide.[24] This option enjoyed very little support.[25]

On the last day of the Diplomatic Conference, the Conference Bureau presented what it considered to be a compromise approach that would "attract the broadest possible support for the statute."[26] This approach, codified in the final text of Article 12 of the Rome Treaty, requires as a precondition for the exercise of jurisdiction that either the territorial state or the state of nationality of the accused be party to the Court's Statute. The United States responded by proposing an amendment to Article 12 that would exempt the nationals of a non–party state from the jurisdiction of the ICC in cases arising from the official actions of the non–party state acknowledged as official by the non–party.[27] The proposed amendment was soundly defeated on a no-action vote.[28]

The United States now argues that under no circumstances can the ICC legitimately exercise jurisdiction over the nationals of non–party states. However, at the Diplomatic Conference the United States did not object to the ICC's exercise of universal jurisdiction over the citizens of non–party states for the crime of genocide, nor did it object to universal jurisdiction over the private citizens of non–party states for crimes against humanity or war crimes. The U.S. delegation's positions in Rome thus undercut the credibility of the current absolutist legal argument.

The Universal Nature of the Crimes within the Rome Statute

Ambassador Scheffer holds that "[n]ot all of the crimes within the subject matter jurisdiction of the Court in fact enjoy universal jurisdiction under customary international law."[29] Thus, he argues that "[i]t is implausible for a state party or a consenting non–party state to delegate to a treaty-based international court the right to prosecute a mixture of crimes, some of which in a domestic setting are crimes of universal jurisdiction but others of which, even in a domestic setting, are not crimes of universal jurisdiction."[30]

Philippe Kirsch has written that "[i]t was understood that the Statute was not to create new substantive law, but only to include crimes already prohibited under international law."[31] This limitation reflected the international maxim *nullem crimen sine lege*, which requires that the ICC try only existing crimes recognized under international law or under the law of the state in whose territory the crime was committed.[32] This is true whether the Security Council refers a case to the Court (in which case the Rome Statute requires the consent of no State)[33] or the Prosecutor or a state refers the case. Although Article 11 of the Rome Treaty limits the ICC's jurisdiction to crimes committed after its entry into force, the *nullem crimen* principle is still relevant because the ICC can prosecute continuing crimes, such as disappearances or forced removal of children from an ethnic group, even if commenced prior to the Court's entry into force. Thus the drafters intended to limit the ICC's subject-matter jurisdiction to prior existing international crimes of universal jurisdiction.

The four offenses within the Rome Statute were considered crimes of universal jurisdiction under customary international law by most states and commentators, "even though their precise definition had not been completely agreed by all States."[34] That is, even without complete accord on the exact definition of each offense, the delegations to the Rome Diplomatic Conference generally seemed confident of the possibility of defining their scope for purposes of the ICC's universal jurisdiction.[35] This was really no different from what the international community had done in 1945, when it enumerated the first definition of *crimes against humanity* in the Nuremberg Charter,[36] or in 1958, when it established the first codified definition of *piracy* in the Law of the Sea Convention[37]—both of which were subsequently viewed as codifications of customary law. Thus, Leila Sadat, who was an observer at the Rome Conference, writes, "It is certainly possible to view the drafters in Rome merely as scribes writing down already existing customary international law, rather than as legislators prescribing laws for the international community."[38]

There are two alternative premises underlying universal jurisdiction.[39] The first involves the gravity of the crime. Many of the crimes subject to the universality principle are so heinous in scope and degree that they offend the interest of all humanity and any state may, as humanity's agent, punish the offender. The second involves the place of the act. Many of the crimes subject to the universality principle occur in territory over which no country has jurisdiction or in situations in which the territorial state is unlikely to exercise jurisdiction because, for example, the perpetrators are state authorities or agents of the State.[40]

The first widely accepted crime of universal jurisdiction was piracy. For over three centuries, states have exercised jurisdiction over piratical acts on the high seas, even when neither the pirates nor their victims were nationals of the prosecuting state. Piracy's fundamental nature and consequences explained why it was subject to universal jurisdiction. Piracy often consists of heinous acts of violence or depredation committed indiscriminately against the vessels and nationals of numerous states.[41] Moreover, pirates can quickly flee across the seas, making pursuit by the authorities of particular victim states difficult.[42] In 1820, the U.S. Supreme Court upheld the exercise of universal jurisdiction by U.S. courts over piracy in *United States v. Smith*.[43] The Court reasoned that "pirates being *hostis humani generis* [enemies of all humankind] are punishable in the tribunals of all nations. All nations are engaged in a league against them for the mutual defence and safety of all."[44]

Although piracy and its land counterpart, brigandage, are the oldest of the crimes of universal jurisdiction recognized under customary international law, until recently there was no authoritative definition of *piracy*. "It was not settled, for example, whether *animus furandi*, an intent to rob, was a necessary element, whether acts by insurgents seeking to overthrow their government should be exempt, as were acts by state vessels and by recognized belligerents, and whether the act had to be by one ship against another or could be on the same ship."[45] It was not until the negotiation of the 1958 Law of the Sea Treaty that a precise definition of piracy was adopted by the international community.[46] The historic debate over the definition of the crime of piracy indicates that disagreement over the precise scope or contours of a universal crime does not deprive the offense of its universal character.

In the aftermath of the atrocities of World War II, the international community extended universal jurisdiction to war crimes and crimes against humanity. Trials exercising this jurisdiction took place in international tribunals at Nuremberg and Tokyo, as well as in domestic courts. Some individuals faced trial in the states in which they had committed their crimes, but others were tried by faraway states where they were later captured, surrendered, or found—including Canada[47] and Australia.[48] Thus, on the basis of universal jurisdiction, Israel tried Adolf Eichmann in 1961[49] and John Demjanjuk in 1988[50] for crimes committed before the existence of the Israeli state.

In extending universal jurisdiction to war crimes and crimes against humanity, an analogy was made between those offenses and piracy. Like piracy, the Nazi and Japanese offenses during the war involved violent and predatory action and typically were committed in locations where they would not be prevented or punished through other bases of jurisdiction.[51] On December 11, 1946, the U.N. General Assembly unanimously affirmed the "principles of international law recognized by the Charter of the Nuremberg Tribunal and the Judgment of the Tribunal,"[52] thereby "codifying the jurisdictional right of all States to prosecute the offenses addressed by the IMT [Nuremberg Tribunal],"[53] namely war crimes, crimes against humanity, and the crime of aggression.[54] The General Assembly subsequently has confirmed that no statute of limitations or asylum may be applied to bar prosecution of such crimes.[55]

In recent years, domestic courts in Spain and the United Kingdom have determined that universal jurisdiction exists to prosecute the former president of Chile for acts of torture committed in Chile in the 1980s,[56] courts of Denmark and Germany have relied on the universality principle in trying Croatian and Bosnian Serb nationals for war crimes and crimes against humanity committed in Bosnia in 1992,[57] and courts in Belgium have cited the universality principle as a basis for issuing arrest warrants against persons involved in the 1994 genocide in Rwanda.[58]

In 1993, the U.N. Security Council established an ad hoc international criminal tribunal with jurisdiction over war crimes, genocide, and crimes against humanity committed in the former Yugoslavia—the ICTY.[59] The ICTY's jurisdiction was conservatively formulated to cover only those crimes that were "beyond any doubt" recognized under customary international law.[60] In *Prosecutor v. Tadic*, the ICTY's Appeals Chamber held that the crimes within the ICTY's Statute (including war crimes in internal armed conflict) are amenable to universal jurisdiction.[61] As Theodor Meron has written, "international humanitarian law has developed faster since the beginning of the atrocities in the former Yugoslavia than in the four-and-a-half decades since the Nuremberg Tribunals and the adoption of the Geneva Conventions of 1949."[62] Customary international law on the definition and scope of war crimes and crimes against humanity has been clarified and crystallized by the promulgation of the statutes of the ICTY and the International Criminal Tribunal for Rwanda (ICTR), the decisions rendered by these tribunals, and the acceptance of the international community of these developments.

Under the Rome Statute, the ICC would have jurisdiction over the same crimes that are within the jurisdiction of the ICTY: genocide, crimes against humanity, and war crimes (although the scope of some of these are defined in slightly different terms). In addition to confining the ICC's jurisdiction to core offenses that have been recognized authoritatively as crimes of universal jurisdiction, the drafters stipulated that the Court is only to exercise its jurisdiction in cases involving "the most serious crimes of concern to the international community as a whole."[63] This gravity requirement means that the crimes within the ICC's jurisdiction will be interpreted narrowly, in the light of the first premise underlying universal jurisdiction. In addition, Article 8(b) of the Rome Statute further limits the interpretation of the ICC's jurisdiction over war crimes to those "within the established framework of international law," which was taken to mean war crimes recognized under existing customary international law.

Conferral of Jurisdiction through a Treaty

Ambassador Scheffer argues that ICC jurisdiction over the nationals of a non–party state would violate the Vienna Convention on the Law of Treaties,[64] which "states rather clearly that treaties cannot bind non–party states."[65] However, it is a distortion to say that the Rome Statute purports to impose obligations on non–party states. Under the terms of the Rome Treaty, the Parties are obligated to provide funding to the ICC, to extradite indicted persons to the ICC, to provide evidence to the ICC, and to provide other forms of cooperation to the Court. Those are the only obligations the Rome Treaty establishes on states, and they apply only to States Parties.

The U.S. argument confuses the concepts of obligations of non–party states and the exercise of jurisdiction over the nationals of such states. To untangle the confusion, Philippe Kirsch wrote that the statute "does not bind non–parties to the Statute. It simply confirms the recognized principle that individuals are sub-ject to the substantive and procedural criminal laws applicable in the territories to which they travel, including laws arising from treaty obligations."[66] However, the United States has responded that the assertion that a treaty could provide the basis for jurisdiction with respect to nationals of states that are not party to the treaty contravened "fundamental principles of treaty law."[67]

However, there is nothing unusual about the conferral of universal jurisdiction over nationals of non–party states through the mechanism of treaty law. The United States is party to numerous international conventions that empower States Parties to exercise jurisdiction over perpetrators of any nationality found within their territory, irrespective of whether the state of the accused's nationality is also a party to the treaty. Such treaties include (in chronological order): the 1949 Geneva Conventions, the 1958 Law of the Sea Convention, the 1970 Hijacking Conven-tion, the 1971 Aircraft Sabotage Convention and its 1988 Airport Security Proto-col, the 1973 Internationally Protected Persons Convention, the 1979 Hostage Taking Convention, the 1984 Torture Convention, and the 1988 Maritime Terror-ism Convention. Most recently, the United States took the lead in negotiating (and has signed but not yet ratified) the 1994 Convention on the Safety of United Nations Peacekeepers and the 1998 International Convention for the Suppression of Ter-rorist Bombings. It is noteworthy that none of these treaties purport to limit their application to offenses committed by the nationals of parties; nor do the U.S. criminal statutes implementing these treaties limit prosecution to the nationals of the treaty parties.[68]

The United States has exercised treaty-based universal jurisdiction over the nationals of non–party states even in cases in which the crime was not previously recognized as subject to universal jurisdiction under customary international law. Consider *United States v. Yunis* (1991)[69] involving hostage taking and hijacking, which had not been recognized as crimes of universal jurisdiction under customary international law. In 1988, the United States indicted, apprehended, and prosecuted Fawaz Yunis, a Lebanese national, for hijacking from Beirut airport a Jordanian airliner whose passengers included two U.S. citizens. The United States asserted jurisdiction on the basis of, inter alia, the Hostage Taking Convention,[70] a treaty that provides jurisdiction over hostage takers, despite the fact that Lebanon was not a party to the treaty and did not consent to the prosecution of Yunis in the United States.[71] The D.C. Circuit Court of Appeals in 1991 upheld its jurisdiction based on the domestic legislation implementing the Hostage Taking Convention that had conferred on it universal and passive personality jurisdiction over this type of terrorist act.[72] As counsel to the State Department's Counter-Terrorism Bureau at the time of the Yunis case, the author recalls that officials in the Department of Justice and the Department of State viewed this confirmation (that the antiterrorism conventions could provide the basis for prosecuting nationals of non–party states) as an important development in the fight against terrorism. The *Yunis* precedent was reaffirmed in *United States v. Ali Rezaq* (1998), in which the United States apprehended and prosecuted a Palestinian national for hijacking an Egyptian airliner, despite the fact that Palestine is not party to the Hague Hijacking Convention.[73]

The *Yunis* Court was not writing on a blank slate. Even before *Yunis*, the United States had exercised treaty-based jurisdiction over the nationals of non–party states with respect to the crews of so-called "stateless" vessels on the high seas engaged in narcotics trafficking. In *United States v. Marino-Garcia* (1982),[74] the U.S. Eleventh Circuit Court of Appeals held that the 1958 Law of the Sea Convention gave the United States jurisdiction[75] to prosecute Honduran and Colombian crew members of two "stateless" vessels (sailing under the flags of two or more states and using a flag according to convenience). The ships were boarded by U.S. Coast Guard officials on the high seas and found to contain thousands of pounds of marijuana. The Court was not troubled by the fact that neither Honduras nor Colombia was a party to the 1958 Law of the Sea Convention nor that customary international law did not authorize prosecution of crew members of a "stateless" vessel.[76]

In light of these precedents, the U.S. position that international law bars the ICC from exercising jurisdiction over the nationals of non–party states is not only unfounded, but it also has the potential to affect negatively existing U.S. law enforcement authority with respect to terrorists and narco-traffickers, as well as torturers and war criminals. Had Ambassador Scheffer's remarks been on the record prior to *Yunis*, *Ali Rezaq*, and *Marino-Garcia*, the defendants in those cases could have cited this "official U.S. position" in an attempt to challenge the U.S. assertion of treaty-based jurisdiction over nationals of non–party states.

Conferral of State Jurisdiction on an International Court: The Nuremberg Precedent

The preceding section gave examples of U.S. acceptance of the legitimacy of a treaty's conferring on a State Party the authority to prosecute nationals of non–party states accused of committing an offense defined by the treaty. The only difference between those precedents and the ICC is that, rather than prosecuting in domestic courts, the state has delegated its authority to prosecute to an international body. A precedent for the collective delegation through a treaty of a mix of territorial and universal jurisdiction to an international criminal court exists in the form of the post–World War II Nuremberg Tribunal.

The Nuremberg Tribunal was established through the London Agreement of August 8, 1945, signed by the United States, Great Britain, the Soviet Union, and France and adhered to by the other Allied countries.[77] The Tribunal was established to try the major German war criminals "whose offenses have no particular geographical location."[78] In his seminal article on crimes against humanity and the Nuremberg Tribunal, Egon Schwelb listed the following features that evince that the Nuremberg Tribunal was not a mere occupation court applying national law, but rather an international judicial body applying universal jurisdiction over the Axis countries' war criminals:

(a) the name given to the court, The International Military Tribunal;

(b) the reference in the Preamble to the fact that the four Signatories are "acting in the interests of all the United Nations";

(c) the provision in Article 5 of the Agreement giving any Government of the United Nations the right to adhere to the Agreement . . . ;

(d) the provision of Article 6 of the Charter, according to which the jurisdiction of the Tribunal is not restricted to German major war criminals, but, in theory at least, comprises the right to try and punish the major war criminals of all other European Axis countries; [and]

(e) the provision of Article 10 of the Charter providing for the binding character, in proceedings before courts of the signatory States, of a declaration by the Tribunal that a group or organization is criminal.[79]

In addressing the propriety of this arrangement, the Nuremberg Tribunal stated:

The Signatory Powers created this Tribunal, defined the law it was to administer, and made regulations for the proper conduct of the trial. In doing so, they have done together what any one of them might have done singly; for it is not to be doubted that any nation has the right thus to set up special courts to administer law. . . .

[I]ndividuals can be punished for violations of international law. Crimes against international law are committed by men, not by abstract entities, and only by punishing individuals who commit such crimes can the provisions of international law be enforced. . . .

[T]he very essence of the Charter is that individuals have international duties which transcend the national obligations of obedience imposed by the individual state.[80]

In construing these passages, both U.S. Prosecutor Robert Jackson[81] and U.K. Prosecutor Sir Hartley Shawcross[82] drew an analogy between the trial of war criminals at Nuremberg and the trial of pirates under international law. While these passages have been subject to varying interpretations, it is of particular significance that the definitive report on the Nuremberg Trials submitted by the U.N. secretary-general in 1949 concluded:

It is . . . possible and perhaps . . . probable that the International Military Tribunal considered the crimes under the Charter to be, as international crimes, subject to the jurisdiction of every State. The case of piracy would then be the appropriate parallel. This interpretation seems to be supported by the fact that the Court affirmed that the signatory Powers in creating the Tribunal had made use of a right belonging to any nation.[83]

In 1992, in its report to the Security Council, the U.N. Commission of Experts on the Former Yugoslavia stated:

States may choose to combine their jurisdictions under the universality principle and vest this combined jurisdiction in an international tribunal. The Nuremberg International Military Tribunal may be said to have derived its jurisdiction from such a combination of national jurisdiction of the States Parties to the London Agreement setting up that Tribunal.[84]

Given the exceptional credentials of the distinguished members of the Commission, its characterization of Nuremberg as a Tribunal of delegated universal jurisdiction should be accorded great weight.[85]

Ambassador Scheffer seeks to distinguish the World War II War Crimes tribunals from the ICC by arguing that "the Nuremberg and Tokyo tribunals actually operated with the consent of the state of nationality of the defendants, even though such consent arose from the defeat of Germany and Japan, respectively."[86] Yet, in none of the judgments of the World War II international war crimes trials do the judicial opinions cite the consent of Germany as the basis for the Tribunal's jurisdiction. The absence of any such reference was explained by Henry King, who had served as one of the junior prosecutors at Nuremberg, in the following terms: "It should be noted that the German armies surrendered unconditionally to the Allies on May 8, 1945. There was no sovereign German government with which they dealt in the surrender arrangements."[87] Writing in 1945, Hans Kelsen pointed out that the occupying powers never sought to conclude a peace treaty with Germany (which could have included a provision consenting to trial of German war criminals). He argued that this was because at the end of the war no such government existed "since the state of peace has been de facto achieved by Germany's disappearance as a sovereign state."[88]

The legal foundation of the Nuremberg Tribunal should be contrasted with that of the Tokyo Tribunal, which was established with the consent of the Japanese government that continued to exist after the war. John Pritchard, the foremost expert on the Tokyo Tribunal, writes: "The legitimacy of the Tokyo Trial, unlike its Nuremberg counterpart, depended not only upon the number and variety of states that took part in the Trial but more crucially upon the express consent of the Japanese state to submit itself to the jurisdiction of such a court, relinquishing or at least sharing a degree or two of sovereignty in the process."[89]

While the Nuremberg Tribunal itself contained only the few implied references to universal jurisdiction quoted earlier, the jurisprudence of several of the subsequent war crimes trials based on the Nuremberg Charter and conducted under the international authority of Control Council Law No. 10 (CCL 10) is more explicit.[90] A prominent example was in re *List*, which involved the prosecution of German officers who had commanded the execution of hundreds of thousands of civilians in Greece, Yugoslavia, and Albania.[91] In describing the basis of its jurisdiction to punish such offenses, the U.S. CCL 10 Tribunal in Nuremberg indicated that the defendants had committed "international crimes" that were "universally recognized" under existing customary and treaty law.[92] The Tribunal explained that "[a]n international crime is . . . an act universally recognized as criminal, which is considered a grave matter of international concern and for some valid reason cannot be left within the exclusive jurisdiction of the State that would have control over it under ordinary circumstances."[93] The Tribunal concluded that a State that captures the perpetrator of such crimes either may "surrender the alleged criminal to the State where the offense was committed, or . . . retain the alleged criminal for trial under its own legal processes."[94]

Other decisions rendered by the CCL 10 Tribunals that similarly rely on the universality principle include the *Hadamar* trial of 1945,[95] the *Zyklon B* case of 1946,[96] and the *Einsatzgruppen* case of 1948.[97] Based on these precedents, the U.S. Sixth Circuit Court of Appeals noted in *Demjanjuk v. Petrovsky* that "it is generally agreed that the establishment of these [World War II] tribunals and their proceedings were based on universal jurisdiction."[98] These tribunals thus provide a compelling precedent for the collective exercise of universal jurisdiction.

The Precedent of the International Criminal Tribunals for the Former Yugoslavia and Rwanda

Like the Nuremberg Tribunal, the ICTY and the ICTR represent a collective exercise of universal jurisdiction of states.[99] In 1993 and 1994, the member states of the Security Council decided to establish these tribunals by means of a binding decision of the Security Council. In doing so, they acted not as individual states on their own behalf, but rather as member states of the U.N. Security Council acting on behalf of the international community of states.

Ambassador Scheffer has stressed that the tribunals are distinguishable from the ICC in their mode of creation: the ICTY and ICTR were created by the Security Council as an enforcement measure under Chapter VII of the U.N. Charter, whereas the ICC is created by the Rome Treaty.[100] Yet on close examination, the foundations of these tribunals are not that different from the ICC. While the tribunals were established pursuant to a Chapter VII Resolution of the Security Council, the underlying authority for the Council's action was a treaty—the U.N. Charter.[101]

Nearly every country on earth is a party to the U.N. Charter; thus, it could be argued that the ICTY and the ICTR exercise jurisdiction over nationals of countries with their implied consent by virtue of their obligations as U.N. members. Yet the ICTY has indicted several officials[102] of one country—Serbia—that the United States and its North Atlantic Treaty Organization (NATO) allies maintain is not a party to the U.N. Charter[103] by virtue of Security Council Resolution 777 and General Assembly Resolution 47/1. Those resolutions rejected the claim of the Federal Republic of Yugoslavia (FRY—Serbia and Montenegro) to be entitled to continue the membership of the Socialist Federal Republic of Yugoslavia in the United Nations.[104] Thus, the ICTY provides modern precedent for a treaty-based international tribunal to issue indictments and arrest warrants for nationals of a country that is not a party to the treaty authorizing the creation of the tribunal. An unintended consequence of the U.S. argument about ICC jurisdiction is to give Slobodan Milosevic a basis for challenging the ICTY's jurisdiction over him and other nationals of the Federal Republic of Yugoslavia.

THE TERRITORIALITY PRINCIPLE OF JURISDICTION

There is nothing novel under international law about a state exercising jurisdiction over the nationals of another state accused of committing any offense in the territory of the former state without the consent of the latter. Thus, Americans expect foreigners to abide by U.S. law while in the United States and expect to be subject to foreign law when they travel abroad. The only difference in the ICC case is that rather than prosecuting in domestic courts, the territorial state has delegated through the Rome Treaty its authority to prosecute to an international body.

The U.S. government does "not believe that the customary international law of territorial jurisdiction permits the delegation of territorial jurisdiction to an international court without the consent of the state of nationality of the defendant."[105] This section examines three questions related to the territoriality principle. First, do the policies underlying the territoriality principle of jurisdiction prevent its delegation to other states and international tribunals? Second, is there any precedent for the delegation of territorial jurisdiction to another state to prosecute an individual without the consent of the state of nationality of the accused? And third, is there any precedent for the delegation of territorial jurisdiction to an international tribunal?

The Policies Underlying Territorial Jurisdiction

It has been suggested that delegation of territorial jurisdiction should not be seen as legitimate because it would undermine those features of territorial jurisdiction that warrant "its pride of place among internationally recognized bases for jurisdiction includ[ing] the presumed involvement of the interests of the state where the crime occurred and, secondarily, the convenience of the forum for the availability of witnesses and evidence and the like."[106] There are several problems, however, with this contention.

First, the United States increasingly has asserted territorial jurisdiction based on the "effects theory," especially with respect to narcotics cases. Here, the United States asserts jurisdiction when the criminal acts occurred abroad but the drugs were intended to be distributed within the United States.[107] In addition, under the legal fiction that a conspiracy takes place wherever a single coconspirator commits an overt act, U.S. courts frequently exercise jurisdiction over coconspirator acts committed abroad.[108] In both of these types of cases, most of the witnesses and evidence are located abroad, thereby undermining the argument about convenience of the forum meriting a doctrine of nondelegation of territorial jurisdiction.

Second, there exists no internationally recognized jurisdictional hierarchy that would give greater weight to a country's assertion of the territorial basis of jurisdiction than to other bases. This is demonstrated by U.S. extradition practice. When the United States receives two requests for extradition of a single fugitive from countries with different bases of jurisdiction, the usual U.S. practice is to extradite to the country that lodged the request first, not to give priority to the territorial state. Similarly, the European Convention on Extradition provides that when extradition is requested concurrently by more than one state for the same offense, the requested state shall make its decision "having regard to all the circumstances" including the respective dates of the requests, the nationality of the person, and the place of commission of the offense.[109] Territoriality does not take precedence over other factors.

For years the United States and Great Britain relied primarily on the territorial basis of jurisdiction because they were separated from much of the world by great seas. These two countries became more aggressive in exercising other bases of jurisdiction in response to the relatively recent explosion of international commerce and tourism. For the Continental European countries—neighbors on the same land mass—the nationality basis of jurisdiction was always as important as the territoriality basis. This remains true as the European countries have promoted their citizens' freedom of movement.[110]

Moreover, a state's interest in punishing war crimes or crimes against humanity that occur abroad can be every bit as significant as its interest in punishing crimes that are perpetrated within its own borders. This is especially true in situations like Bosnia and Kosovo, where NATO countries have committed troops to peace-restoration operations whose success is in part dependent on the prosecution of indicted war criminals.

Third, while the other bases of jurisdiction do not have the advantages of territoriality in terms of the location of witnesses and physical evidence, the international community has developed modes of judicial cooperation to overcome that handicap.[111] Thus, the European countries have adopted the European Convention on Mutual Assistance in Criminal Matters,[112] and the United States has entered into two dozen bilateral Mutual Legal Assistance Treaties to facilitate obtaining evidence and witnesses from abroad.[113] Similar types of judicial assistance would be employed for the ICC.[114]

Finally, potential for abuse may be reduced where the jurisdiction is transferred not to an individual state but to a collective court. Ambassador Scheffer has expressed concern about the case of France delegating jurisdiction to try an American to Libya. But, in the case of delegation of a case to an international court, the court shares the interest of the party that triggered its jurisdiction as well as the interest of the international community in punishing grave international crimes.

The Relevance of the Transfer of Proceedings Convention

While acknowledging the precedent of the 1972 European Convention on the Transfer of Proceedings in Criminal Matters, the United States has argued that the Convention only permits transfer of proceedings with the consent of the state of nationality. Ambassador Scheffer has asserted that "there seem to be no precedents for delegating territorial jurisdiction to another state when the defendant is a national of a third state in the absence of consent by that state of nationality."[115] However, a close examination of the text of the European Convention,[116] its legislative history,[117] and the writings of experts on its application reveal that the Convention does in fact permit transfer of proceedings in the absence of the consent of the state of nationality and therefore provides the very precedent that the United States asserts is missing.

The 1972 European Convention on the Transfer of Proceedings in Criminal Matters embodies the "representation" principle.[118] It operates as the reverse of extradition. The Convention is usually employed in cases in which an accused offender has fled the state in whose territory the offense was committed and is present in the requested state, which, pursuant to the authority of the Convention, is willing to prosecute the offender on the request of the territorial state.[119] Instead of requesting the fugitive for trial in the state in which an offense occurred, that state "deputizes" the custodial state with its authority to prosecute the offender.[120]

According to the legislative history of the Convention, "usually—but not always," the offender is a national of the requested state,[121] in which case transfer takes place with the consent of the state of nationality. In fact, there have been cases in which the transferred person is a national of a third state, whose consent is not requested because it is not relevant under the Convention.[122] The Convention is intended to apply, for example, where the offender is a national of a third state who is a resident alien of the requested state or who is present in the requested state due to criminal proceedings against him on an unrelated offense committed in the requested state.[123] In such cases, the Convention does not require the consent of the state of the offender's nationality as a prerequisite for the transfer of proceedings to the requested state.[124]

Nuremberg and the Territoriality Principle

As demonstrated earlier, one of the bases for the Nuremberg Tribunal's jurisdiction was the universality principle, collectively exercised on behalf of the Allied nations. A second basis for the Nuremberg Tribunal's jurisdiction was the territoriality principle, in that the Tribunal was set up by the occupying powers who had assumed the sovereign functions of the state of Germany. Thus, Roger Clark writes, "[T]he power of the Allies to set up the Tribunal may be said to flow either from their authority as the de facto territorial rulers of a defeated Germany, or, more congenially, as exercising the authority of the international community operating on a type of universal jurisdiction."[125]

The territorial authority of the occupying powers was described in 1945 by Hans Kelsen in the following terms:

> The unconditional surrender signed [on June 5, 1945,] by the representatives of the last legitimate Government of Germany may be interpreted as a transfer of Germany's

sovereignty to the victorious powers [who are] signatories to the surrender treaty. . . . Since the German territory together with its population has been placed under the sovereignty of the occupant states, the whole legislative and executive power formally exercised by the German government has been taken over without any restriction by the governments of the occupant states.[126]

In the Einsatzgruppen Trial, the CCL 10 Tribunal indicated that its jurisdiction (and that of the Nuremberg Tribunal) was based on a mixture of the universality principle and the territoriality principle:

> In spite of all that has been said in this and other cases, no one would be so bold as to suggest that what occurred between Germany and Russia from June 1941 to May 1945 was anything but war and, being war, that Russia would not have the right to try the alleged violators of the rules of war on her territory and against her people. And if Russia may do this alone, certainly she may concur with other nations who affirm that right.[127]

As previously discussed, at the time of the unconditional surrender of the German army, there existed no sovereign German state to provide consent for the trial of the major German war criminals at Nuremberg. Nor, as Kelsen explained, could the German people be deemed to be nationals of the occupying powers: "Since the occupant state does not intend to annex the occupied territory placed under its sovereignty, it will not confer upon the former citizens of the occupied state political rights with respect to its own legislative or executive organs, nor will the occupant state impose upon them military duties. Consequently they are not to be considered as 'citizens' of the occupant state."[128] Therefore, the creation of the Tribunal did not amount to the consent of the state of nationality of the accused. Consequently, in addition to universal jurisdiction, the Nuremberg and CCL 10 tribunals exercised the delegated territorial jurisdiction of their members without the consent of the state of the accused's nationality—providing a strong historic foundation for the ICC's jurisdictional reach.

CONCLUSION

The foregoing analysis of historic precedents and principles of international law has shown the ICC's jurisdiction over the nationals of nonparty states to be well grounded in international law. The legitimate exercise of such jurisdiction can be based on a mix of the universality principle and the territoriality principle. The core crimes within the ICC's jurisdiction—genocide, crimes against humanity, and war crimes—are crimes of universal jurisdiction. The negotiating record of the Rome Treaty indicates that the consent regime was layered on the ICC's jurisdiction over these crimes, such that with the consent of the state in whose territory the offense was committed, the Court has the authority to issue indictments against the nationals of non–party states accused of committing these universal crimes. The Nuremberg Tribunal and the ad hoc ICTY provide precedent for the collective delegation of universal jurisdiction to an international criminal court without the consent of the state of the nationality of the accused. In addition, international law recognizes the authority of the state where a crime occurs to delegate its territorial-based jurisdiction to a third state or international tribunal. Careful analysis of the European Convention on the Transfer of Proceedings indicates that the consent of the state of the nationality of the accused is not a prerequisite for the delegation of territorial jurisdiction under the Convention. Finally, there are no compelling policy reasons why territorial jurisdiction cannot be delegated to an international court, and the Nuremberg Tribunal provides the precedent for the collective exercise of territorial as well as universal jurisdiction.

In the final analysis, there is scant basis for convincing the Parties to the Rome Treaty that they must refrain from exercising the universal and territorial jurisdiction of the ICC over the nationals of non–party states as a matter of international law. Since the ICC can legitimately indict U.S. officials for crimes committed in the territories of State Parties to the Rome Treaty, the United States actually preserves very little by remaining outside the treaty regime—and could protect itself better by signing the treaty.

In its refusal to recognize this reality, the executive branch of the U.S. government has resorted to a legal interpretation that is not only based on selective use of the historic record and incomplete analysis of the guiding precedents, but also has the potential of undermining important U.S. law enforcement interests. Unless the executive branch abandons or significantly modifies its legal argument, Ambassador Scheffer's sweeping statement that a treaty cannot legitimately provide the basis for jurisdiction with respect to nationals of non–party states will almost certainly be cited by accused terrorists, torturers, war criminals, and drug traffickers to block U.S. efforts to exercise treaty-based jurisdiction over such persons who are nationals of non–party states.

NOTES

1. Coordinator for Counterterrorism, U.S. Department of State, *Fact Sheet: U.S. Strike on Facilities in Afghanistan and Sudan*, U.S. Information Agency, August 21, 1998, available: <http://www.usia.gov/topical/pol/terror/98082112.htm> (April 20, 1999); Letter from the Permanent Representative of the United States of America to the United Nations Addressed to the President of the Security Council, U.N. Doc. S/1998/760, August 20, 1998.

2. Michael Barletta, "Report: Chemical Weapons in the Sudan," *The Nonproliferation Review* 6 (1998); Colum Lynch, "Allied Doubts Grow about U.S. Strike on Sudanese Plant," *Boston Globe*, September 24, 1998, A2.

3. Barletta, "Report: Chemical Weapons," at n. 41; Lynch, "Allied Doubts Grow," A2.

4. Statute, reprinted in M. Cherif Bassiouni, *The Statute of the International Criminal Court* (Irvington-on-Hudson, N.Y.: Transnational, 1998), 39.

5. Congressional Research Service/The Library of Congress, *The International Criminal Court Treaty: Description, Policy Issues, and Congressional Concerns* (January 6, 1999), 9.

6. David Scheffer, "The United States and the International Criminal Court," *American Journal of International Law* 93 (1999): 12, 19.

7. David Scheffer, "Hearing Before the Subcommittee on International Operations of the Committee on Foreign Relations of the United States Senate" (statement made before the 105th Cong., 2nd. sess., S. Hrg. 105–724, July 23, 1998), 13.

8. David Scheffer, "International Criminal Court: The Challenge of Jurisdiction" (address at the Annual Meeting of the American Society of International Law, March 26, 1999), 1.

9. Scheffer, "International Criminal Court: The Challenge," 4.

10. Scheffer, "International Criminal Court: The Challenge," 4.

11. Scheffer, "International Criminal Court: The Challenge," 4–5.

12. H.R. 2381, 106th Cong., 1st sess., June 29, 1999.

13. Kenneth C. Randall, "Universal Jurisdiction under International Law," *Texas Law Review* 66 (1988): 785, 786.

14. Randall, "Universal Jurisdiction," 787.

15. Scheffer, "International Criminal Court: The Challenge," 3.

16. Scheffer, "International Criminal Court: The Challenge," 3.

17. Scheffer, "International Criminal Court: The Challenge," 3.

18. Philippe Kirsch and John T. Holmes, "The Rome Conference on an International Criminal Court: The Negotiating Process," *American Journal of International Law* 93, no. 2 (1999), 12 n. 19.

19. Kirsch and Holmes, "The Rome Conference," 9.

20. Leila Sadat and S. Richard Carden, "The New International Criminal Court: An Uneasy Revolution," *Georgetown Law Journal* 88 (forthcoming 2000).

21. Kirsch and Holmes, "The Rome Conference," 7 n. 19.

22. Kirsch and Holmes, "The Rome Conference," 7.

23. Kirsch and Holmes, "The Rome Conference," 7.

24. Kirsch and Holmes, "The Rome Conference," 7.

25. Kirsch and Holmes, "The Rome Conference," 9.

26. Kirsch and Holmes, "The Rome Conference," 9.

27. U.N. Doc. A/CONF.183/C.1/L.90 (1998); Theodor Meron, "The Court We Want," *Washington Post,* October 13, 1998, A15; Scheffer, "The United States and the International Criminal Court," 19.

28. U.N. Doc. A/CONF.183/C.1/L.90 (1998); Meron, "The Court We Want," A15.

29. Scheffer, "International Criminal Court: The Challenge," 3.

30. Scheffer, "International Criminal Court: The Challenge," 3.

31. Kirsch and Holmes, "The Rome Conference," 12 n. 19.

32. International Covenant on Civil and Political Rights, December 16, 1966, art. 15, 999 U.N.T.S. 171; *Nazi Conspiracy and Aggression: Opinion and Judgment* 49 (Washington, D.C.: U.S. Government Printing Office, 1947).

33. Report of the Secretary-General Pursuant to Paragraph 2 of Security Council Resolution 808 (1993), U.N. Doc. S/25704, par. 34 (1993).

34. Sadat and Carden, "The New International Criminal Court."

35. Sadat and Carden, "The New International Criminal Court."

36. Agreement for the Prosecution and Punishment of the Major War Criminals of the European Axis and the Charter of the International Military Tribunal annexed thereto, August 8, 1945, art. 1, 82 U.N.T.S. 279.

37. Geneva Convention of the High Seas, April 29, 1958, arts. 5, 14, and 19, 13 U.S.T. 2312, T.I.A.S. no. 5200, 450 U.N.T.S. 82.

38. Sadat and Carden, "The New International Criminal Court."

39. Lee A. Steven, "Genocide and the Duty to Extradite or Prosecute: Why the United States Is in Breach of Its International Obligations," *Virginia Journal of International Law* 39 (1999): 425, 434.

40. Sadat and Carden, "The New International Criminal Court."

41. Hari M. Osofsky, "Domesticating International Criminal Law: Bringing Human Rights Violators to Justice," *Yale Law Journal* 107 (1997): 191.

42. Daniel Bodansky, "Human Rights and Universal Jurisdiction," in *World Justice? U.S. Courts and International Human Rights*, ed. Mark Gibney (Boulder, Co.: Westview, 1991), 9.

43. *United States v. Smith*, 18 U.S. (5 Wheat.) 153 (1820).

44. *United States v. Smith*, 18 U.S. (5 Wheat.) 153, 156 (1820); *U.S. v. Klintock*, 18 U.S. (5 Wheat.) 144, 147–48 (1820).

45. Malvina Halberstam, "Terrorism on the High Seas: The *Achille Lauro*, Piracy, and the IMO Convention on Maritime Safety," *Amererican Journal of International Law* 82 (1988): 269, 272.

46. "Geneva Convention of the High Seas," art. 5, April 29, 1958, 13 U.S.T. 2312, T.I.A.S. No. 5200, 450 U.N.T.S. 82.

47. *R. v. Imre Finta*, 28 C.R. (4th) 265 (S.C.) (Canada) (1994).

48. *Polyukhovich v. Commonwealth*, 172 C.L.R. 501 (Australia) (1991).

49. *Attorney General of Israel v. Eichmann*, 36 I.L.R. 277, 299, 304 (Isr. Sup. Ct. 1962).

50. *Demjanjuk v. Petrovsky*, 776 F.2d 571 (6th Cir. 1985); Cr. A. 347/88, *Demjanjuk v. State of Israel* (Special Issue), 395–96; Mordechai Kremnitzer, "The Demjanjuk Case," in *War Crimes in International Law*, ed. Yoram Dinstein and Mala Tabory (Cambridge, Mass: Martins Nijhoff, 1996), 321, 323.

51. Randall, "Universal Jurisdiction," 793.

52. G.A. Res. 95, U.N. Doc. A/64/Add.1, at 188 (1946).

53. Randall, "Universal Jurisdiction," 834.

54. Agreement for the Prosecution and Punishment of the Major War Criminals of the European Axis and the Charter of the International Military Tribunal annexed thereto, August 8, 1945, art. 6, 82 U.N.T.S. 279.

55. See, e.g., Declaration on Territorial Asylum, G.A. Res. 2312, U.N. GAOR Supp. 22 no. 16, 81, U.N. Doc. A/6716 (1967); United Nations Resolution on War Criminals, G.A. Res. 2712, U.N. GAOR Supp. 25, no. 28, 78–79, U.N. Doc. A/8028 (1970); G.A. Res. 2840, U.N. GAOR Supp. 26, no. 29, 88, U.N. Doc. A/8429 (1971); United Nations Resolution on Principles of International Cooperation in the Detection, Arrest, Extradition, and Punishment of Persons Guilty of War Crimes and Crimes against Humanity, G.A. Res. 3074, GAOR Supp., no. 30, 79, U.N. Doc. A/9030 (1973).

56. *Regina v. Bow Street Metropolitan Stipendiary Magistrate, ex parte Pinochet Ugarte* [1999] *W.L.R.* 2, 272 (H.L.), reprinted in *ILM* 38 (1999): 430.

57. Mary Ellen O'Connell, "New International Legal Process," *American Journal of International Law* 83 (1999): 334, 341; *International Law Update* 5 (May 1999): 52; *Kadic. v. Karadzic*, 70 F.3d 232, 240 (2d Cir. 1995).

58. Theodor Meron, "International Criminalization of Internal Atrocities," *American Journal of International Law* 89 (1995): 554, 576.

59. Statute of the International Tribunal for the Prosecution of Persons Responsible for Serious Violations of International Humanitarian Law Committed in the Territory of the Former Yugoslavia Since 1991, annexed to *Report of the Secretary-General Pursuant to Paragraph 2 of Security Council Resolution 808 (1993)*, U.N. Doc. S/25704, Annex (1993).

60. *Report of the Secretary-General Pursuant to Paragraph 2 of Security Council Resolution 808 (1993)*, U.N. Doc. S/25704, par. 34 (1993).

61. *Prosecutor v. Tadic*, Appeal on Jurisdiction, No. IT-94-1-AR72, par. 94 (October 2, 1995), *ILM* 35 (1996): 32; Geoffrey R. Watson, "The Humanitarian Law of the Yugoslavia War Crimes Tribunal: Jurisdiction in *Prosecutor v. Tadic*," *Virginia Journal of International Law* 36 (1996): 687, 707.

62. Theodor Meron, *War Crimes Law Comes of Age* (New York: Clarendon Press, 1998), 297.

63. Statute, art. 1, Statute, Preamble, par. 5.

64. Vienna Convention on the Law of Treaties, May 23, 1969, U.N. Doc. A/Conf. 39/27, (1969): 289, 1155 U.N.T.S. 331.

65. Scheffer, "International Criminal Court: The Challenge," 3.

66. Philippe Kirsch, "The Rome Conference on the International Criminal Court: A Comment," *ASIL Newsletter* 1 (November/December 1998).

67. David J. Scheffer, speech at the Twelfth Annual U.S. Pacific Command International Military Operations and Law Conference, Honolulu, Hawaii, February 23, 1999, available: <http://www.state.gov/www/policy-remarks/1999/990223-Scheffer-hawaii.html>. Accessed May 25, 1999.

68. See, e.g., 18 U.S.C. 32 (1994) (destruction of aircraft); 18 U.S.C. 37 (1994) (violence at international airports); 18 U.S.C. 112, 878, 1116 (1994) (threats and violence against foreign officials); 18 U.S.C. 1203 (1994) (hostage taking); 18 U.S.C. 1653 (1994) (piracy); 18 U.S.C. 2280-81 (1994) (violence on or against ships and fixed platforms); 21 U.S.C. 960 (1994) (drug trafficking); 49 U.S.C. 46502 (1994) (hijacking), 18 U.S.C.A. 2340 (West Supp. 1997) (torture).

69. *United States v. Yunis*, 924 F.2d 1086 (D.C. Cir. 1991).

70. Convention for the Suppression of Unlawful Seizure of Aircraft, Dec. 16, 1970, 22 U.S.T. 1643, T.I.A.S. No. 7192.

71. *United States v. Yunis*, 1092; *Treaties in Force*, U.S. Department of State Publication 9453 (1990), 291.

72. *United States v. Yunis*, 1091.

73. *United States v. Ali Rezaq*, 134 F.3d 1121, 1130 (D.C. Cir. 1998).

74. *United States v. Marino-Garcia*, 679 F.2d 1373, 1383, 1386-87 (11th Cir. 1982).

75. 21 U.S.C. Section 955b(d) includes stateless vessels, as defined by Article 6 of the 1958 Convention on the High Seas, as vessels subject to the jurisdiction of the United States.

76. *Treaties in Force*, 345.

77. Agreement for the Prosecution and Punishment of the Major War Criminals of the

European Axis and the Charter of the International Military Tribunal annexed thereto, August 8, 1945, art. 1, 82 U.N.T.S. 279.

78. Agreement for the Prosecution and Punishment of the Major War Criminals of the European Axis and the Charter of the International Military Tribunal annexed thereto, August 8, 1945, art. 1, 82 U.N.T.S. 279.

79. Egon Schwelb, "Crimes against Humanity," *British Year Book of International Law* 23 (1946): 178, 209.

80. *Trial of the Major War Criminals before the International Military Tribunal 22* (Lake Success, N.Y.: United Nations, 1949), 461, 466.

81. Robert. H. Jackson, *The Nuremberg Case* 88 (1947, 2d printing 1971).

82. *Trial of the Major War Criminals*, 106.

83. *The Charter and Judgment of the Nuremberg Tribunal* 80, U.N. Doc. A/CN.4/5, U.N. Sales No. 1949V.7 (1949) (memorandum submitted by the Secretary General).

84. *Interim Report of the Independent Commission of Experts Established Pursuant to Security Council Resolution 780* (1992), at par. 73, U.N. Doc. S/25274 (1993).

85. Yoram Dinstein and Mala Tabory, eds., *War Crimes in International Law* (Tel Aviv: Tel Aviv University, Buchmann Faculty of Law, 1996), 155; Henry T. King Jr., "The Limitations of Sovereignty from Nuremberg to Sarajevo," *Canada–U.S. Law Journal* 20 (1994): 167; Telford Taylor, *Nuremberg and Vietnam: An American Tragedy* (Chicago, Ill.: Quadrangle Books, 1970), 80.

86. Scheffer, "International Criminal Court: The Challenge," 3.

87. King, "The Limitations of Sovereignty," 167, 168.

88. Hans Kelsen, "The Legal Status of Germany according to the Declaration of Berlin," *American Journal of International Law* 39 (1945): 518, 524.

89. R. John Pritchard, "The International Military Tribunal for the Far East and Its Contemporary Resonances: A General Preface to the Collection," in *The Tokyo Major War Crimes Trial*, ed. R. John Pritchard (Lewiston, N.Y.: Edwin Mellen Press, 1998), xxxi.

90. Matthew Lippman, "The Other Nuremberg: American Prosecutions of Nazi War Criminals in Occupied Germany," in *Ind. Int'l & Comp. L. Rev.* 3, no. 1 (1992): 8. CCL 10 and the Rules of Procedure for the CCL 10 proceedings are reproduced in Virginia Morris and Michael P. Scharf, *The International Criminal Tribunal for Rwanda* (Irvington-on-Hudson, N.Y.: Transnational, 1998), 494, 497.

91. *Trials of War Criminals* 11 (1946–1949), 757 (U.S. Mil. Trib.—Nuremberg 1948).

92. *Trials of War Criminals* 11 (1946–1949), 1235 (U.S. Mil. Trib.—Nuremberg 1948).

93. *Trials of War Criminals* 11 (1946–1949), 1241 (U.S. Mil. Trib.—Nuremberg 1948).

94. *Trials of War Criminals* 11 (1946–1949), 1242 (U.S. Mil. Trib.—Nuremberg 1948).

95. *Law Reports of Trials of War Criminals* 1 (1949), 46 (U.S. Mil. Commission—Wisbaden 1945).

96. *Law Reports of Trials of War Criminals* 1 (1949), 93 (British Mil. Ct.—Hamburg 1946).

97. *United States v. Otto Ohlendorf*, reprinted in *IV Trials of War Criminals before the Nuernberg Military Tribunals under Control Council Law*, no. 10 (1950), 411, 462.

98. *Demjanjuk v. Petrovsky*, 776 F.2d 571, 582 (6th Cir. 1985).

99. *Prosecutor v. Dusko Tadic*, International Tribunal for the former Yugoslavia, IT-94-1-AR72, Decision on the Defence Motion for Interlocutory Appeal on Jurisdiction (Appeals Chamber, October 2, 1995), at par. 58; Geoffrey R. Watson, "The Humanitarian Law

of the Yugoslavia War Crimes Tribunal: Jurisdiction in *Prosecutor v. Tadic,*" *Virginia Journal of International Law* 36 (1996): 687, 707.

100. Scheffer, "International Criminal Court: The Challenge," 4.

101. Charter of the United Nations, June 26, 1945, 59 Stat. 1031, T.S. No. 993, 3 Bevans 1153, arts. 2(6), 25, and 103.

102. *Prosecutor v. Slobodan Milosevic, Milan Milutinovic, Nikola Sainovic, Dragoljub Ojdanic, and Vlajko Stojiljkovic,* indictment issued May 22, 1999; available: <http://www.un.org/icty/indictment>; accessed May 25, 1999.

103. In April 1999, the Federal Republic of Yugoslavia (FRY—Serbia and Montenegro) instituted proceedings before the International Court of Justice against ten NATO countries, accusing them of bombing Yugoslav territory in violation of their obligation not to use force against another state; International Court of Justice, Press Communique 99/17, April 29, 1999; available: <www.icj.-cij.org>; accessed May 25, 1999. Several of the respondents, including the United States and the United Kingdom, argued that the FRY was not a party to the United Nations by virtue of Security Council Resolution 777 (1992) and United Nations General Assembly Resolution 47/1 (1992) and therefore could not bring a case before the ICJ. International Court of Justice, Press Communiqué 99/25, June 2, 1999; available: <http://www.icj.law>; accessed August 16, 1999.

104. S.C. Res. 777, U.N. SCOR, 47th Sess., 3116th mtg. at 1, U.N. Doc. S/RES/777 (1992); Michael P. Scharf, "Musical Chairs: The Dissolution of States and Membership in the United Nations," *Cornell International Law Journal* 28 (1995): 29–69.

105. Scheffer, "International Criminal Court: The Challenge," 4.

106. Madeline Morris, "Exercise of ICC Jurisdiction over Nationals of Non-Party States," *Law and Contemporary Problems* (forthcoming), 11.

107. Jordan Paust, et al., *International Criminal Law, Cases and Materials* (Durham, N.C.: Carolina Academic Press, 1996), 1270 (citing cases from the U.S. First, Second, Third, Fifth and Ninth Circuit Courts of Appeals).

108. Jordan Paust, et al., *International Criminal Law, Cases and Materials* 1270.

109. European Convention on Extradition, Europ. T.S. no. 24, art. 17 (1957).

110. Christopher L. Blakesley, "Extraterritorial Jurisdiction," in M. Cherif Bassiouni, *International Criminal Law: Procedural and Enforcement Mechanisms,* 2d ed., (Irvington-on-Hudson, N.Y.: Transnational, 1999), 63.

111. Ekkehart Muller-Rappard, "Inter-State Cooperation in Penal Matters within the Council of Europe Framework," in Bassiouni, *International Criminal Law,* 331; Allan Ellis and Robert L. Pisani, "The United States Treaties on Mutual Assistance in Criminal Matters," in Bassiouni, *International Criminal Law,* 403.

112. European Convention on Mutual Assistance in Criminal Matters of 1959, Europ. T.S. No. 30 (1959), reproduced in Bassiouni, *International Criminal Law,* 381; Additional Protocol to the European Convention on Mutual Assistance in Criminal Matters of 1978, Europ. T.S. No. 99 (1978), reproduced in Bassiouni, *International Criminal Law,* 389.

113. Ellis and Pisani, "The United States Treaties on Mutual Assistance," 406–7.

114. Statute, arts. 86–102.

115. Scheffer, "International Criminal Court: The Challenge," 4.

116. European Convention on the Transfer of Proceedings in Criminal Matters, Europ. T.S. No. 73, reproduced in Bassiouni, *International Criminal Law,* 661.

117. Council of Europe, "Explanatory Report on the European Convention on the Transfer of Proceedings in Criminal Matters," (Strasbourg: Council of Europe, 1985), 20.

118. Council of Europe, "Extraterritorial Criminal Jurisdiction," reprinted in *Criminal Law Forum* 3 (1992): 441, 452.

119. Julian Schutte, "The European System," in Bassiouni, *International Criminal Law,* 661.

120. Schutte, "The European System," 648.

121. Council of Europe, "Explanatory Report," 20.

122. According to Professor Andre Klip of the University of Utrecht, who was one of the drafters of the Council of Europe's "Explanatory Report on the European Convention on the Transfer of Proceedings in Criminal Matters," no statistics have been compiled on the number of times the Convention has been used to transfer a national of a third state, but "such cases are not unheard of." Interview with Andre Klip, Siracusa, Sicily, September 15, 1999.

123. Council of Europe, "Explanatory Report," 32; Schutte, "The European System," 648.

124. Council of Europe, European Convention on the Transfer of Proceedings in Criminal Matters, 661.

125. Roger Clark, "Nuremberg and Tokyo in Contemporary Perspective," in *The Law of War Crimes: National and International Approaches*, ed. Timothy McCormack and Gerry Simpson (The Hague: Kluwer Law International, 1997), 172.

126. Kelsen, "The Legal Status of Germany," 518, 519, 520.

127. *United States v. Otto Ohlendorf*, 411, 462.

128. Kelsen, "The Legal Status of Germany," 518, 523.

14

The ICC and the Future of the Global Legal System

Abram Chayes and Anne-Marie Slaughter

If an appraisal of U.S. national interest begins with the military dimension, it cannot end there. The United States has traditionally maintained the importance for its own national security of an international system governed by the rule of law. Skeptics have often dismissed this invocation of an international rule of law as the utopian rhetoric of a few internationalists. In the post–Cold War world, however, it is hardheaded realism. An increasingly interdependent world is bound together by law. Much of what the United States can and must do to enhance its own prosperity and well-being depends on reliably functioning legal frameworks.

The processes involved in the globalization of the economy—international funds transfers, trade in goods and services, investment, worldwide air transport, telecommunications, and much more—all operate within well-defined regimes of law. Much has been made of the importance for globalization of deregulation and free markets. But it is elementary that a necessary condition for the operation of markets is the rule of law, not only to enforce contracts but also to establish norms defining what practices are permissible and what transactions are appropriate. Without this legal infrastructure, economic globalization would not work.

The requirement of the rule of law is not limited to the global economy. Efforts to deal with major environmental problems—climate change, the protection of the ozone layer, maintenance of fish stocks, management of waste—all operate within a legal framework that defines the rights and the obligations of public and private actors. Closer to traditional national security areas, the attempts to control drug traffic, to defend against terrorism, and to prevent the spread of nuclear, chemical, and biological weapons proceed against a highly developed international legal backdrop defining prohibited activities and establishing modalities for cooperation.

Of particular importance in recent years has been the strengthening of human

237

rights and the humanitarian laws of war. This responds to the most fundamental demand of a legal system: that it should protect the physical security of those who live under it. The development of human rights norms in the second half of the twentieth century bespeaks a growing sense that individuals live under the international legal system and must necessarily have rights and obligations flowing from it. It is true that these relatively recent international norms are not infrequently violated. The response to violation, as in the domestic field, should be to improve the legal system rather than to resort to vigilantism and self-help. The movement for the International Criminal Court (ICC) is just such an effort.

These various bodies of law do not emanate from a single legislative institution. Some of the rules are comprised in formal treaties among states. More are to be found in agreements and understandings among administrative bodies and even private or quasi-private actors. But all of these regimes are interlinked in many ways. Most fundamentally, they all depend on an underlying respect for law and the legal order.

It is difficult to say with assurance how this respect is generated and maintained. But one essential factor must be the element of reciprocity embodied in the idea of equality under the law. Exemption of any nation—especially the richest and most powerful—from important legal requirements strikes at this foundation notion of equal treatment under law. In the case of the ICC, this claim of U.S. exceptionalism manifests itself both in the decision not to sign the Rome Statute and in the underlying reason for that refusal, namely that American citizens might in some circumstances, however unlikely, be subject to prosecution without U.S. consent.

A realistic evaluation of the U.S. position on the ICC must count this erosion of the international rule of law as a heavy cost.

THE PRICE OF OPTING OUT

The impact of the U.S. failure to support to the ICC Statute is only partly symbolic—a high-profile rejection of a major initiative for the rule of law in international affairs. The treaty reflects and embodies many of the larger current trends in the evolution of international legal institutions. These trends did not begin with the negotiations for the ICC, and they will persist whatever the future of the Court may be. But the detailed course these trends take will be shaped in significant part by the evolving experience with the Court.

Thus there are more specific costs to the United States in standing aside from this process of evolution. The United States has worked hard to formulate and to implement a strategy for the twenty-first century that includes a vision of global governance, international institutions, a proper balance between national and global interests, and mechanisms for delegating the many dimensions of government to different levels of responsibility appropriate to the tasks. Participation in the ICC would mean that the United States would have a major role in shaping the evolution of the Court in ways that further this vision of the future of the international legal system. Conversely, staying out of the ICC and clinging to the architecture of the past may mean that a critical aspect of the development of the international legal system—with which we will have to live in any case—takes place without U.S. input. If the ICC goes forward in the face of U.S. opposition and proves to be an institution that continues to command the support of a majority of the world's nations, including many of the most powerful, then prospects for realization of a coherent U.S. vision will be correspondingly blunted. The U.S. decision to oppose the Statute will thus undercut its larger effort to effectuate its distinctive vision of international governance for the twenty-first century.

This chapter briefly reviews some of the most important of the more specific issues that are at stake.

INDIVIDUALS AT THE BAR OF INTERNATIONAL LAW

Traditional international law was an affair of states. It was said to govern relations among states and to prescribe rights and duties binding on them. In the International Court of Justice (ICJ), only states can appear as litigants in a case. Contemporary international law, however, increasingly recognizes and makes room for the coexistence of individual and state actors within the same international regime. For two decades now, U.S. courts have been deciding cases involving violations of human rights brought against foreign officials by their victims.[1] This trend is highlighted in the ICC treaty itself, which builds on the human rights insistence of holding governments accountable for their treatment of individuals by seeking to hold individuals accountable for the actions of governments.

More generally, the debate about the future of international law and, indeed, world politics often frames a false dichotomy between traditional statists and new medievalists, all arguing over whether the state is here to stay or rather is doomed to wither away. Many commentators, observing the rise of a host of nonstate actors—a category that includes regional and local governments, nongovernmental organizations (NGOs), individuals, and international and supranational institutions—conclude that the state is being displaced.[2] Traditionalists point to the present international scene as evidence that the state is alive and well and that, if anything, state power is needed more than ever to anchor and to check this diverse array.[3]

The ICC treaty, by contrast, envisions a regime in which state and the individual participate side by side. Defendants before the Court would be natural persons. But when a case is brought, it is assumed that both the defendant and his or her state will respond.[4] The state can of course choose to disavow the individual; conversely the individual could presumably choose to leave the conduct of the case entirely to his or her government. But the presumption is that both will want to be heard, and the Statute provides both with an opportunity to do so.

This emerging phenomenon also characterizes other "mixed regimes" like the North American Free Trade Agreement (NAFTA) and the World Trade Organization (WTO), in which both individuals and state officials participate—either directly or indirectly—in dispute resolution proceedings.[5] In those institutions, individuals play a role analogous to their function as "private attorneys general" in the United States, helping ensure that those with the greatest interests in seeing the law implemented are at least partially responsible for its enforcement. The same principle operates in the right of individual petitions in human rights regimes such as the European Convention on Human Rights and the Inter-American Convention on Human Rights. In the ICC, the same principle of mixed representation applies. States represent the accused individuals while simultaneously allowing them to represent themselves. This is very different from the traditional image of international diplomacy, but it is one that is quite consistent with the multiple roles played by both governments and individuals in liberal democracies.

A Shrinking Conception of Domestic Jurisdiction

If international law establishes rights and duties of individuals, it implies a radical reconstruction of the concept of domestic jurisdiction. The international architecture of 1945 preserved an insulated and carefully protected sphere of domestic affairs. Article 2 (7) of the U.N. Charter provides: "Nothing contained in the present Charter shall authorize the United Nations to intervene in matters which are essentially within the domestic jurisdiction of any state."[6]

Although the provision reads only against the United Nations (and even then had an exception for enforcement measures adopted by the Security Council under Chapter VII), it has been read more generally to instate the general prohibition of the Westphalian system against interference by one state in the internal affairs of another. And as the U.S. Senate promptly proclaimed in the 1945 Connally reservation to the U.S. submission to the jurisdiction of the World Court, governments could and did reserve to themselves the decision as to what matters fell within the scope of domestic affairs.[7]

But only three years after the adoption of the Charter, the Universal Declaration of Human Rights foreshadowed a contrary movement that has burgeoned in recent years. The existence of exclusive domestic jurisdiction is now increasingly conditional on conformity with international rules and principles, especially human rights norms. As evidenced by the intervention in Kosovo, the international community is no longer prepared to stand aside while a government commits gross violations of fundamental human rights under the rubric of internal affairs.

The contingent nature of domestic sovereignty is not confined to the field of human rights. It follows from the increasingly coextensive scope of domestic and international regulation. In the areas of economic integration, trade, environmental affairs, and internal conflict, international and domestic law now often regulate the same conduct. Laws drafted and implemented at both levels organize and constrain the behavior not only of states but also of the individuals and groups within them. National jurisdiction may be primary, but it is no longer exclusive.

The ICC Statute can be seen as a natural product of this development. Within the ICC framework, if the national law enforcement system actively and effectively prosecutes crimes within ICC jurisdiction, the ICC (and by extension the international community) will not interfere.[8] But should the national legal system fail, the international system will take over.

The Role of Nongovernmental Organizations

Without the NGO community, the ICC treaty might not have been concluded. Organizations devoted to human rights, women's rights, humanitarian assistance, social justice, and the eradication or at least the diminution of the myriad forms of oppression, all organized, lobbied, drafted, and negotiated to push governments in their desired direction.[9] Moreover, it is already apparent that NGOs will have a major part in providing impetus for the ratification of the Statute in many states and in Statute implementation. Indeed, Article 15 specifically provides that the Prosecutor may seek information from NGOs in evaluating the seriousness of information he or she has received concerning possible crimes within the jurisdiction of the Court.

This phenomenon of major NGO input in treaty drafting and negotiation surfaced earlier in the context of the Land Mine Convention and numerous environmental treaties like the Framework Convention on Climate Change.[10] As a result, NGOs increasingly are recognized as independent participants in the process of international lawmaking.[11] This development too gained new ground in the ICC negotiating process. NGOs have not displaced states, but states can no longer reckon without them.

The United States has long encouraged this development. NGOs are vibrant participants in U.S. civil society. Under a different guise as Alexis de Tocqueville's "voluntary associations," they have been the backbone of American democracy.[12] Private groups, from the American Civil Liberties Union (ACLU) to the American Manufacturers Association are a familiar part of domestic politics and lawmaking at all levels. In the past four decades, NGOs here and abroad have been regarded as a force for global democracy. In many cases, indigenous NGOs appear as more legitimate representatives of their countries than the governments they expose and denounce and that seek to repress and stifle them.

Domestic NGOs working within the liberal democratic society of the United States play a well-established part in the political system. In the United States, it is automatically assumed that they have a similar role to play in developing U.S. foreign policy, as gadflies and representatives of voices otherwise unheard in the decision-making process. Thus, although U.S. opposition to the ICC is easily framed as "the United States versus the world," the division is just as sharp between U.S. government officials and the leaders of the myriad U.S.-based NGOs who fought so hard for the Treaty.

It is usual to think of NGOs as the fiber of both domestic and transnational civil society. Yet the new role of NGOs has its own problems. Their operation in the domestic context raises questions of accountability and democratic representation. These questions are intensified in the field of international affairs.[13] Indeed, since the strongest and the richest NGOs are organized in the United States and other industrialized countries, their activities in the foreign policy field are often regarded by others as simply another manifestation of the West's power. Figuring out a new framework to encompass state and nonstate actors as both principals and agents in the international legal system is an important task for the twenty-first century.

A NEW JUDICIAL PARTNERSHIP

The ICC also reflects a growing interrelationship between national and international courts. The central concept is *complementarity*, under which the ICC will have jurisdiction over a case only if the Judges determine that national legal authorities are "unable or unwilling" to prosecute the case themselves. This concept provides a framework for a new relationship and perhaps even for a partnership between national and supranational judges. Although the most obvious implication of this arrangement is that supranational judges must evaluate the quality and the sincerity of their national counterparts, the relationship need not be and is unlikely to be primarily confrontational. Instead of the supranational tribunal seeking to encroach on national jurisdiction by carving out specific issues or doctrinal areas for its own, this arrangement instead assumes that national courts have primary jurisdiction and indeed presumes that national courts will be fully up to the task of doing justice. It is only in exceptional circumstances where this assumption does not hold that jurisdiction will devolve to the supranational level.

At the same time, national courts will increasingly be inclined to look to the ICC for guidance in the developing area of war crimes law. The ICC will not be hierarchically superior to national tribunals, and its decisions will not be binding on them. But ICC judgments are likely to carry great persuasive authority.

This authority will be enhanced by the mandated composition of the ICC, which includes more specialists in criminal law than in international law.[14] In this respect the ICC illustrates that international law is no longer the exclusive province of internationalists. Five Judges must be distinguished international law specialists, but nine must be criminal law specialists. In the International Criminal Tribunal for the Former Yugoslavia (ICTY), where a similar selection procedure is used, each group learned from the other after an initial period of adjustment, just as judges from civil and common law systems on the European Court of Justice (ECJ) have educated one another.[15]

By ensuring that the members of the ICC are not drawn from an elite, specialized, and often insulated group of international law professors and practitioners, the treaty ensures a broader base of legitimacy for the Court. National judges and prosecutors will see their former colleagues on the Court and assess the Court's judgments accordingly. Above all, as international law becomes simply "law," interpreted and applied by both supranational and national judges and shaped by their respective training and expertise, it becomes much less remarkable and much more effective.

The most developed judicial partnership between national and supranational tribunals at present is that between the ECJ and the national courts of European Union member states. The ECJ, in effect, "recruited" national courts, first to refer cases and then to abide by and carry out the resulting decisions. The judges on the ECJ crafted their judgments to appeal both to individual litigants and to national courts; the court itself also held seminars and other training sessions for national judges.[16] In so doing, the ECJ created an independent base for the construction of a European Community legal system. At the same time, it gave national courts a role in enforcing and developing a body of supranational rules that they had never before known.

The parameters of this partnership are still developing. The German Constitutional Court, for instance, recently served notice that there are limits to its willingness to be a junior rather than a senior partner. In a case brought by a group of German litigants challenging the constitutionality of the Maastricht Treaty establishing the European Monetary Union, the ECJ held that the treaty was constitutional, but only so long as the competences granted the European Union do not infringe the guarantees of democracy assured all German citizens through their Constitution.[17] In the process, the Court proposed a "cooperative relationship" with the ECJ, whereby the German court would establish a threshold of constitutional guarantees and the ECJ would adjudicate the application of these and additional guarantees on a case-by-case basis.[18] The ultimate outcome of this controversy and the exact place where the line between the supremacy of the two systems will be drawn remain uncertain. Nevertheless, the combination not only of supranational and national law but also of supranational and national adjudication has been uniquely successful and effective and is firmly established.

The European Court of Human Rights has a much less structured relationship with the national courts of the member states within its jurisdiction. However, in effect it judges states' handiwork in the sense that an individual cannot appear before it without first seeking redress in national tribunals without success. In any case, the jurisprudence of the European Court of Human Rights is increasingly cited by European national courts, again as persuasive rather than coercive authority.[19]

Similarly, the decisions of other specialized supranational courts will become part of the sources of national law. National courts will naturally turn to the decisions of WTO dispute-resolution panels for guidance in applying General Agreement on Tariffs and Trade (GATT) principles or perhaps in construing their own national trade law. The Law of the Sea Tribunal may serve the same purpose in its field. Supranational courts can thus become catalysts for increased uniformity and coherence in areas of the law in which they have particular expertise or a valuable bird's-eye global perspective, while in other cases remaining as the court of last resort.

Seen in this perspective, the ICC does not appear as a novel or a frightening departure. It is only the latest example of partnerships between national and supranational judicial authorities, developing the applicable law by a familiar process of interaction among courts dealing with the same subject matter. Within this conception of supranational adjudication, no court or tribunal is likely to truly become a world court, but the courts of the world will interact in many different ways.

CONCLUSION

To return to the initial question, is support for the ICC in the U.S. national security interest? Weighing the costs and benefits of support for or opposition to the ICC requires a sense not only of its specific strengths and weaknesses as an institution, but also of its larger place in the evolution of international legal rules and institutions. This chapter has sought to situate the ICC in that larger context.

An important element of the U.S. conception of its national interest, from the outset, has been the development and maintenance of an international rule of law. The importance the Framers gave to international law is reflected in the Constitution itself. In the twentieth century, the United States was a leading force in the establishment of the Permanent Court of Arbitration at The Hague. Woodrow Wilson was the prime proponent of the League of Nations, even though he was ultimately unable to convince the Senate to approve U.S. participation. After World

War II, the United States was the chief architect of the United Nations, the International Monetary Fund (IMF), the World Bank, and associated international institutions. All of them bear many of the marks of the American political and legal experience. More recently, U.S. trade negotiators pushed steadily for the increasing legalization of the GATT and ultimately the creation of the World Trade Organization. Over the past fifty years, the United States has been a major participant in these institutions, exercising a predominant influence in their implementation and evolution.

The international institutions of the 1940s reflected the spirit of their time. They had an important normative content—most prominently the prohibition of the use of force against another state. But they also embodied a realism born of the experience of the interwar years, a recognition of the continuing importance of power. They thus gave the most powerful states that emerged from World War II the principal responsibility to address a discrete set of international security problems. They were state-centric and intergovernmental, primarily oriented to the relatively limited set of problems that the experience of the previous three decades had demonstrated could not be left to the unmediated interactions of national governments.

The international institutions of the 1990s reflect the new spirit and the new problems of these times. These new institutions are often unwieldy and unsatisfying. They challenge common preconceptions and do not fit the analytical categories carried over from the Cold War period. They are born of a complex process in which states, individuals, and NGOs all participate. They are supranational as well as intergovernmental. They are universal and legislative rather than voluntary and contractual. They blur the line between international and domestic law.

But although these new institutions embody in a general way the emerging tendencies in international law, the specific form they will take will only become clear with practice over time. Like the post–World War II legal structure, the ultimate shape of today's new institutions will depend on the continued participation of all those actors in the implementation of the rules that are adopted and the standards that are set. The balance between power and equal treatment remains to be struck. The respective roles of state and nonstate actors remain to be defined. Operating procedures that ensure both domestic participation and domestic support for the new institutions remain to be worked out. The solutions that are developed for these problems will affect not only the detailed contours of the ICC, but also the broader evolution of the global legal system of the twenty-first century.

Consistent with its own conception of its global position, the United States should be taking the lead in shaping these new institutions. It is not too late. By signing the treaty, even if prospects for early ratification look dim, the United States would strengthen its ability to participate as an observer in the early phases of implementation. If the United States stands aside from the process, it will miss an opportunity of serious dimensions. And the loss will have an impact on U.S. national interests far beyond the work of prosecuting war crimes.

NOTES

Abe Chayes died while this volume was in press. His contribution to the whole volume as well as this essay was great and expressive of the dedication to promoting the law over force in international relations that marked his academic and public career.
The authors would like to thank David Bosco for his research assistance.

1. John F. Murphy, "Civil Liability for the Commission of International Crimes as an Alternative to Criminal Prosecution," *Harvard Human Rights Journal* 12, no. 1 (1999).

2. Jessica T. Mathews, "Power Shift," *Foreign Affairs* (January/February 1997): 50; Susan Strange, *The Retreat of the State: The Diffusion of Power in the World Economy* (New York, N.Y.: Cambridge University Press, 1996).

3. John Mearsheimer, "The False Promise of International Institutions," *International Security* (Winter 1994/95): 5.

4. Statute (July 17, 1998), arts. 18 and 19 (giving the state of nationality the right to object to the admissability of the case).

5. Richard Shell, "The Trade Stakeholders Model and Participation by Nonstate Parties in the World Trade Organization," *University of Pennsylvania Journal of International Economic Law* 17 (1996): 359; Philip M. Nichols, "Participation of Nongovernmental Parties in the World Trade Organization: Extension of Standing in World Trade Organization Disputes to Nongovernment Parties," *University of Pennsylvania Journal of International Economic Law* 17 (1996): 295.

6. U.N. Charter, art. 2, par. 7.

7. 92, *Congressional Record*, 79th Cong. 2d sess., 1946, 10, 694.

8. Statute, n. 4, art. 17.

9. Roger S. Clark and Ved P. Nanda, "An Introduction to the Symposium," *Transnational Law and Contemporary Problems* 5, No. 2, i, iv–vi (1995); Charles Truehart, "Clout without a Country: The Power of International Lobbies," *Washington Post*, June 18, 1998, A32.

10. Kal Raustiala, "The 'Participatory Revolution' in International Environmental Law," *Harvard Environmental Law Review* 21 (1997): 537.

11. Raustiala, "The 'Participatory Revolution,'" 537–39.

12. Alexis de Tocqueville, "Democracy in America," trans. George Lawrence (New York: Harper and Row, 1988): 513–24.

13. Peter J. Spiro, "New Global Potentates: Nongovernmental Organizations and the 'Unregulated' Marketplace," *Cardozo Law Review* 18 (1996): 957.

14. Statute, n. 4, art. 36.

15. Symposium, "War Crimes Tribunals: The Record and the Prospects: *The Prosecutor v. Dusko Tadic*," *American University International Law Review* 13 (1998): 1441 (with then president of the ICTY Gabrielle Kirk McDonald noting the mix of legal systems in the tribunal's work); Thijmen Koopmans, "The Birth of European Law at the Crossroads of Legal Traditions," *American Journal* 39 (1991): 493; David Edward, "How the Court of Justice Works," *European Law Review* 20 (1995): 539.

16. Joseph H. H. Weiler, "The Transformation of Europe," *Yale Law Journal* 100 (1991): 2403; Anne-Marie Burley and Walter Mattli, "Europe before the Court: A Political Theory of Legal Integration," *International Organization* 47 (Winter 1993): 41.

17. "*Brunner v. The European Union Treaty*," *Bundesverfassungsgericht* (2. Senat), October 12, 1993, *Common Market Law Review* 1, 57 (F.R.G.).

18. "*Brunner v. The European Union Treaty*," 79.

19. Laurence R. Helfer and Anne-Marie Slaughter, "Toward a Theory of Effective Supranational Adjudication," *Yale Law Journal* 107 (1997): 273.

Appendix

Bringing a Case to the ICC: Pathways and Thresholds

Bartram S. Brown

Step I: Ratification of the ICC Statute

The Statute must be ratified by 60 States to take effect and establish the ICC. (Article 126(1))

The ICC will have jurisdiction only over crimes committed after the Statute enters into effect. (Article 11(1))

Step II: Preconditions to the exercise of the ICC's jurisdiction

Before the ICC can act, its jurisdiction must be accepted by either: (Article 12(2))

The Territorial State	The State of Nationality of the Accused
(where crime was allegedly committed)	(the United States in the case of U.S. nationals)

"A State which becomes a Party to this Statute thereby accepts the jurisdiction of the Court with respect to the crimes referred to in article 5." (Article 12(1))

When necessary, other states may also accept ICC jurisdiction by declaration. (Article 12(3))

Step III: Initiation of investigations and prosecutions

Who can initiate investigations leading to possible ICC prosecutions?
Three possibilities under Article 13:

Referral of a situation by a **State-Party**	Referral of a situation by the **U.N. Security Council**	Initiation of an investigation by the **Prosecutor** on his or her own authority
A basic right of Parties to the Statute.	**No need for precondition in Step II to be met in this case.** Based on the special role of the Council under the U.N. Charter in maintaining international peace and security. Could involve the Security Council in enforcing the ICC's requests for cooperation from states. (Article 87(7))	**Special limits apply** to the Prosecutor's initiation of an investigation *proprio motu.* (Article 15) Pre-Trial Chamber of the ICC must approve any investigation initiated by the Prosecutor by finding: "reasonable basis to proceed with an investigation." that the case "appears to fall within the jurisdiction" of the ICC.

Step IV: Admissibility/Complementarity
The deference of the ICC to the jurisdiction of national courts

---

The most general and effective jurisdictional limit on the ICC lies in its relationship to national courts.

The jurisdiction of the ICC "shall be complementary to national criminal jurisdictions." (Article 1)

An additional threshold of "admissibility" applies to ensure that the ICC will have jurisdiction only in exceptional cases, as a "safety net" to prevent impunity for serious international crimes.

The Standard of Admissibility (Article 17):

The ICC shall not proceed with any case if:	The only exception to (a) and (b) is if:
(a) It **is being investigated or prosecuted by a State** that has jurisdiction.	The state concerned "**is unwilling or unable genuinely to carry out the investigation or prosecution.**"
(b) It **has been investigated** by a State that has jurisdiction over it and the State has decided not to prosecute the person concerned.	**Unwillingness standard** considers whether:
	National proceedings or decision made for the **purpose of shielding the person from criminal responsibility.**
	Unjustified delay in the proceedings is inconsistent with an intent to bring the person concerned to justice.
(c) The **person has already been tried** for the same conduct.	**Proceedings not being conducted independently or impartially,** and conducted in a manner that, in the circumstances, is inconsistent with an intent to bring the person concerned to justice.
(d) The **case is not of sufficient gravity to justify further action** by the Court.	**Inability standard** considers whether:
	"due to **a total or substantial collapse or unavailability of its national judicial system, the State is** unable to obtain the accused or the necessary evidence and testimony or otherwise **unable to carry out its proceedings.**"

Admissibility can be challenged at various stages, but only once by any person or state. (Article 19(4))

Preliminary Ruling on Admissibility at the Initiation of a Case
Any state with jurisdiction over the case can assert its superior right to exercise that jurisdiction. (Article 18)

The ICC **Prosecutor must notify all states** with jurisdiction of any investigations commenced.

States have one month to notify Prosecutor of their own investigation of the persons concerned.

ICC **Prosecutor must defer to any State's investigations,** unless a Pre-Trial Chamber decides to authorize the investigation (i.e., finds the case to be admissible).

The State may appeal the Pre-Trial Chamber's decision.

Other challenges to the admissibility of a case (Article 19)

Admissibility **may be determined by the ICC on its own motion,** or

An **accused** may bring a challenge, or

A **state with jurisdiction,** may also bring a challenge on the **ground that it is investigating or prosecuting the case or has already done so.**

A **state whose acceptance of jurisdiction is required, as a precondition** of the exercise of jurisdiction under Article 12 may refuse to accept ICC jurisdiction.

Step V: Possible deferral pursuant to decision of the Security Council

"No investigation or prosecution may be commenced or proceeded with under this Statute for a period of 12 months after the Security Council, in a resolution adopted under Chapter VII of the Charter of the United Nations, has requested the Court to that effect; that request may be renewed by the Council under the same conditions." (Article 16)

Step VI: Investigation/Evaluation by the Prosecutor

After the referral of a situation by a State Party or by the Security Council, the Prosecutor evaluates the information made available to him or her.

Prosecutor makes a preliminary decision whether to proceed with the investigation based on whether: (Article 53)

(a) The information available to the Prosecutor provides a reasonable basis to believe that a crime within the jurisdiction of the Court has been or is being committed;

(b) The case is or would be admissible under article 17; and

(c) Taking into account the gravity of the crime and the interests of victims, there are nonetheless substantial reasons to believe that an investigation would not serve the interests of justice.

If the Prosecutor decides not to proceed, it notifies the Pre-Trial Chamber and the referring Party— either the State Party or the Security Council.

Decision there is no reasonable basis to proceed	**Otherwise Prosecutor proceeds to investigate**
Referring Party and Pre-Trial Chamber are notified.	Collects evidence, seeks testimony, seeks cooperation of states and international organizations.
Pre-Trial Chamber may review the decision at the request of the referring party or on its own initiative.	Is to respect rights of persons during the investigations. (Article 55)
Process may end here.	

Step VII: Pre-Trial Chamber decides on the issuance of orders and warrants requested by Prosecutor for purposes of investigation (Articles 57-58)

Summons to appear, measures to preserve evidence, arrest warrants.

Article 58 sets out the standards for issuance of an arrest warrant.

Ideally the arrest warrant leads to either:

> Arrest by the custodial state and surrender to the ICC, or
> Voluntary appearance before the ICC of the person whose arrest is sought.

Step VIII: Confirmation of charges before trial (Article 61)

Within a reasonable time after the person's surrender or voluntary appearance before the Court or in the absence of the person charged if the presence of that person cannot be secured:

> After informing the person charged, and/or his or her counsel, of all charges and evidence, the Pre-Trial Chamber holds a hearing to determine whether to confirm the charges.
>
> Document setting out the charges must be provided to the person and his or her counsel.
>
> At the hearing, the Prosecutor shall support each charge with sufficient evidence to establish substantial grounds to believe that the person committed the crime charged.
>
> Pre-Trial Chamber confirms or dismisses each charge.

Index

255

About the Contributors

Gary Jonathan Bass is an assistant professor of politics and international affairs at Princeton University. He is the author of a book on the politics of war crimes tribunals, forthcoming from the Princeton University Press. A former reporter for the *Economist*, he has also written about international justice in the *New York Times*, *Washington Post*, and *New Republic*.

Bartram S. Brown is an associate professor of law, Chicago-Kent College of Law, Illinois Institute of Technology. He was legal adviser in June and July 1998 to the Delegation of the Republic of Trinidad and Tobago to the U.N. Diplomatic Conference of Plenipotentiaries on the Establishment of an ICC, Rome, Italy. He also served as a law clerk from 1995 to 1996 at the International Criminal Tribunal for the Former Yugoslavia, The Hague, Netherlands.

Abram Chayes was the Felix Frankfurter Professor of Law Emeritus at Harvard Law School where he taught international law. He served as legal adviser in the Department of State in the Kennedy administration from 1961 to 1964. In the 1980s, he represented Nicaragua in the World Court case against the United States. His book, *The New Sovereignty, Compliance with Treaties in International Regulatory Regimes,* coauthored with his wife, Antonia H. Chayes, was published in 1995 by Harvard University Press.

Robinson O. Everett is a professor at Duke Law School where he founded the Center on Law, Ethics, and National Security. He served on active duty during the Korean War in the Judge Advocate General's department and in 1978 retired as a colonel from the Air Force Reserve. From 1955 to 1980, he was engaged in private law practice. He has served as a counsel to the Subcommittee on Constitutional Rights of the Senate Committee on the Judiciary. In April 1980, Judge Everett joined the U.S. Court of Military Appeals as Chief Judge. He now serves as a senior judge of that Court. He has edited many symposia and written many articles and a book, *Military Justice in the Armed Forces of the United States.*

Richard J. Goldstone is a justice of the Constitutional Court of South Africa. From 1991 to 1994, he served as chairperson of the Commission of Inquiry regarding Public Violence and Intimidation (the Goldstone Commission). He is also chairperson of the Standing Advisory Committee of Company Law. From August

1994 to September 1996, he served as the chief prosecutor of the U.N. International Criminal Tribunals for the Former Yugoslavia and Rwanda.

Carl Kaysen is the David W. Skinner Professor of Political Economy Emeritus. He is a member of the Security Studies Program at Massachusetts Institute of Technology (MIT) and chairman of the Committee on International Security Studies at the American Academy of Arts and Sciences. Professor Kaysen served as deputy special assistant to the president for national security affairs from 1961 to 1963. He has written and lectured on a variety of arms control and security topics.

Madeline Morris is a professor of criminal law and international criminal law at Duke University where she is Duke faculty director of the Duke/Geneva Institute in Transnational Law. She served as adviser on justice to the president of Rwanda, 1995 to 1997. She was coconvenor, in 1996 and 1997, of the Inter-African Cooperation on Truth and Justice program and served in 1997 as consultant and adjunct faculty member of the U.S. Naval Justice School. Professor Morris served as special consultant to the secretary of the army in 1997. Professor Morris is director of the Duke Law School Pro Bono Projects on International Criminal Law.

William L. Nash (Major General, U.S. Army, Retired) is the Mitrovica regional administrator for the U.N. Interim Administration Mission in Kosovo. He is also the director of Civil-Military Programs for the National Democratic Institute for International Affairs in Washington, D.C. In 1998, he was a fellow and visiting lecturer at the John F. Kennedy School of Government, Harvard University. General Nash was commanding general of the U.S. Army's 1st Armored Division from June 1995 to May 1997. In 1996, he was the commander of Task Force Eagle, a multinational division supporting the Dayton Peace Accord in northeastern Bosnia-Herzegovina.

Samantha Power is executive director of the Carr Center for Human Rights Policy at the John F. Kennedy School of Government. From 1993 to 1996, she covered the wars in the former Yugoslavia as a reporter for *U.S. News and World Report* and the *Economist*. In 1996, she worked as a political analyst for the International Crisis Group (ICG) in Bosnia. She is currently writing a book examining American responses to genocide since the Holocaust.

Leila Nadya Sadat (formerly Leila Sadat Wexler) in 1992 became a professor at Washington University School of Law (St. Louis). She previously had practiced international commercial law in Paris. She was admitted to the Paris Bar as an *avocat* in 1992 and is a member of the Louisiana, American, and International

Bar Associations. Her study of the Barbie, Touvier, and Papon prosecutions and their significance has been the subject of several articles and book chapters, and her work on crimes against humanity was cited by the International Criminal Tribunal for the Former Yugoslavia in the *Tadic* decision. She received a Treiman Fellowship from the Law School to pursue her work on the three prosecutions and her work on the permanent International Criminal Court.

Michael P. Scharf is a professor of law and director of the Center for International Law and Policy at the New England School of Law. He previously served as the attorney-adviser for U.N. Affairs in the U.S. State Department's Office of the Legal Adviser where he helped create the International Criminal Tribunal for Yugoslavia. He serves as chair of the International Institutions Committee of the International Law Section of the American Bar Association and chair of the International Organizations Committee of the American Society of International Law. Professor Scharf's books include *The International Criminal Tribunal for Rwanda* (1998), which was awarded the American Society of International Law's Certificate of Merit for Outstanding Book in 1999, and *Balkan Justice: The Story behind the First International Criminal Trial since Nuremberg* (1997), which was nominated for the Pulitzer Prize in Letters.

David J. Scheffer since 1997 has served as the first-ever ambassador-at-large for war crimes. In 1993, he was appointed senior adviser and counsel to then-Ambassador Albright. Until 1997, Ambassador Scheffer was an adjunct professor of international law at Georgetown University Law Center. Ambassador Scheffer also worked as an attorney at Coudert Brothers from 1979 to 1986. He was a senior associate in international and national security law at the Carnegie Endowment for International Peace (1989–1992) and a senior consultant on the Committee on Foreign Affairs, U.S. House of Representatives (1987–1989).

Sarah B. Sewall served as deputy assistant secretary of defense for peacekeeping and humanitarian assistance during the first Clinton administration and previously spent six years as senior foreign policy adviser to Senate Majority Leader George Mitchell. Currently, she is program director at the Carr Center for Human Rights Policy at Harvard's Kennedy School of Government. She was associate director of the Committee on International Security Studies at the American Academy of Arts and Sciences from 1999 to 2000. She also has been a visiting scholar at the Harvard Program on Negotiation as a Council on Foreign Relations international affairs fellow and a defense analyst at several Washington, D.C., organizations and has taught international affairs for Stanford University.

Anne-Marie Slaughter is the J. Sinclair Armstrong Professor of International, Foreign, and Comparative Law and director, graduate and international legal studies. Professor Slaughter currently is working on a book about the formation of transnational networks of government institutions and the implications of these networks for global governance. She has also written widely on the relationship between supranational tribunals and national courts and the effectiveness of supranational adjudication.

Ruth Wedgwood is professor of law at Yale Law School and senior fellow for international organizations and law at the Council on Foreign Relations in New York City. Professor Wedgwood is also a member of the secretary of state's advisory committee on international law and the board of editors of the *American Journal of International Law* and a vice president of the International Law Association (American Branch). She was the Charles Stockton Professor of International Law at the U.S. Naval War College from 1998 to 1999 and also has served as amicus curiae in *Prosecutor v. Blaskic* at the International Criminal Tribunal for the Former Yugoslavia. She was a federal prosecutor in the Southern District of New York and law clerk to Justice Harry A. Blackmun on the U.S. Supreme Court.

Lawrence Weschler has been a staff writer for *The New Yorker* since 1981. He has variously covered Poland, Yugoslavia, Czechoslovakia, Iraq, Latin America, and South Africa. His books of political reportage include *The Passion of Poland* (1984); *A Miracle, A Universe: Settling Accounts with Torturers* (1990); *Calamities of Exile: Three Nonfiction Novellas* (1998); and the forthcoming *Vermeer in Bosnia*. He has taught variously at Princeton, Columbia, Vassar, Sarah Lawrence, Bard, and the University of California at Santa Cruz. A two-time winner of the George Polk Award, he was also awarded a 1998 Lannan Literary Prize.